touch
WOOD

The Rediscovery of a Building Material

Imprint
The Deutsche Bibliothek is registering this publication in the
Deutsche Nationalbibliographie; detailed bibliographical infor-
mation can be found on the internet at http://dnb.ddb.de

ISBN 978-3-938780-50-3

© 2008 by Verlagshaus Braun
www.verlagshaus-braun.de

1st edition 2008

Editorial staff:
Julia Goltz, Sophie Steybe
Draft texts by the architects. Text editing: Dirk Meyhöfer
Translation:
Stephen Roche, Hamburg
Graphic concept and layout:
Michaela Prinz

touch WOOD

The Rediscovery of a Building Material

BRAUN

Touch Wood

Hamburg, a city largely defined by its red brick architecture, recently passed a new building regulation which stipulated that all new children's daycare centers built within the city boundaries must be constructed of wood. The reasoning behind this measure is clear: Children are the most sensitive users of architecture, and wood is a material with child-like characteristics; it is natural, captivating and emotional.

Touch Wood entices readers to do just what the title says. Wood is a material that begs to be touched. It is held in high regard for its integrity and warmth. Wood is a natural material, and most likely it was the first material used by humans in a systematic and constructive way to create dwellings and functional buildings. But wood has far greater significance. For many architects building with wood represents both a philosophy and a great challenge.

Yet wood has often been the victim of prejudice; it tends to be associated with poverty and traditional, rural styles of building. In China, for example, wood is frowned upon by the nouveaux riches, who identify it as common, old-fashioned, and rural. Similarly, in twentieth-century Europe wood was widely regarded as an outmoded material, best suited for building barns and stables. People became accustomed to living in houses made of stone, and were greatly attached to the sense of security this gave them.

But times have changed greatly. Because wood creates a healthy interior climate and therefore a higher quality of living, it is not surprising that wooden homes are becoming more and more popular. This is a worldwide trend. For example in Germany roughly fifteen percent of all single-family and duplex homes are now being built of timber, and the trend is upwards.

Wood is like healthy food. You really can't go far wrong with it. In terms of its load-bearing properties wood is not a material of superlatives. The tallest wooden buildings are modest, and for expansive structures such as trade fair centers and airport terminals architects generally rely on steel and concrete. When they work with wood they create buildings that are small-scale yet honest. With wood there is no need to conceal details. Wood is omnipotent. Timber construction systems are also highly adaptable to different requirements and conditions. Wood can be used to build bridges and hunting stands; and the very first halls besides churches, namely barns, were likewise built of wood. Wood is essentially the only material that can provide a complete architectural solution, providing the material for every part of a house bar the window panes. Wooden houses are often built of nothing but wood.

In this age of climatic upheaval a further benefit of wood is being rediscovered. These days wood is the most sensible and responsible material one can use. Unlike stone, wood can be planted and harvested. Clearly it enjoys special status among building materials. All timber construction methods have one thing in common: assuming professional planning and execution, there is little difficulty meeting regulatory requirements for damp-proofing, thermal and noise insulation. Particularly when it comes to thermal insulation, which is becoming ever more important with the rise of energy prices, all forms of timber construction have a huge advantage over other materials. For centuries architects have known and

made use of the versatility of timber construction. And now they have taken that knowledge into the twenty-first century.

Timber buildings can generally be divided into massive and lightweight constructions. The traditional prairie or block houses are typical examples of massive timber construction. The outer shell is built of solid planks or boards. The solid wood walls provide both structural stability and excellent thermal insulation. Lightweight timber construction can take the form either of timber panel or wood skeleton constructions. These methods involved combining wood with other materials. The best-known historical form of lightweight timber construction is the half-timbered house made of wood and clay.

The master builders of the Middle Ages understood that wood was as much an ornamental as a structural material. To this day, the centers of many old European cities testify to this builders' craft, with impressive wooden carvings and images looking down from cantilevered façades. The interiors of these buildings display even greater audacity: an artificial supporting structure of beams and columns produced magnificent spacious interiors, reminding modern users that timber construction is the mother of all structural engineering. Modern architecture in wood can justifiably be described as the perfect mixture of ecological sense and architectural vision. Wood is the material that marries sensible houses with daring sculptures.

This effect is very well depicted in this book. Architects and many of their clients, whether in California or Norway, Japan or Switzerland, want to build with and in wood. Wood is a global building material, though naturally it is best used in those regions where it is also extensively grown. Its spectrum of application is incredibly broad. Even the simplest mountain cabins built to provide protection from wind and rain have a robust elegance. A good example of this type of structure is the experimental house in County Leitrim, Ireland designed and built by the architect Dominic Stevens. In the end, this home evolved into a gesamtkunstwerk or total work of art. But wood is far more than just a sensible building material. Two-hundred kilometers south of Leitrim the architects Buchholz McEvoy have ably demonstrated that wood can also achieve loftier ambitions; it can be made to soar and dance. Their building that houses the offices of Limerick County Council plays with the motif of the Irish wind by creating a sail-like façade. These are but two examples of many in this book that convincingly demonstrate the manifold uses of wood in contemporary architecture.

Dirk Meyhöfer

CONSTRUCTIVE

Birdwatching tower, 2005
Address: Graswarder Nature Reserve, Germany.
Client: NABU Heiligenhafen. **Design:** Meinhard
von Gerkan. **Project manager:** Volkmar Sievers.
Gross floor area: 48 m². **Materials:** wood (Siberian
larch) and zinc-galvanized sheeting.

Abstract bird

ARCHITECTS: gmp – Architekten
von Gerkan, Marg und Partner

The Graswarder peninsula that projects into the Baltic Sea not far from the Baltic Sea spa resort of Heiligenhafen is a bird sanctuary which attracts not only ornithologists, but also tourists and casual visitors. In order to allow these visitors to observe the birds without impacting the unspoiled environment, the management of the bird sanctuary decided to construct an appropriate observation tower. The architect devised a wooden post and beam structure that fits both its purpose and its surroundings. The structure is reinforced by diagonal beams, resulting in a filigree and transparent sculpture of an abstract birdlike figure in a sitting posture. The tower provides a spacious, glazed viewing cockpit at a height of 15 meters that is reached via two flights of stairs.

03

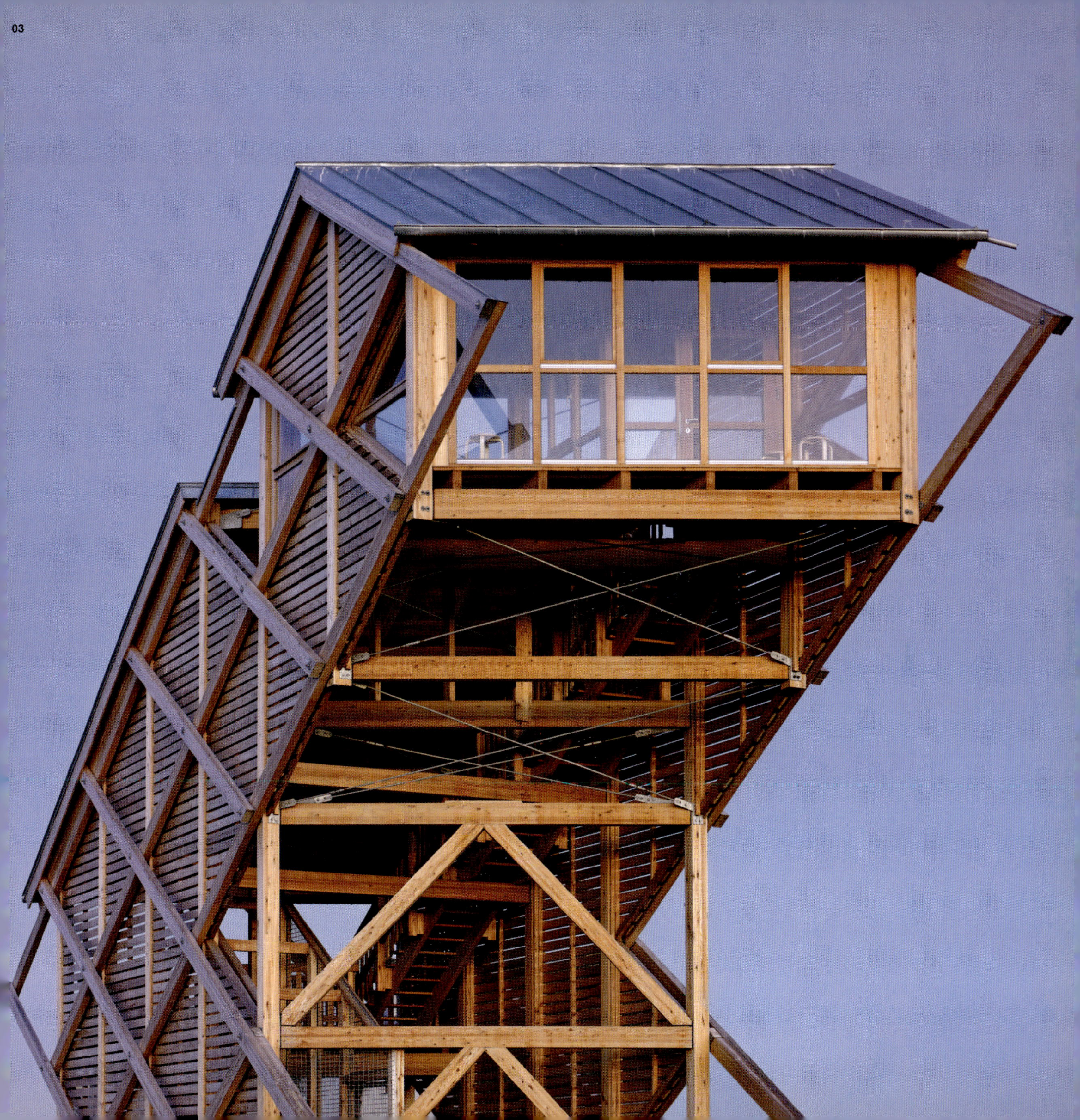

01 Interior view panorama space
02 Total view **03** Exterior view **04**
Elevation **05** Section **06** Exterior
view panorama space

04

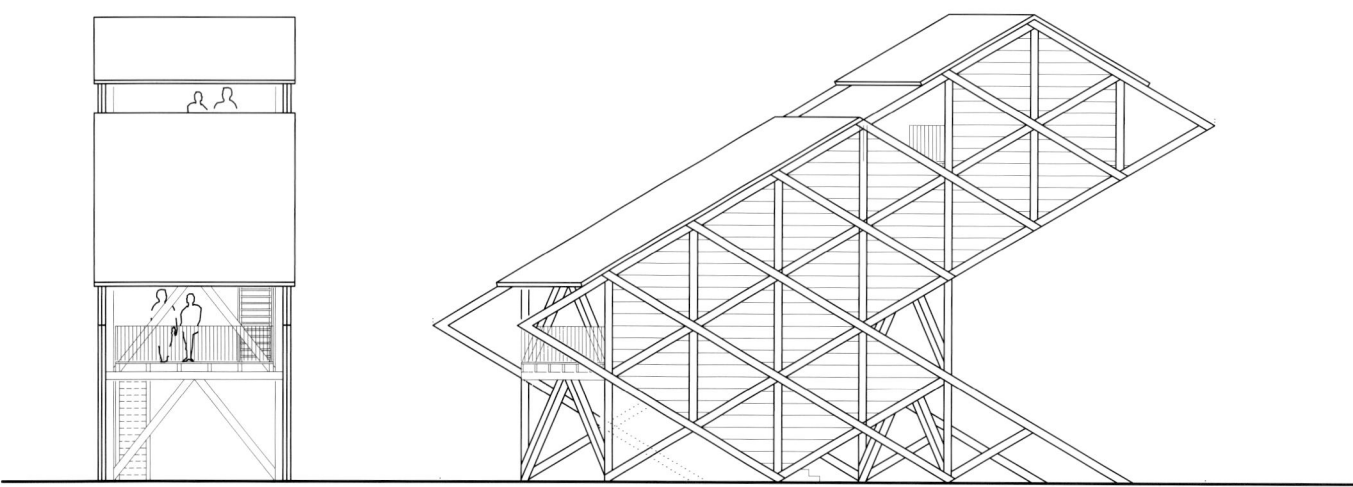

05

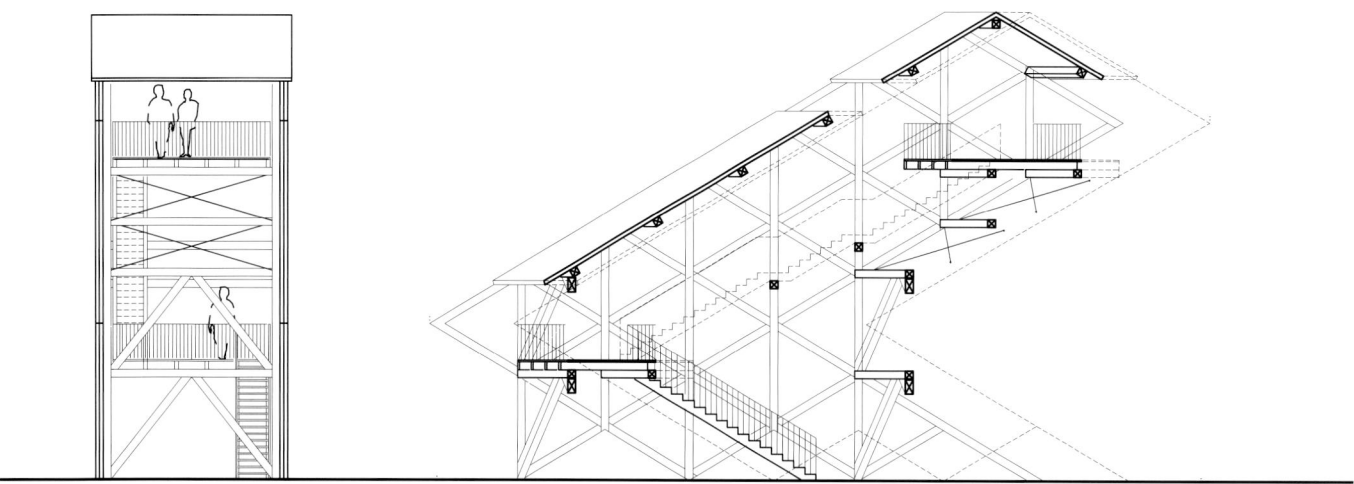

Cliff tree house, 2007
Address: New York, USA. **Client:** private. **Gross floor area:** cabin 10 m², terrace 14 m². **Materials:** wood, stainless steel.

Ship's hatch in a treetop

ARCHITECTS: baumraum / Andreas Wenning

This tree house is located on an east-facing cliff on a spectacular private property near the Hudson river in upstate New York. The main body of the tree house projects over the cliff and is supported closest to the cliff edge by two short posts, and at the overhanging edge by a long, slanting fork. The weight of the terrace is borne by steel cables suspended from the Canadian maple. The lateral walls of the tree house have been constructed as framed supports. They have been clad on the interior with oak shuttering, mineral wool insulation and windproof foil sheeting, and on the outside with ventilated, horizontal panelling. Broad, rough-sawn larch boards, painted silver, were used for the exterior cladding. The interior furnishing of the tree house is sparse, comprising merely a reclining area and a wooden bench. There are windows on all four sides, fitted on the outside with high-quality insect screens. The tree house also includes a skylight that is reminiscent of a ship's hatch.

04

05

06

07

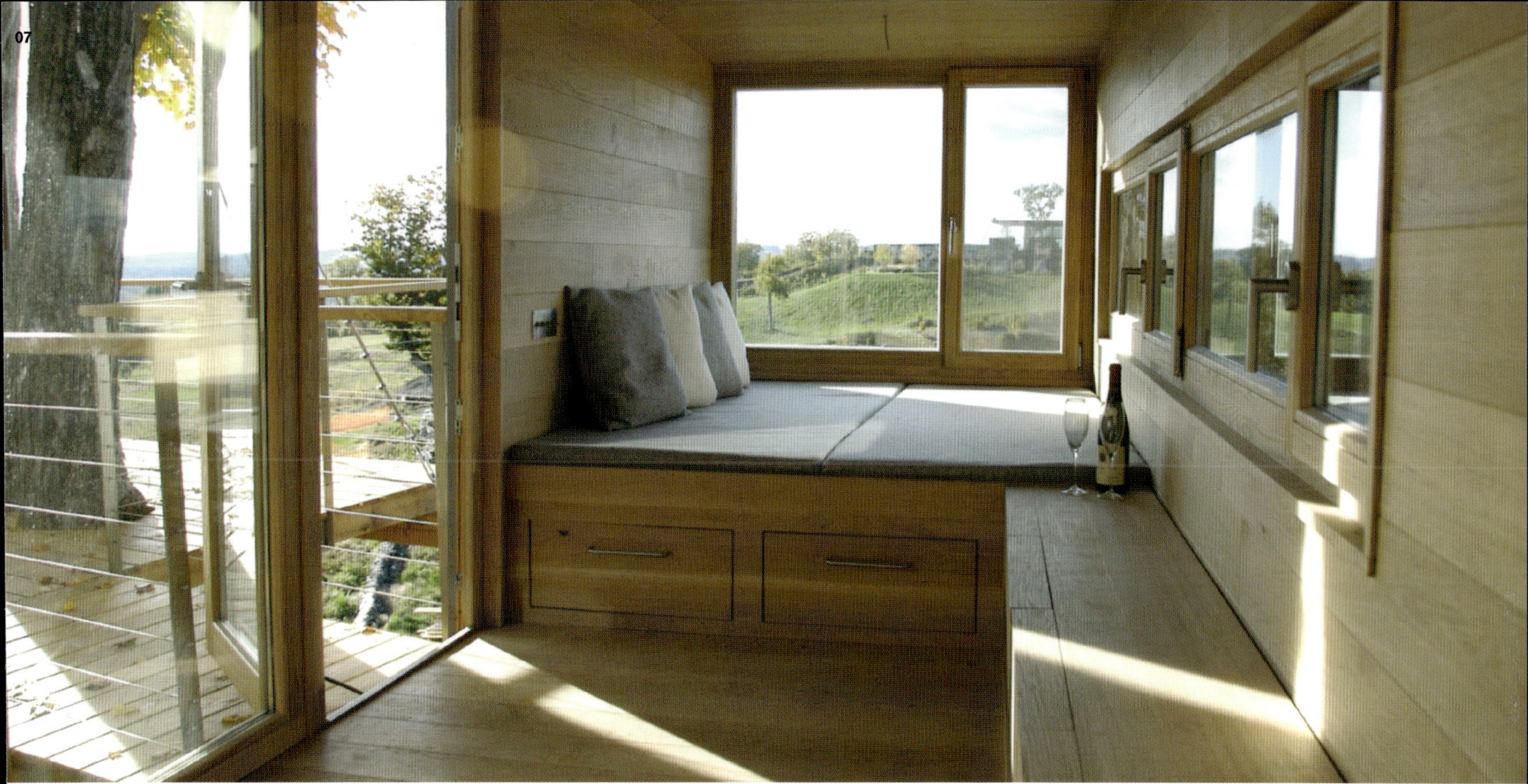

08

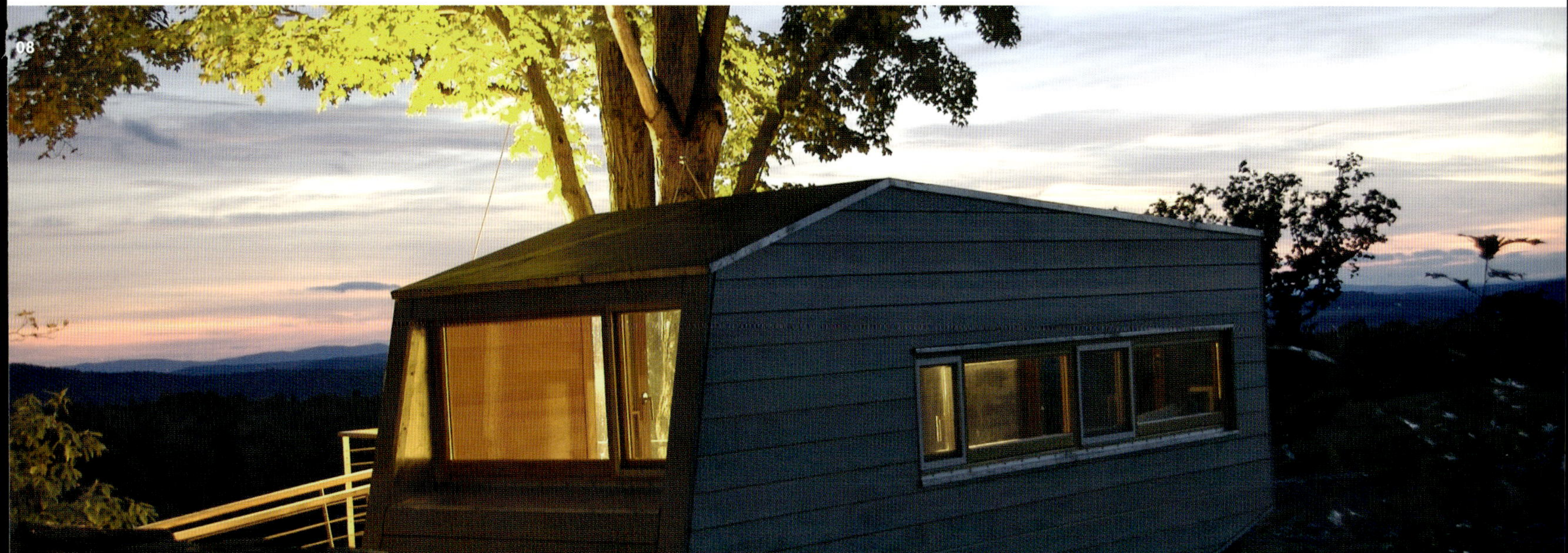

Poolhouse, 2001
Address: 4182 Old Adobe Road, Palo Alto, CA 94306, USA. **Client:** Richard and Victoria Burt. **Gross floor area:** 71 m². **Materials:** Douglas fir posts and beams.

Butterfly roof for the pool

ARCHITECTS: Min | Day

The site is a one-acre hillside lot in Palo Alto, adjoining open space with views to the south and west. The project involves a total reworking of the rear yard, which includes an existing home built in the 1970s. The new poolhouse building consists of a series of interlocking spaces organized within an uniformly repeated structure of Douglas-fir posts and beams set eight feet (2.44 meters) on center. Closest to and most visible from the main house is the screened porch, which evokes a summer cabin; next is a small kitchen that is strategically located between the terrace and screened porch on one side and the main living space on the other. A Douglas-fir butterfly roof opens the room to sunlight, as well as revealing views to the south and the steep landscaped slope at the rear. Three different types of wood were used: Douglas-fir, Western Red Cedar, and Maple. Douglas-fir was used throughout for the structure of the building, Cedar for cladding exterior and interior walls and protecting the structure, and Maple for cabinetry and millwork.

04

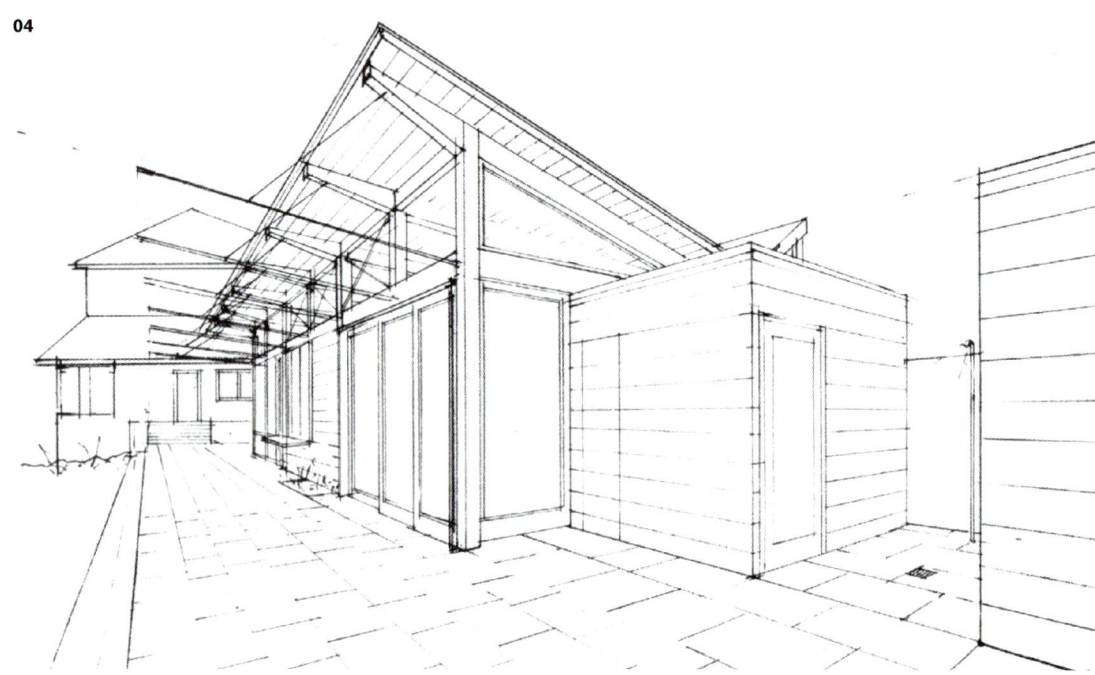

01 View of the kitchen 02 View of cedar-clad mechanical sauna volume 03 Screened porch view 04 Sketch 05 Section through poolhouse, site and existing pool 06 View of maple AV cabinet 07 Screened porch in the evening

05

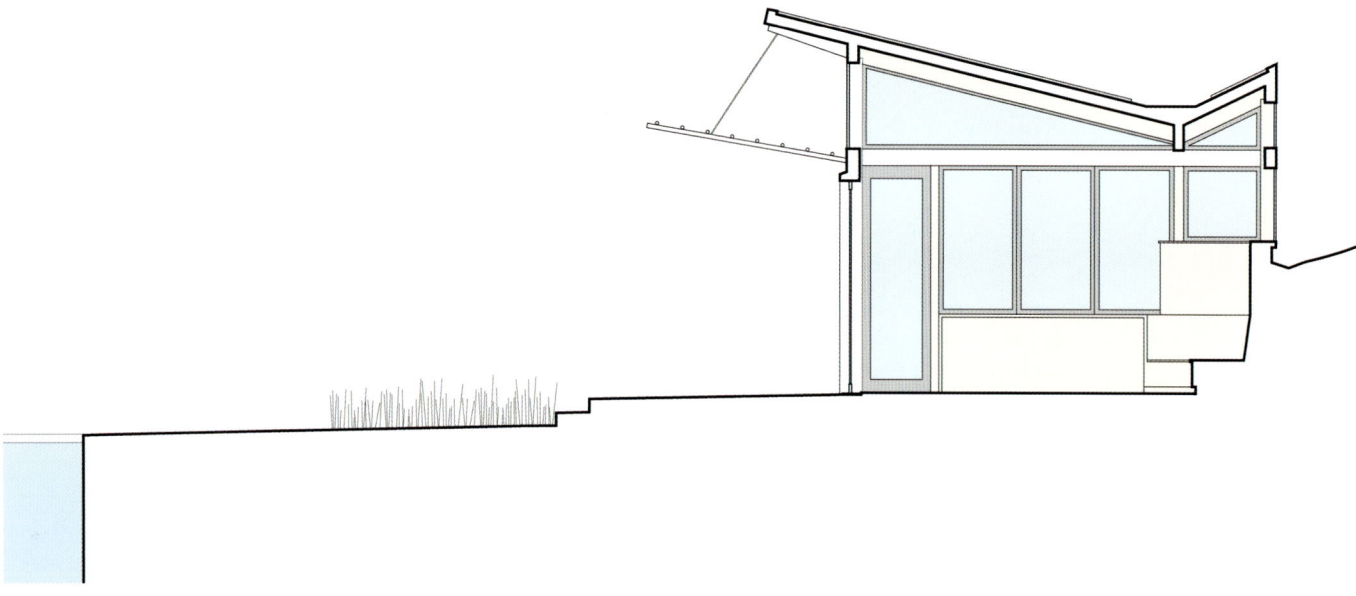

06

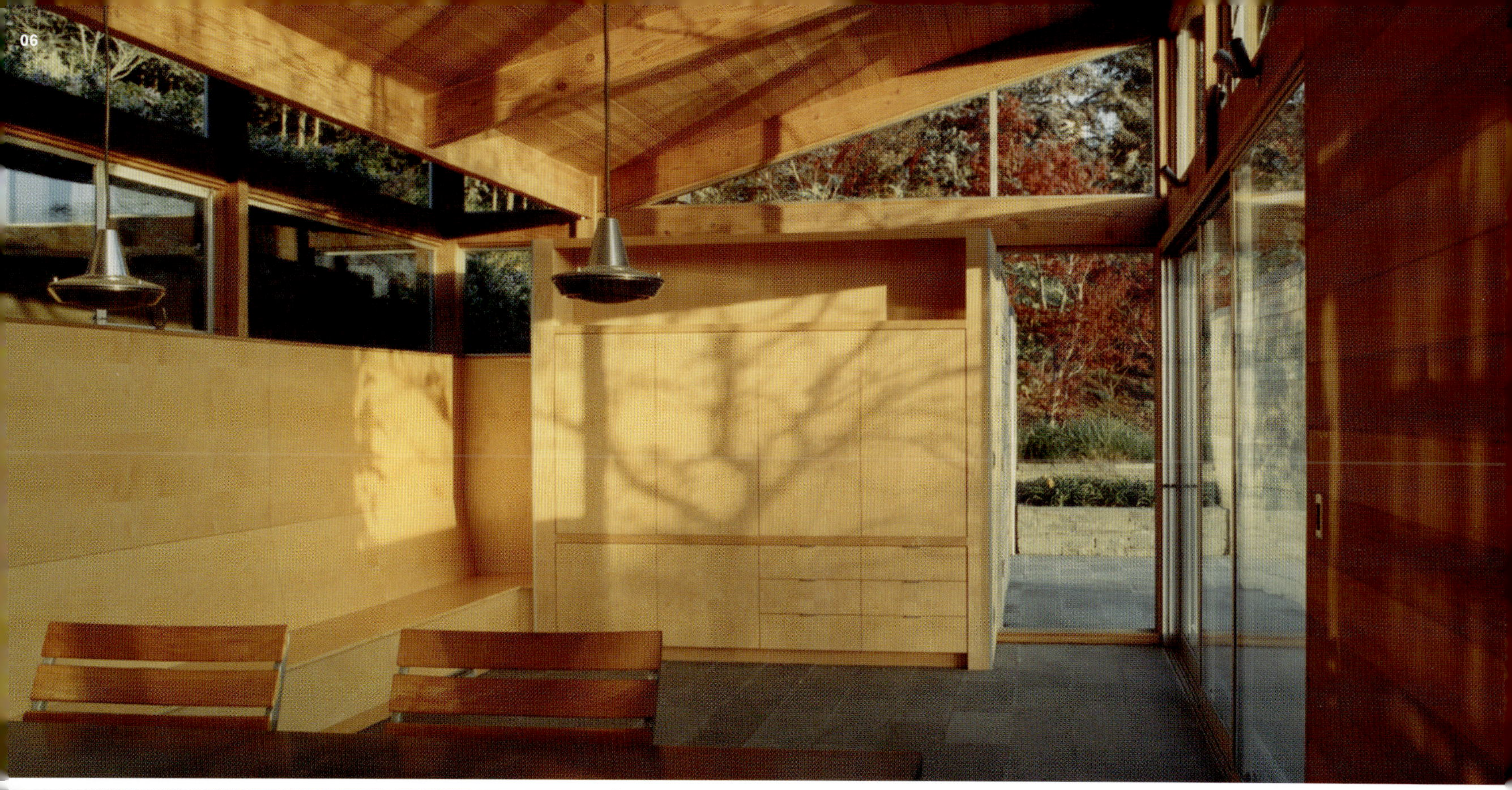

07

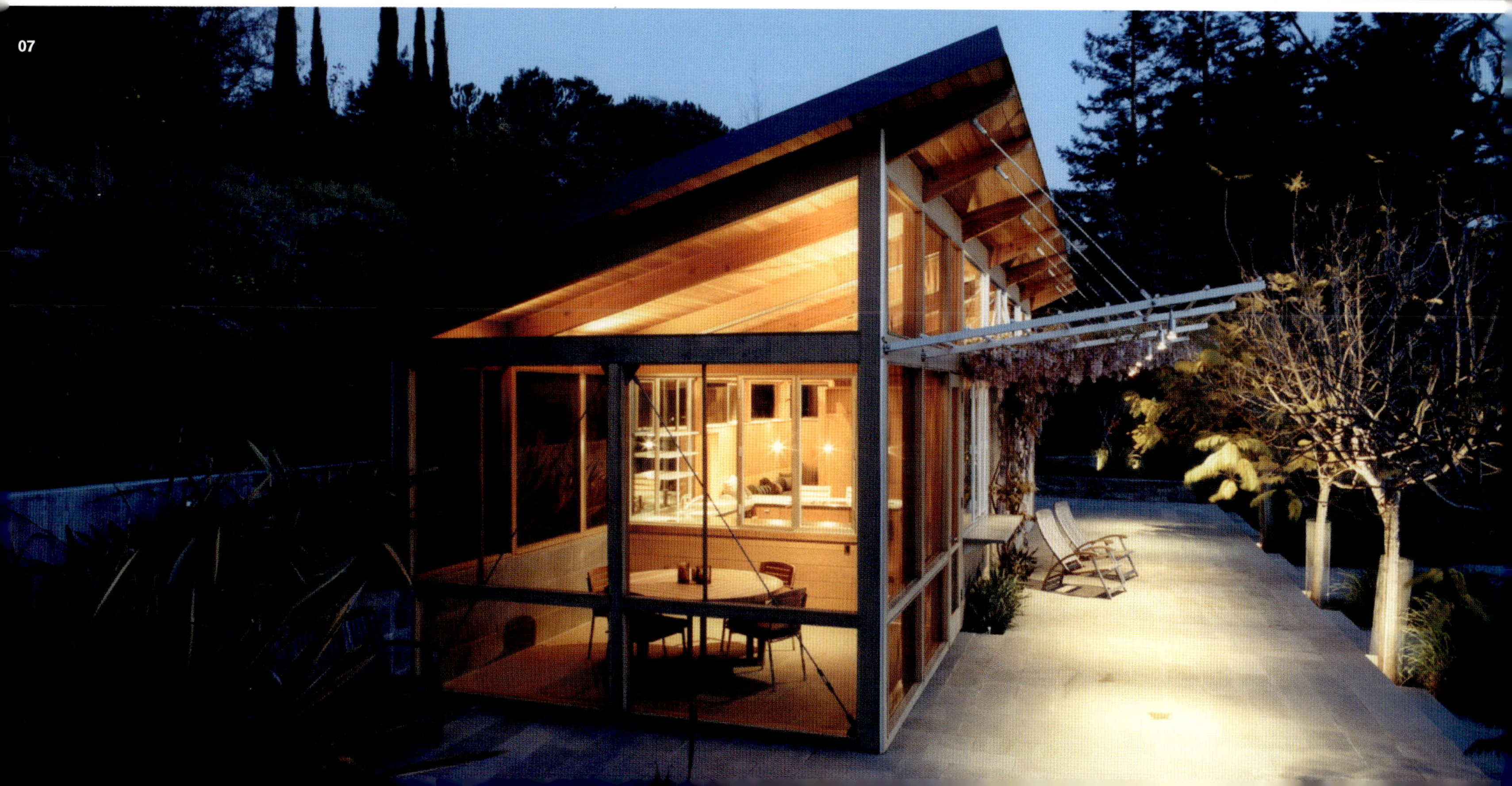

Writing with Light House, 2004
Address: Eastern Long Island, New York, USA. **Client:** private. **Gross floor area:** 511 m² including basement.
Materials: Exterior: weathered cedar slats over cedar boards and vertical cedar batten; Interior: stained concrete floors, pine wood floors, plastered walls.

Seven in Eight

ARCHITECTS: Steven Holl Architects

The concept of this linear wooden beach house was inspired by its close proximity to the studio of the painter Jackson Pollock. Several free-form designs were made based on the 1949 painting "Seven in Eight". Opening up the interior to the bay and the north view of the Atlantic Ocean required closing the south side for privacy. The final scheme brackets the internal energy in an open frame, through which the sun projects lines. The strips of white light inscribe and seasonally bend internal spaces dynamically with the daily cycle. The balloon frame construction is comparable to the strip wood sand dune fencing along the ocean. Guest rooms swirl around the double level living room. From the upper court, the ocean is visible. The exterior skin of the house consists of T1-11 boards, an economical plywood siding material, with vertical red cedar spacers on top, onto which the horizontal red cedar slats are mounted. The decking and rails are also in red cedar.

04

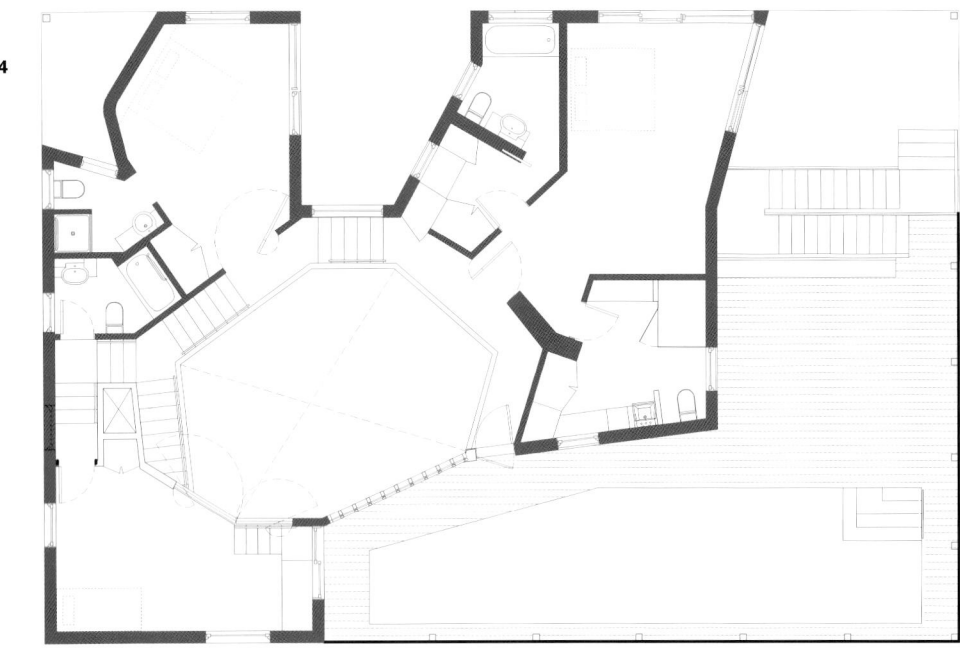

05

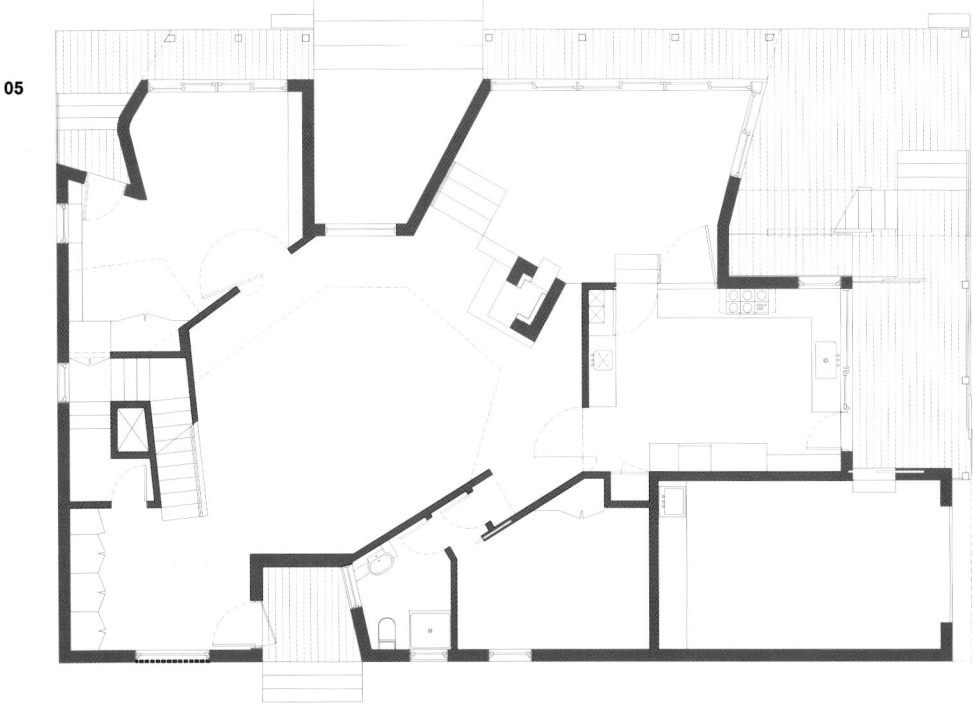

Service building – sports grounds, 2003
Address: 73326 Deggingen, Germany. **Client:** Turn-verein Deggingen. **Gross floor area:** 580 m². **Materials:** wood panel construction.

An innovative energy system
ARCHITECTS: Mario Hägele

The design of this building is as simple as the construction brief – to build an attractive wooden structure as a sports service building. The building forms a harmonious relationship to the surrounding landscape, the access path naturally following the existing contours of the site. Visitors approach the clubhouse, with its pulpit-like veranda, by crossing a stream. The effect is like passing through a gateway that clearly defines the entrance to the sports ground. The building is pre-equipped to utilize an innovative energy system, which was not installed immediately due to budgetary constraints – pipes have been laid in the grounds to facilitate a geothermal heat exchange system. This system fulfills three functions: room heating in winter with a connected heat pump; spatial cooling in summer, if necessary with the help of the heat pump system but principally using mechanical ventilation; and year-round heating of water for showers, using the heat pump.

04

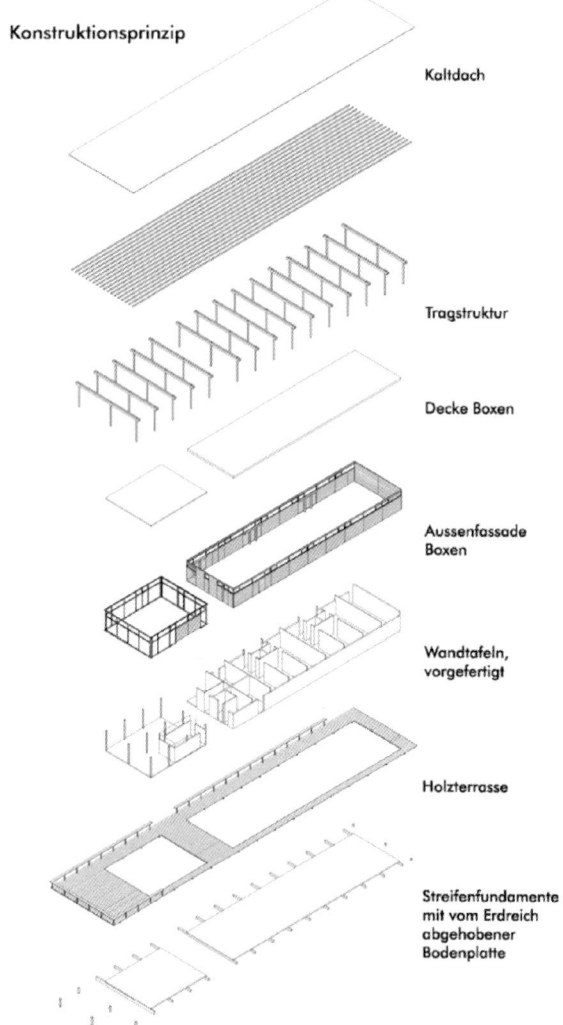

Konstruktionsprinzip

Kaltdach

Tragstruktur

Decke Boxen

Aussenfassade Boxen

Wandtafeln, vorgefertigt

Holzterrasse

Streifenfundamente mit vom Erdreich abgehobener Bodenplatte

05

Lager — Umkleide 2 — Dusche 2 — Umkleide 2 — Umkleide 1 — Dusche 1 — Umkleide 1 — Technik — Lager — Schiri — Clubraum

Kupla – the Bubble, 2002
Address: Korkeasaari Zoo, Helsinki, Finland. **Client:** Korkeasaari Zoo. **Gross floor area:** 82 m². **Materials:** timber.

Like an eggshell

ARCHITECTS: HUT Wood Studio / Ville Hara, architect SAFA

The site is eighteen meters above sea level, giving the tower a prominence when viewed from the Helsinki sea line. The free form is inspired by its natural setting: it follows the existing low stone wall and skirts around a small birch grove. From January to May 2001 students at the Wood Studio workshop developed the draft design. As the irregular form proved difficult to manage, the architect first molded a plastoline model. Digital images of the model then functioned as a basis for the AutoCAD drawings. Finally, between June and August 2002, the tower was erected by an international group of eight architecture students. The hot, sunny summer dried the timber, and the duct pipes that were used for steaming proved useful. The structure behaves like an eggshell; even if the gridshell, which consists of over 600 joints, were punctured it would continue to bear the load. The load bearing gridshell structure consists of 72 gluelam battens, with timber sections of 60 x 60 mm bent and twisted on site from seven preformed types. As the tower has no structural protection against weathering, it was treated with a linen-oil-based wood balm with UV-screen.

05

+28180

+24160

+21280

+18400

01

Viikki Church, 2005
Address: Agronominkatu 5, Helsinki, Finland. **Client:** Helsinki Parishes, Markku Koskinen. **Gross floor area:** 1,566 m². **Materials:** glulam beams and columns, prefabricated timber wall and ceiling elements.

God's rock – in wood

ARCHITECTS: JKMM Architects:
Samuli Miettinen, Asmo Jaaksi, Teemu Kurkela,
Juha Mäki-Jyllilä, Päivi Meuronen

This church combines modern and ancient building methods, sophisticated and rough-hewn surfaces, location and purpose, temporality and eternity. The intention of the client was to create a modern successor to the long tradition of Finnish wooden churches, while taking into account the principles of ecology and sustainability that are practiced throughout the Viikki area. The architectural choices on which this building is based were guided by prefabrication, as the church was built entirely of factory-made components. The building was braced by attaching insulated outer wall elements to the pillars, and ceiling panels to the glulam beams. The paneling was attached to the plate stiffener of the inner walls in the factory. The untreated and gray-aged façade has been clad in cleft aspen shingles and fine-sawn drop siding. The interior lining of spruce was treated with a lye wash, making it easier to clean and restore. Form-pressed veneer elements were added to the false ceiling to improve the acoustics.

02

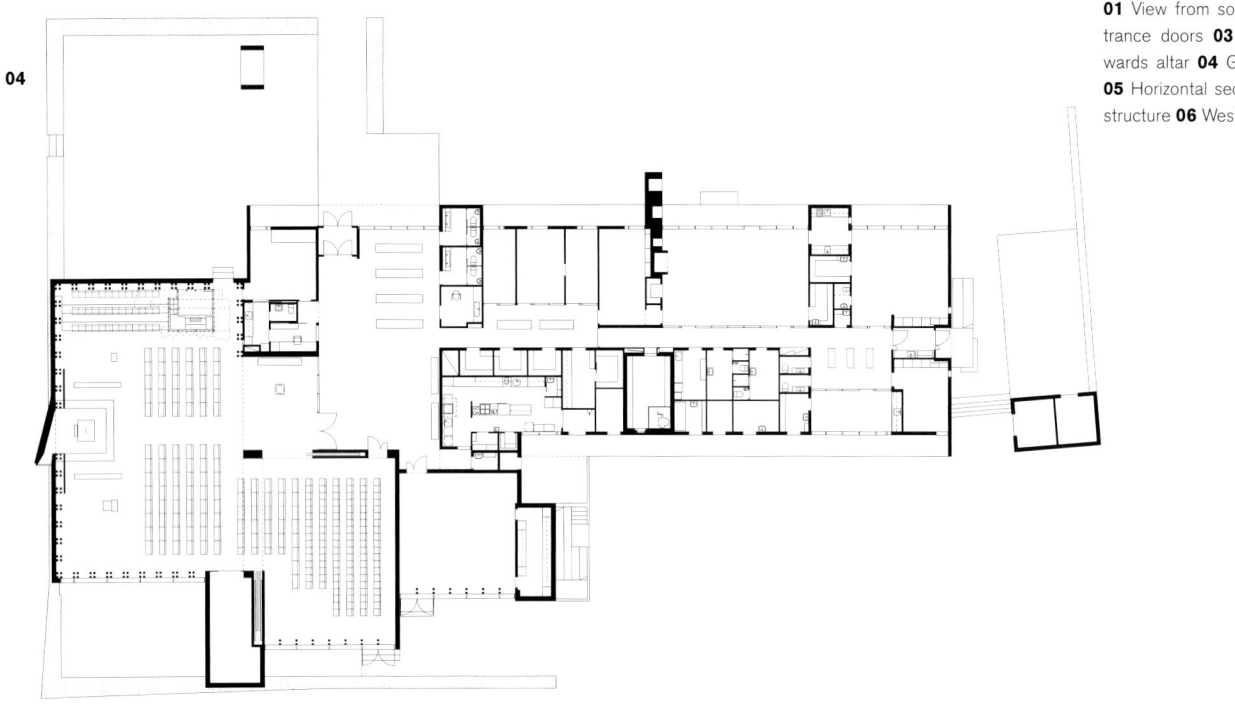

04

01 View from south **02** Main entrance doors **03** Church hall towards altar **04** Ground floor plan **05** Horizontal section of the wall-structure **06** West façade

05

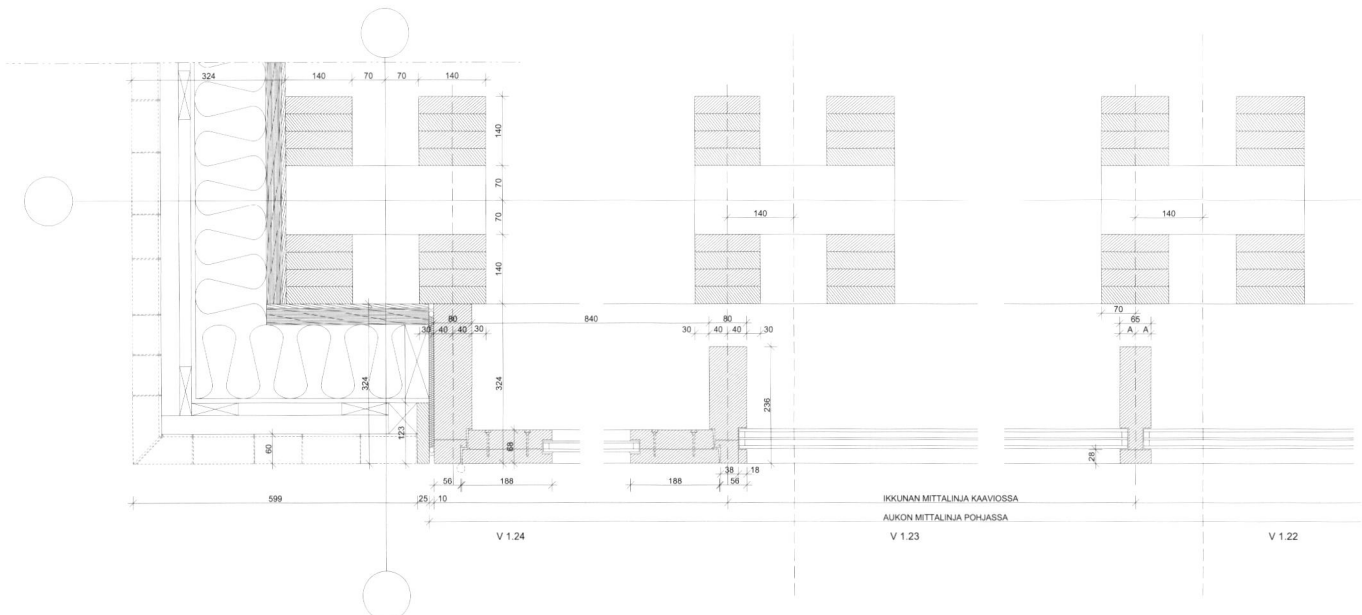

IKKUNAN MITTALINJA KAAVIOSSA
AUKON MITTALINJA POHJASSA

V 1.24   V 1.23   V 1.22

Information and Visitor Center, Renaissance Zoo at Schloss Raesfeld, 2005
Address: Hagenwiese 40, 46348 Raesfeld, Germany.
Client: Trägerverein Tiergarten Schloss Raesfeld e. V.
Gross floor area: 912 m². **Materials:** structural framework of glue-laminated timber, larchwood wall panels, wall and ceiling lining in larchwood slats.

A sense of dialectic

ARCHITECTS: Farwick + Grote

Architects & Urban Planners

The Information and Visitor Center at the Schloss Raesfeld Renaissance Zoo is located at the edge of a forest within view of the palace itself. Any building located so close to a forest will necessarily be inclined to conduct a dialogue between nature and culture. In this case, the architectural design is also influenced by a sense of dialectic: Openness and restriction, light and shadow define this building. The key feature here is a double façade of glass and wood. Thanks to reflections on the glass surface, the building becomes a medium for the natural surroundings. The building is thus transformed by changes in the seasons, daylight and position of the sun. The reflections of the neighboring forest produce the effect of visually merging interior and exterior, building and forest.

03

Ausstellung

Naturklasse

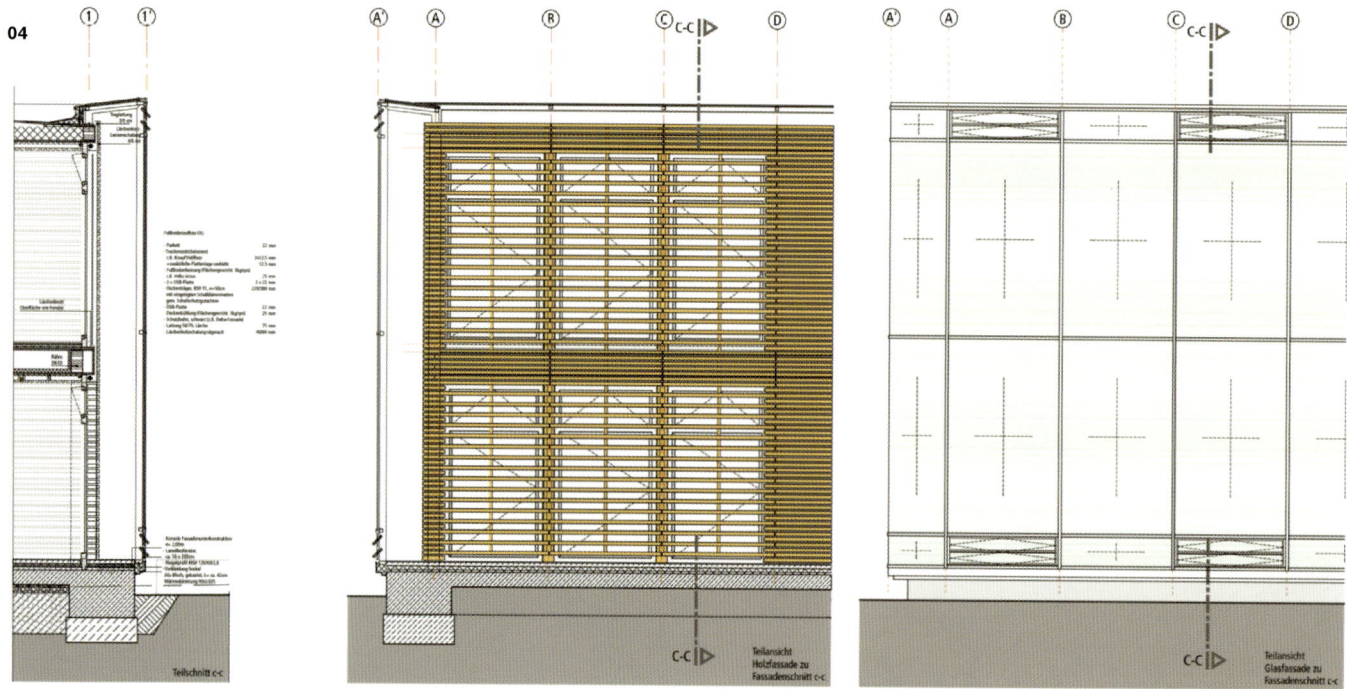

04

Teilschnitt c-c

C-C ▷ Teilansicht Holzfassade zu Fassadenschnitt c-c

C-C ▷ Teilansicht Glasfassade zu Fassadenschnitt c-c

Children's day-care center, 2005
Address: Kaiser-Friedrich-Ufer 5, 20259 Hamburg, Germany. **Client:** Vereinigung Hamburger Kindertagesstätten GmbH (Association of Children's Day-care Centers in Hamburg). **Gross floor area:** 1,180 m². **Materials:** wooden pre-fabricated structure / horizontal stiffening in reinforced concrete.

Siberian larch

ARCHITECTS: Wacker Zeiger Architekten

This day-care center replaced temporary buildings, which explains why the authorities in Hamburg issued a building permit in a designated parkland area in the leafy district of Eimsbüttel. The architects designed a slim elongated structure that minimizes the building's imprint in this green zone, and neither blocks nor detracts from the view of the canal. Because of budgetary constraints and the desire for rapid completion, a new building regulation in Hamburg requires that day-care centers be constructed in wood. For this reason, timber panels were used as the load-bearing structure — for the exterior walls and ceilings a frame of diffusion-tight paneling on the inside and diffusion-open sheeting on the outside was used. Interior walls are made of timber framing with dry-lined infilling. This allows the room partitioning to be easily changed as required. The sculptural façade is constructed from strips of Siberian larch in a curtain-like form, and mounted on a low sub-structure. The larch quickly assumed its distinctive silver-gray patina.

03

04

05

01 Main entrance **02** Inside-outside view **03** View from southwest **04** North elevation **05** South elevation **06** East elevation **07** West elevation **08** Front court **09** Exterior view

06

07

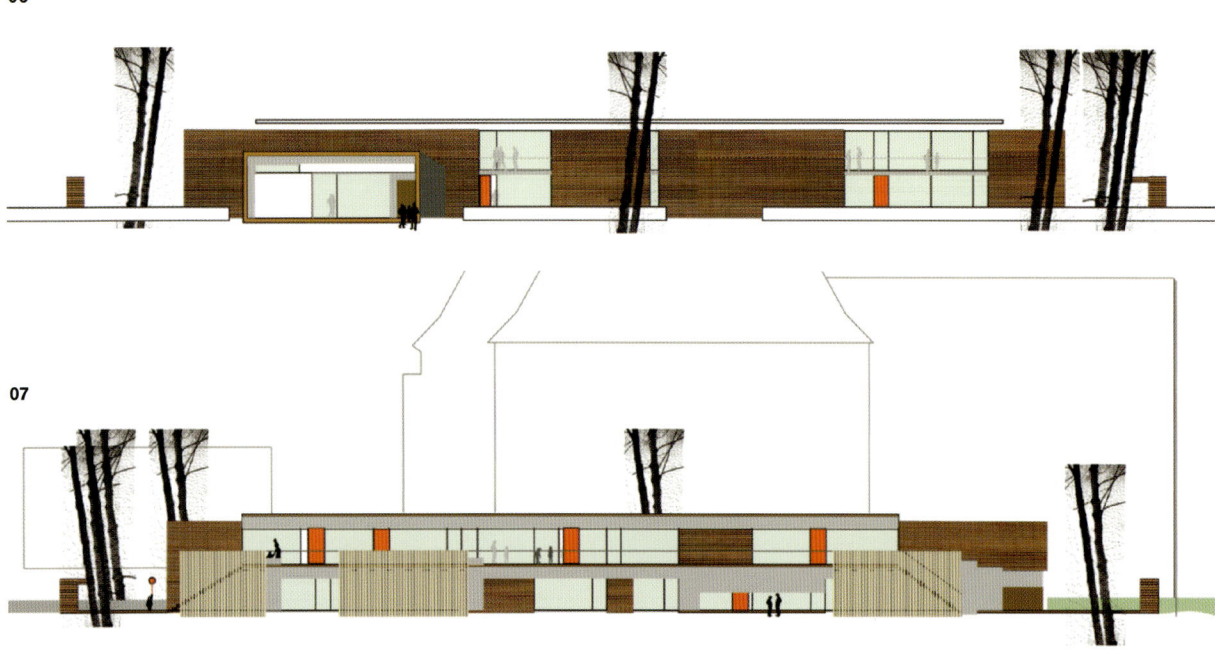

08

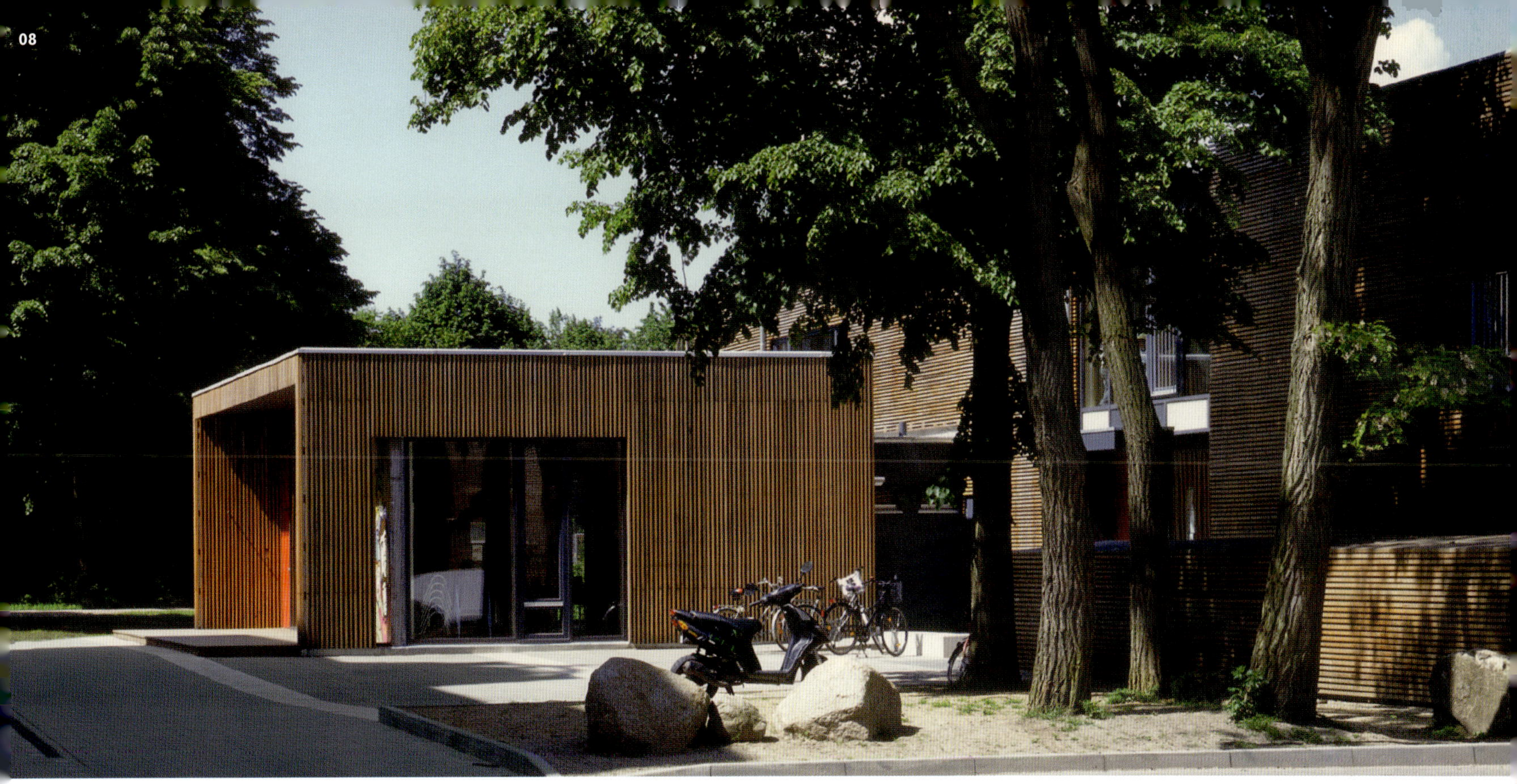

09

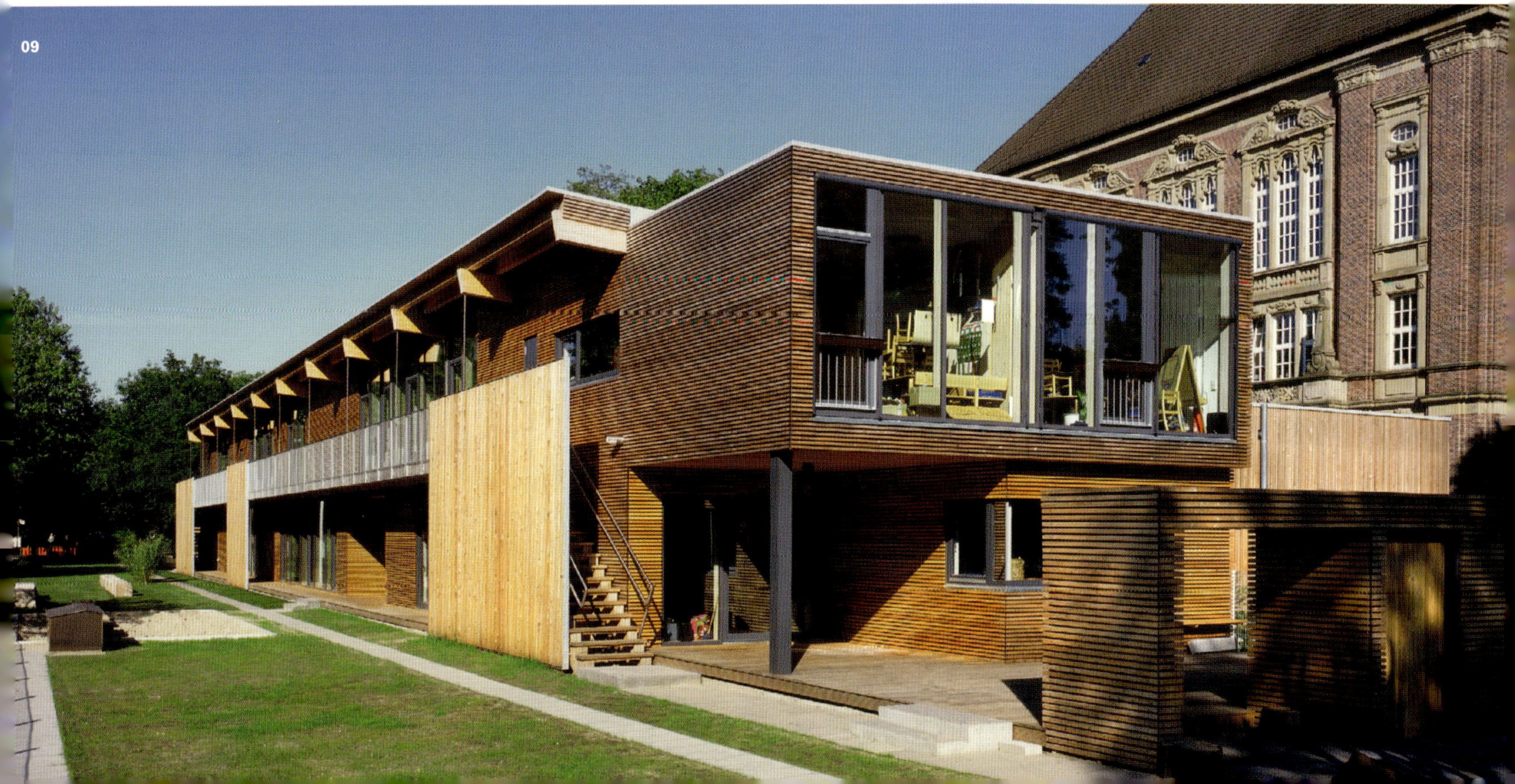

01

Retirement and nursing home, 2005
Address: 10. Oktoberstraße 30, 9754 Steinfeld, Austria. **Client:** Sozialhilfeverband (social services association) Spittal/Drau. **Gross floor area:** 3,658 m². **Materials:** timber construction.

Cast from a mould

ARCHITECTS: Dietger Wissounig

The scenic beauty of the Drava valley forms the backdrop for this unusual retirement home. The elongated building looks like it was cast from a mould. The architect resolved the issue of spatial integrity by including two corridors that run the full length of the building. The volume between these two corridors — the core of the building — becomes a multi-story atrium. Apart from bridges on the first and second floors connecting the east and west sides of the building, this atrium does not contain any structures. Yet it serves to visually unite every level of the building. The atrium is gradually turning into a miniature jungle, which functions as a climatic buffer. From there, pre-warmed or pre-cooled air is captured in ground collectors and channeled into the living spaces. The Steinfeld retirement and nursing home is a low-energy house with heating energy requirements of approx. 15 kWh per square meter.

02

04

05

48

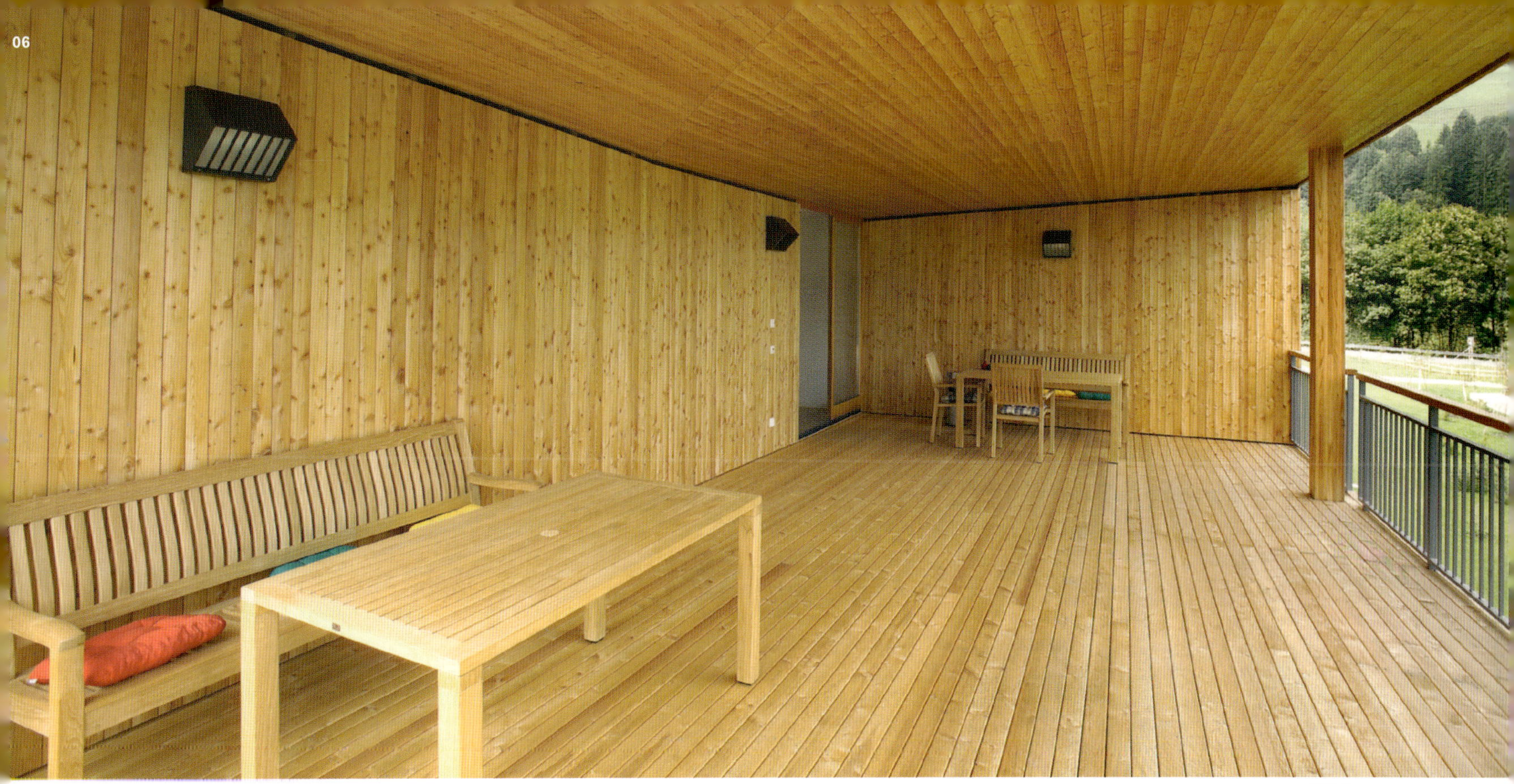
06

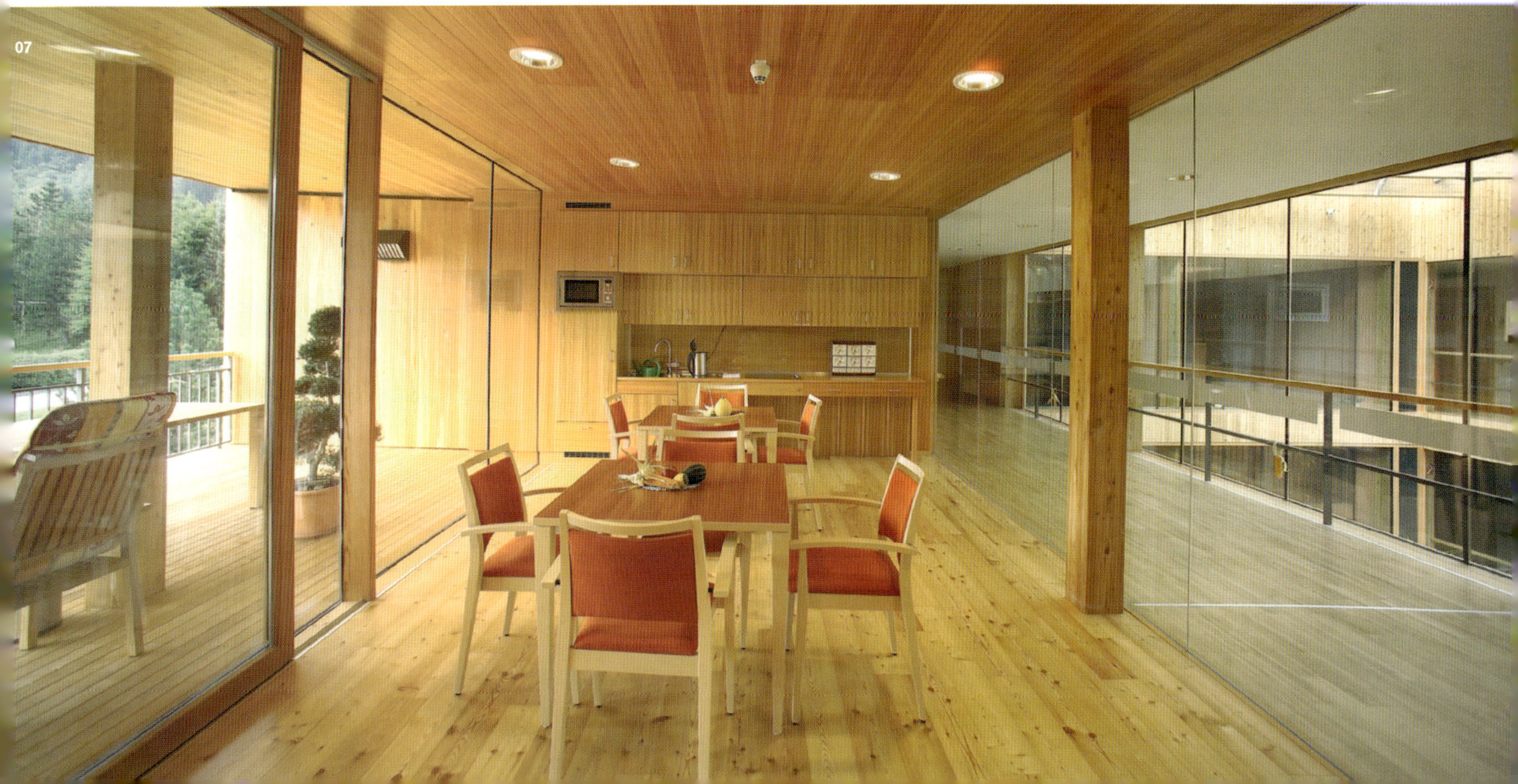
07

Revital Nussdorf, 2004
Address: Nussdorf 71, 9900 Nussdorf-Debant, Austria.
Client: Maria Mietschnig & Klaus Michor. **Net floor
area:** 419 m². **Materials:** energy-saving wood skeleton
construction.

A multi-sensual material

ARCHITECTS: Architekturbüro Steinklammer

This new office building for one of Austria's landscape planning firms is built on a south-facing slope
with a commanding view of the Lienz Valley. The building reflects the activities of its occupants: it is located
in open countryside, and constructed of timber. Tiered,
veranda-like spaces are incorporated into each of the
building's three floors. In addition to open spaces the offices also offers many niches and enclosed spaces. The
east-facing side of the building is closed off by a slanting, oak-paneled stairwell. This external stairwell allows
the building to later be converted into three separate
living units. Revital's work involves landscape planning
and sustainable, forward-looking ecological solutions.
Wood is, essentially, this firm's model material. That
is why wood is used wherever possible in this building – as a structural material, as floor covering and as
paneling for walls and ceilings. Wood, with its great
variety of form and appearance, is a truly sensual
material: its texture appeals to our sense of touch, its
appearance to our visual sense, and its fragrance to our
sense of smell.

02

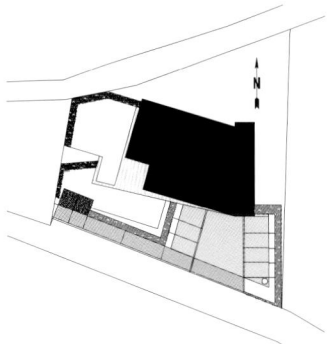

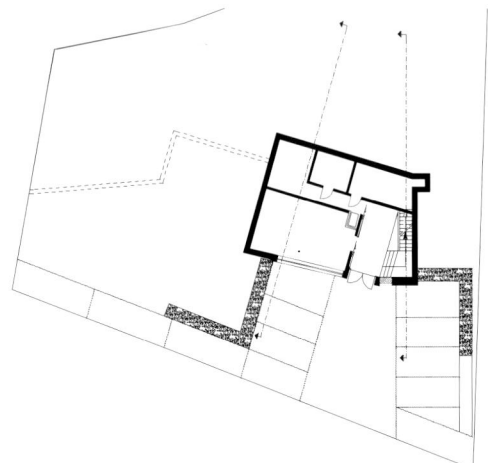

GRUNDRISS KELLERGESCHOSS

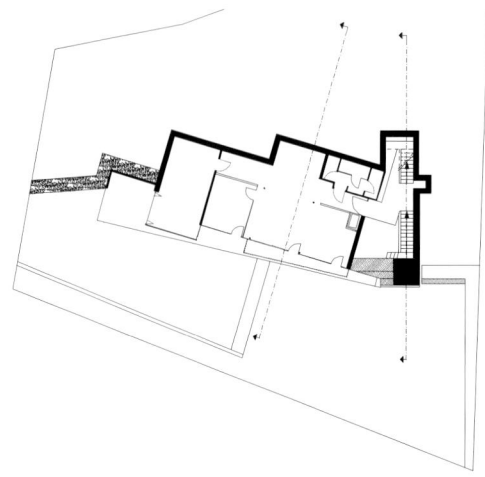

GRUNDRISS ERDGESCHOSS

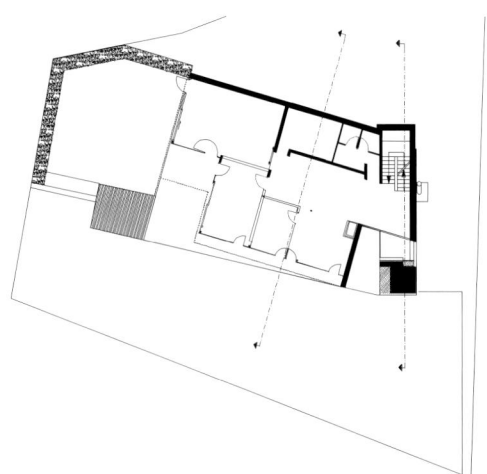

GRUNDRISS 1.OBERGESCHOSS

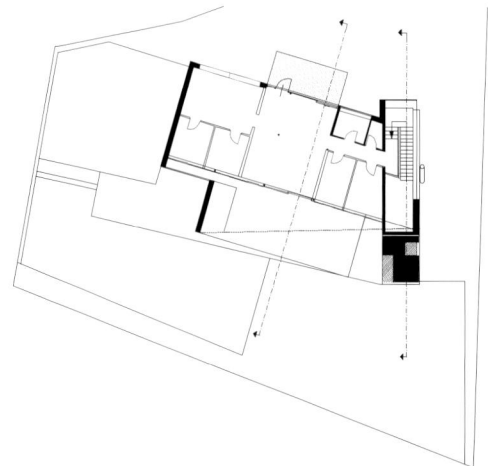

GRUNDRISS 2.OBERGESCHOSS

Rucksack House, since 2004
Site: as a temporary, "parasitic" structure the Rucksack House can be installed on various urban façades.
Client: Stefan Eberstadt / plan project. **Dimensions:** 2.5 x 3.6 x 2.5 meters. **Materials:** Structure: welded steel cage; Exterior: weather-resistant laminated plywood, steel cables; Interior: birch veneer; Plexiglas windows.

Rucksack House

ARCHITECTS: Stefan Eberstadt

With his "Rucksack House" project, the artist Stefan Eberstadt addresses contemporary architectural issues such as mobility and flexibility, thereby reacting to the changing conditions of modern life. Because this structure is so unique – a room suspended by steel cables from the façade of another building – Rucksack House has attracted at lot of interest and attention. As its name suggests, the Rucksack House functions according to the same principle as a backpack; it hangs from its "host", creating a separate and private space within the realm of the public space. Rucksack House attracted huge public and media attention when it was first installed at the former cotton mill (Baumwollspinnerei) in Leipzig in 2004. From there it has been moved and attached to an apartment building in Cologne between September 2005 and March 2006.

02

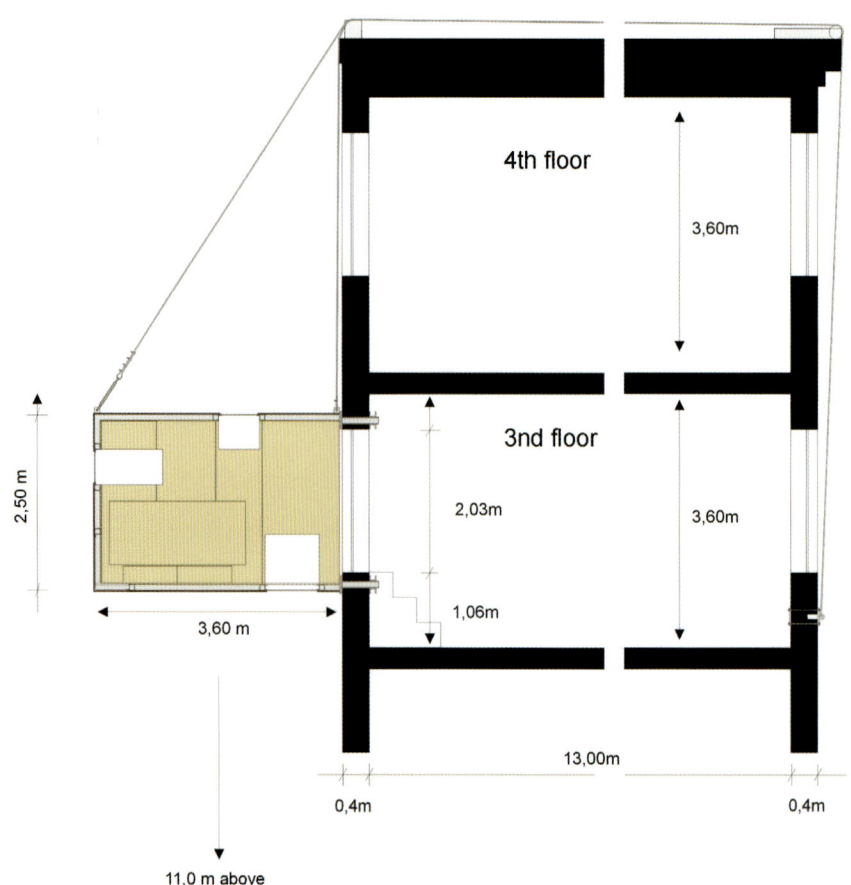

4th floor

3,60m

3nd floor

2,03m

3,60m

2,50 m

1,06m

3,60 m

13,00m

0,4m

0,4m

11,0 m above
ground level

01 View of façade **02** Cross section **03** Exterior view, cube

Espace Gruyère, 2000
Address: Rue de Vevey 136–144, 1630 Bulle, Switzerland. **Technical direction:** Atelier d'architecture A3 – Maillard – Francey – Grandjean, Bulle. **Client:** SI Espace Gruyère SA (Municipality of Bulle, Agrarian association, Market of Gruyère). **Gross floor area:** 8,400 m². **Materials:** wood and steel.

Ice rink in a cowshed
ARCHITECTS:

O. Galletti & C. Matter with Yves Jaccot

The principal purpose of this building is to accommodate up to 500 cows or bulls when the main cattle markets are held. However, the building also accommodates an ice rink / theater, as well as trade fairs and exhibitions. The covered market acts as an interface between region, town and district. It is composed of two volumes that interpenetrate one another. The second volume, in copper, houses the theater, ice rink and service building, and also acts as the entrance to the market. Because of its position, this volume reconstructs the north face of the Place des Albergeux and creates a relationship with the village. The introverted, horizontal space of the market / exhibition hall is defined by a wooden enclosure that creates the rural atmosphere specified in the brief. Its roof also provides the natural lighting and ventilation needed by the animals. The main elements that define the image and ambience of the building are in wood: the façade and roof of the exhibition hall; the façade and structure of the ice rink / theater.

01 View from south 02 Terraces of
the presentation hall 03 Ice rink 04
Floor plan, entrance level 05 Cross
section through presentation hall
06 Covered market

04

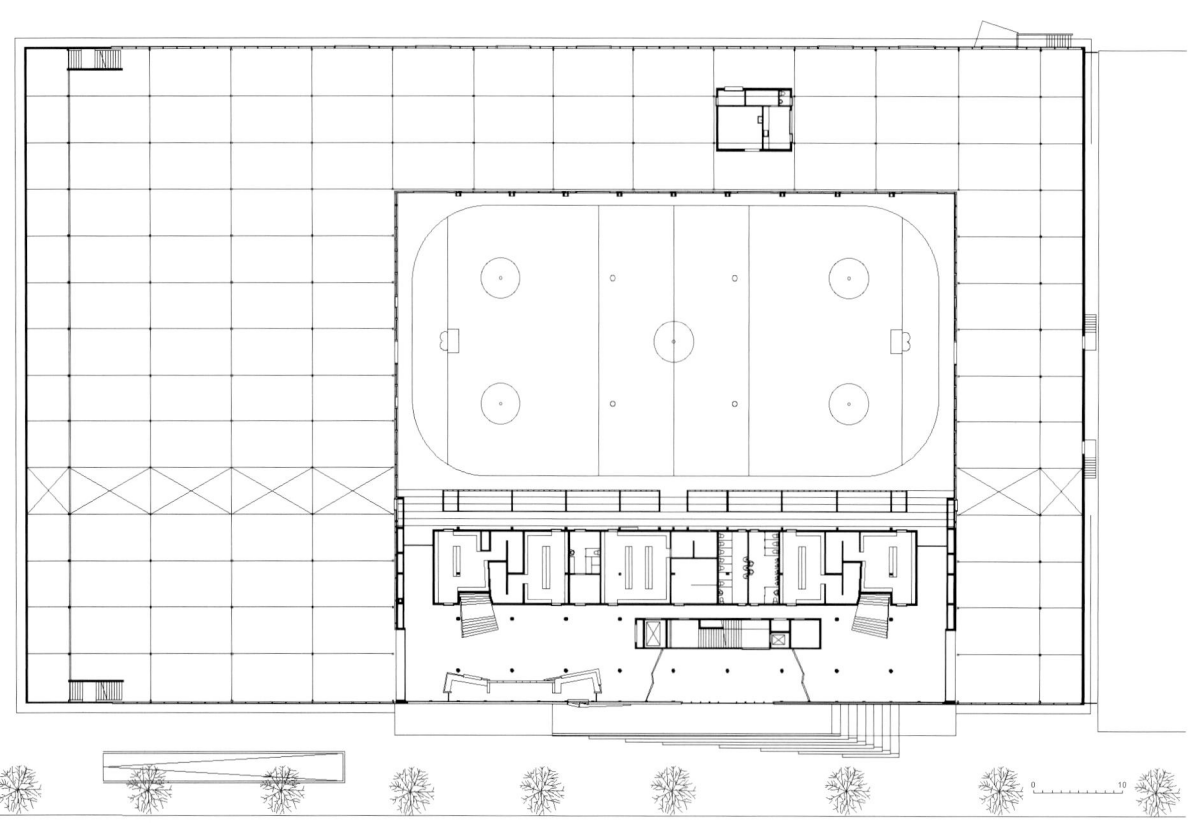

05

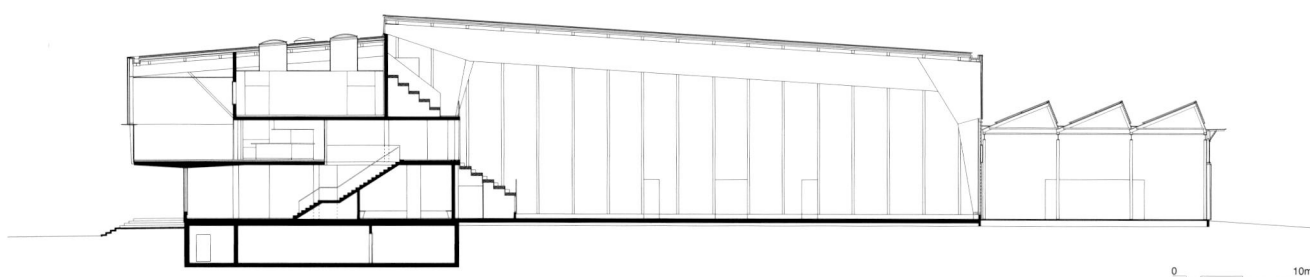

58

Montessori Werkhaus der Generationen (Generational Workshop), 2006
Address: Zusmarshauser Straße 19, 86637 Wertingen, Germany. **Client:** GbR Krug – Dohrn, Augsburg. **Net floor area:** 853 m². **Materials:** solid wood ceilings and walls.

A window to nature

ARCHITECTS: Eberle Architekten

The key concept behind this building was to create a feeling of being within nature. This is achieved thanks to a wood and glass façade that gives each room a "window to nature". Wood is the predominant material in this building. The idyllic setting of the meadowlands that border the Zusam river called for a sensitive architectural response. The architect Werner Eberle chose to reduce the optical impact of this building by designing a recessed upper floor. The building thus adopts a terraced appearance that imitates the natural contour of the surrounding terrain as it runs down to the river. This effort to adapt to the environment is also evidenced in the grass roof and a color scheme on the façade that reflects the seasonal changes in color tone of the surrounding foliage.

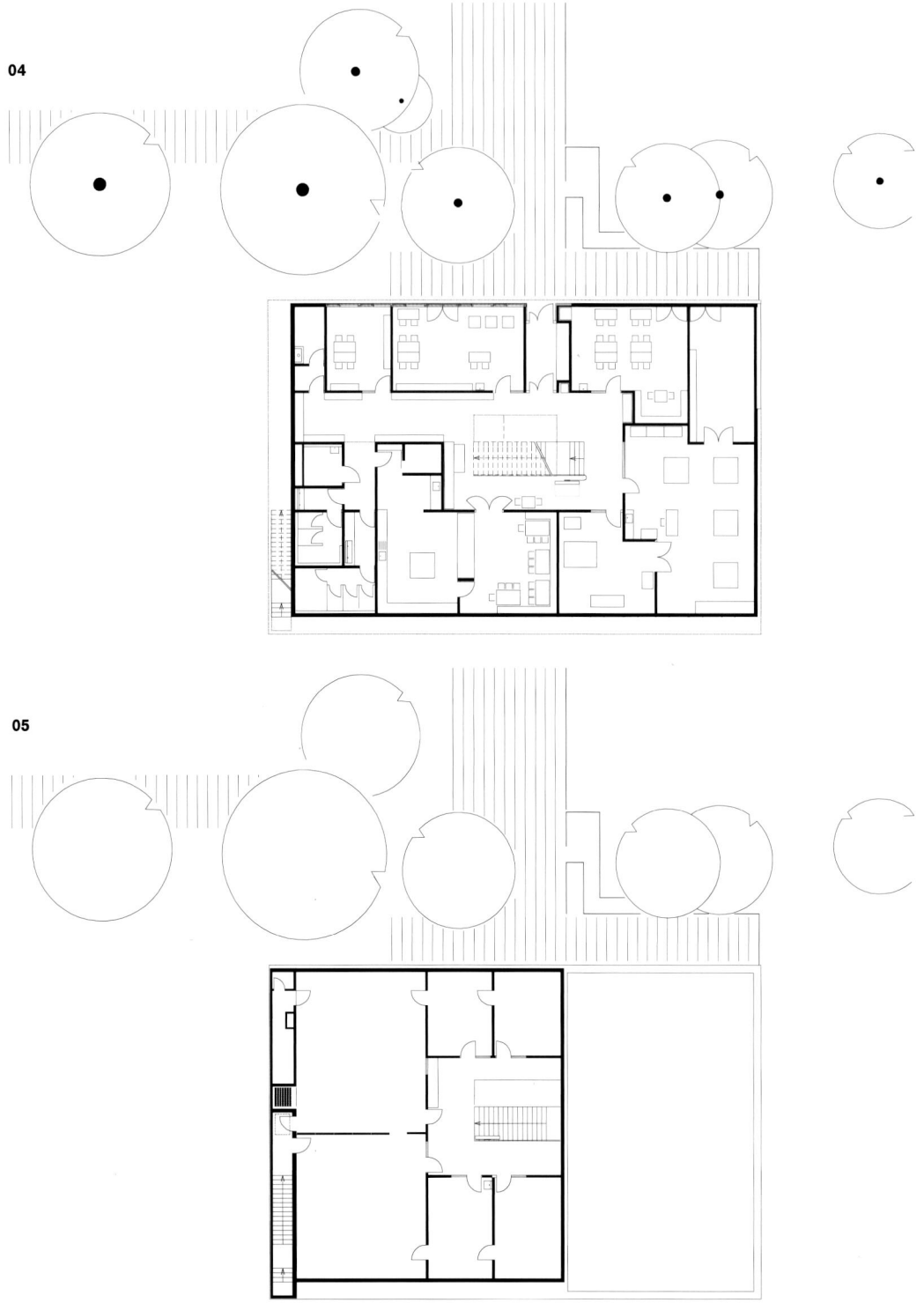

04

05

01 General view **02** View from the garden **03** Exterior view **04** Ground floor plan **05** First floor plan **06** Interior view, veranda **07** Interior view, stairway to the gallery

06

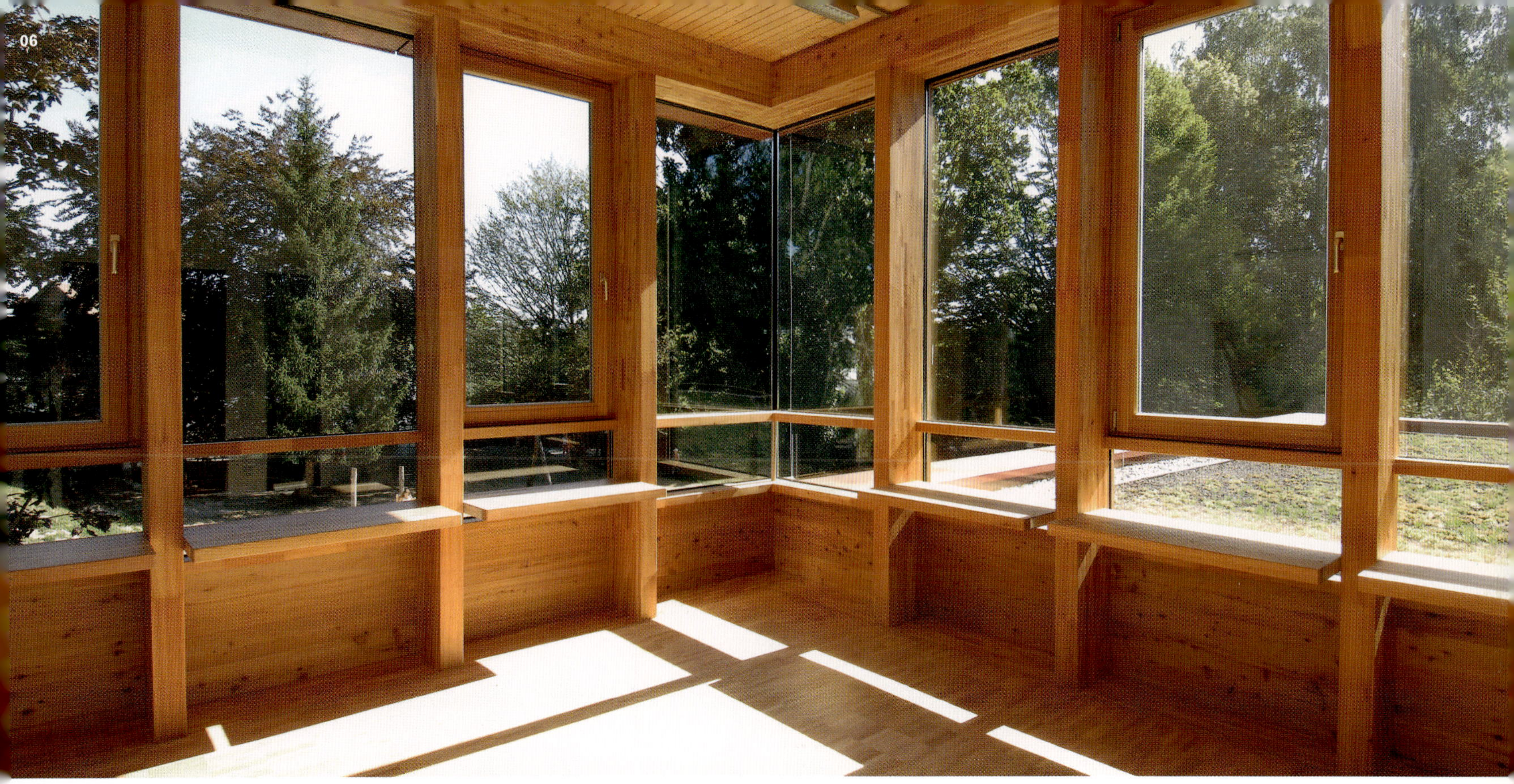

07

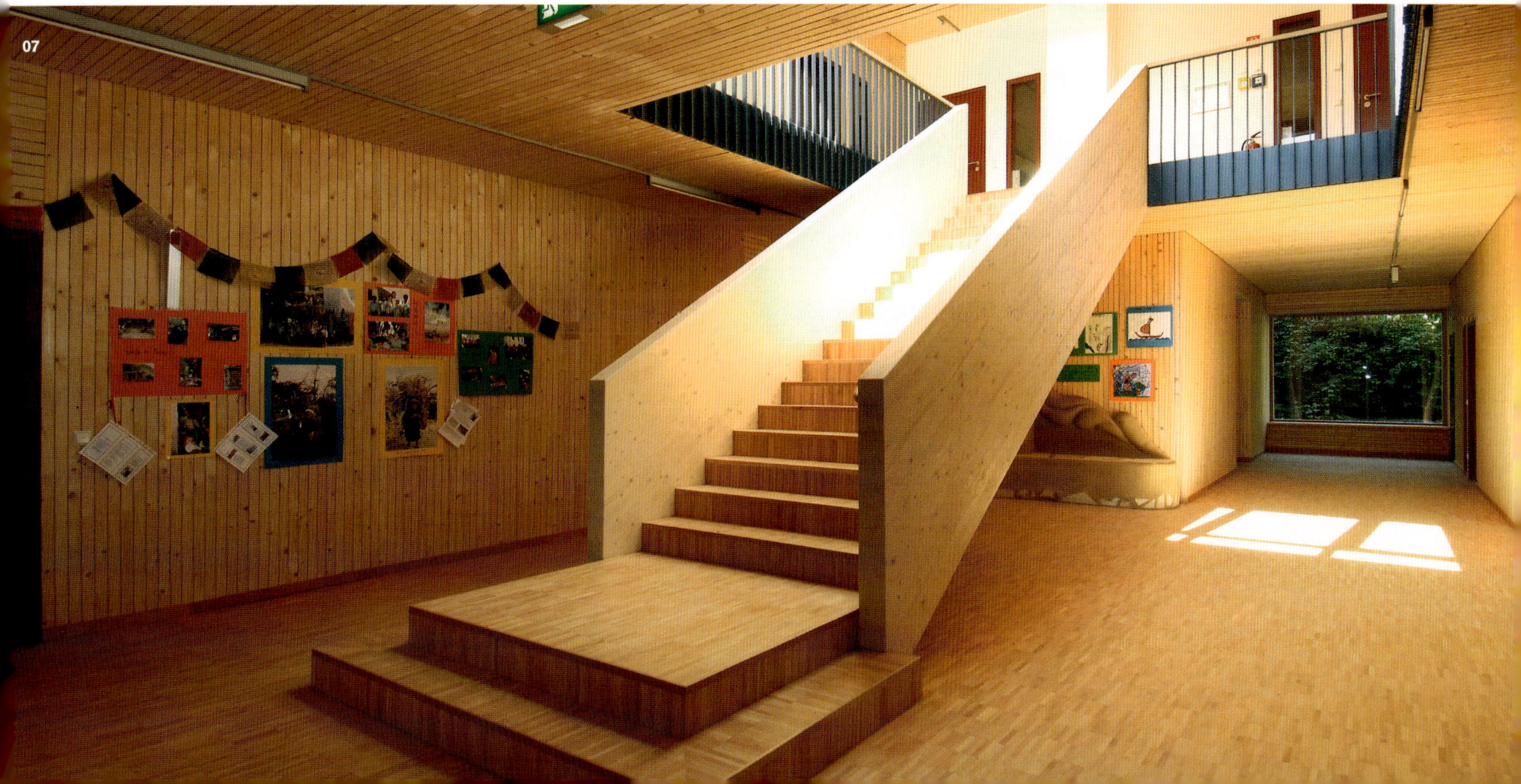

"Arcadia" housing, 2002
Address: Berliner Straße / Lyonel-Feininger-Weg, 71679 Asperg, Germany. **Client:** Strenger Bauen und Wohnen GmbH (real estate development). **Gross floor area:** 1.4 hectares total site area; 10,280 m² living space; 84 residential units in a variety of forms (townhouses, single-family detached homes, semi-detached and apartment buildings and loft apartments).

Urban village

ARCHITECTS: Joachim Eble Architektur
with Lasuveda Color Design Studio
and Atelier Dreiseitl

This housing estate was inspired by the garden city movement, taking it a step further to develop the milieu of an "urban village". All of the residential buildings are developed around a "village square" in a natural configuration that preserves the intimate seclusion of individual units. The health and comfort of residents was a primary consideration in the selection of building materials and the installation of building services. The synthesis of natural and emission-free materials combined with well-designed ventilation and heating strategies in the interiors promise a healthy indoor climate. Wood, more than any other material, unites the various dimensions and forms of these buildings, creating a unified structure within the estate. The homogenous use of detail and color in the wooden arcades as well as the balconies, balustrades and slatted screens gives this estate its unified character.

04

05

Südansicht

Ostansicht EFH 8

06

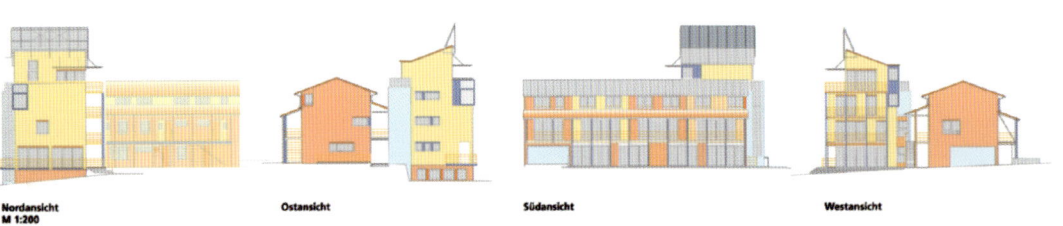

Nordansicht
M 1:200

Ostansicht

Südansicht

Westansicht

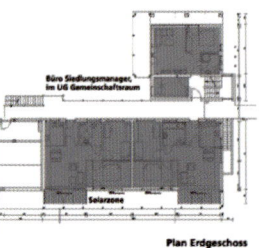

Plan Erdgeschoss

01

Representation Center of the State of North Rhine-Westphalia to the Federation in Berlin, 2002
Address: Hiroshimastraße 12–16, Berlin, Germany.
Client: NRW Ministry of Urban Development, Culture and Sport. **Gross floor area:** 5,550 m². **Materials:** wood, glass and steel.

Technology and symbolism
ARCHITECTS:

Thomas Pink | Petzinka Pink Architekten

The new building that houses the Berlin representative offices of the state of North Rhine-Westphalia is distinguished by a combination of sustainable architecture, state-of-the-art technology and unique symbolism. The result is a powerful overall design. The decision to move the technically indispensable bracing to the façade, and its overstatement in the form of a parabola-like wooden structure, symbolizes the synergetic use of technology that gives this building its specific character. A particularly unusual and innovative feature is the use of hollow ceilings in a four-story public building of this size. This building is sustainable in a special sense – not just because of its multi-functionality, but because it succeeds in developing the technologies it uses into a culturally legible expression of identity.

02

04

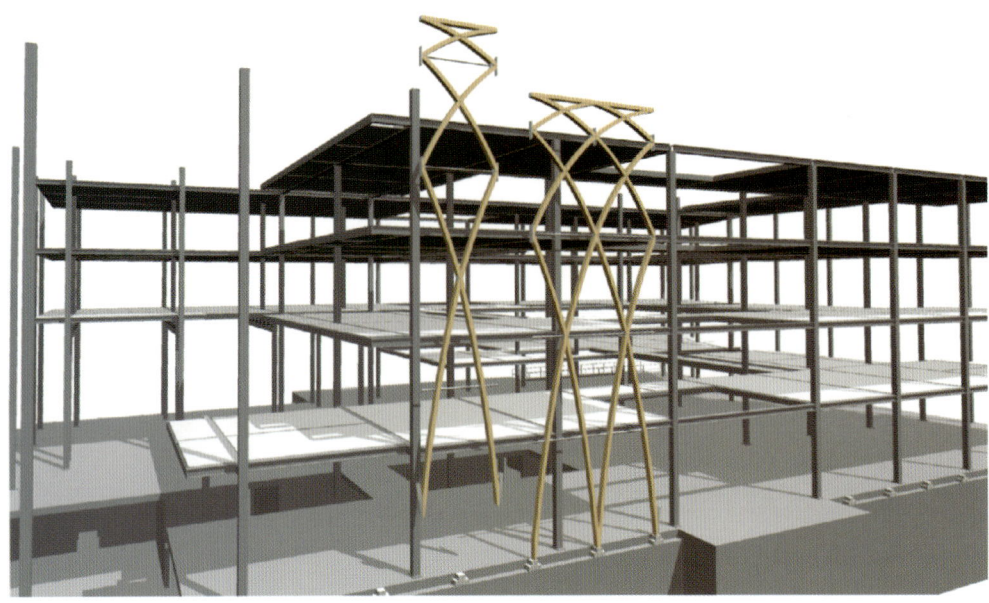

05

06

SKIN

Limerick County Council Headquarters, 2003
Address: Dooradoyle, County Limerick, Ireland.
Client: Limerick County Council. **Gross floor area:**
7,000 m². **Materials:** timber, concrete, glass, steel.

Timber and glass

ARCHITECTS: Bucholz McEvoy Architects

This low energy and naturally ventilated office building of the local government is located in the Limerick city suburb of Dooradoyle, directly adjacent to a large shopping center and the small public library. The environment created by the building acts as a "hinge" between the semi-natural open space that follows the Ballinacurragh creek, and the shopping center. The building is linked to the open space by the sloping green planes on the western portion of the site; these planes are planted with naturally occurring vegetation. The gesture of the tilting timber screen is towards the sky; the gesture of the land, its inclination towards the building, held by timber retaining walls, links the sky and the land. The timber Atrium Screen both shades the atrium and supports it. It consists of 25 three-by-fifteen-meter timber trusses spanning from a galvanized steel structure that is supported by the concrete frame at the top to a precast concrete column at the bottom.

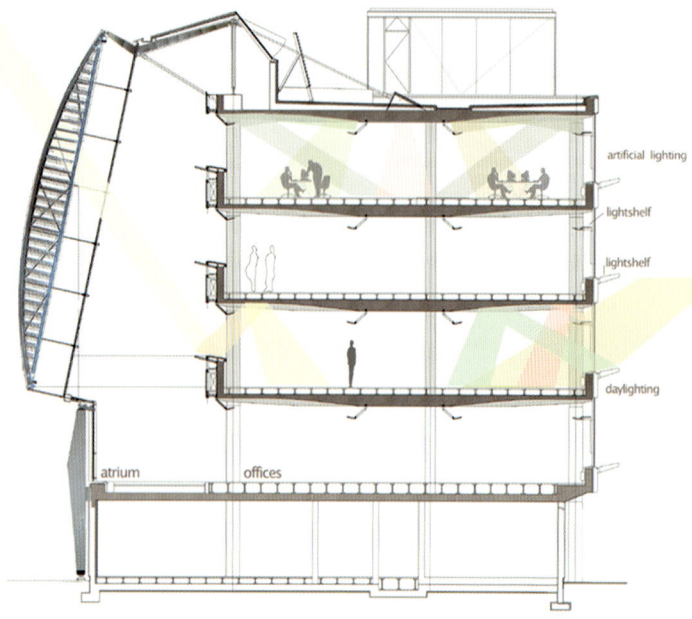

artificial lighting

lightshelf

lightshelf

daylighting

atrium   offices

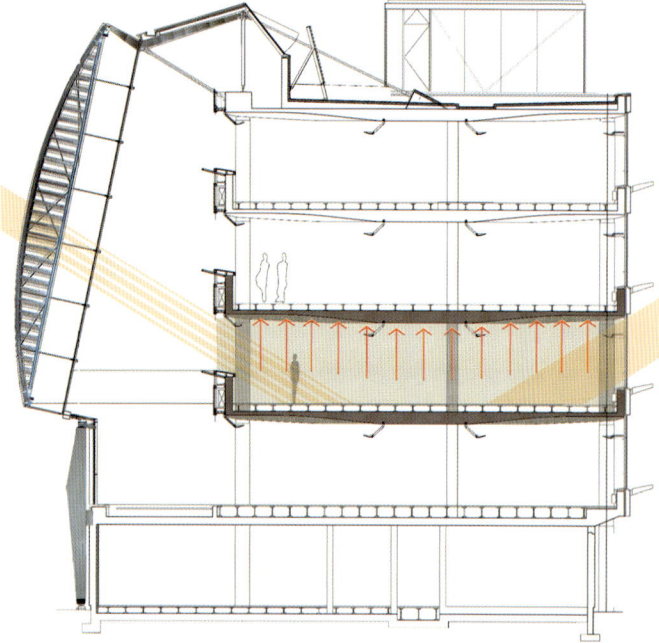

01 Building frontage **02** External atrium screen **03** External atrium screen **04** Atrium with screen **05** Environmental section – daylight **06** Environmental section – heat gain **07** Atrium, offices

Pergola Residence, 2004
Address: St. Kassianweg 40, 39022 Algund (Lagundo), Italy. **Client:** Josef and Ruth Innerhofer. **Gross floor area:** 2,536 m². **Materials:** wood, stone.

Living on a slope, living with vines

ARCHITECTS: Matteo Thun & Partners

A sloping site is always an opportunity. It begs the question: How can architectural design save energy? And also: Can architecture and wine-growing borrow each other's forms? Both of these questions have been answered in Algund near Merano. Departing from the clichés of Alpine architecture and Southern Tirolean grandiosity, Matteo Thun has created something unique in this wine-growing region: a hotel in the form of a pergola, using only wood, stone and living vines. As the vines grow, the building itself recedes from view, concealing an expansive 2,800 m² complex composed of 12 residential units with adjacent terraces, two luxury suites, a breakfast room and a spa equipped with pools and saunas. Wooden structures, identical to those of the centuries-old neighboring vineyards, have been used to create pergolas above the terraces that border the living rooms. This is both an aesthetic and ecological stroke of genius.

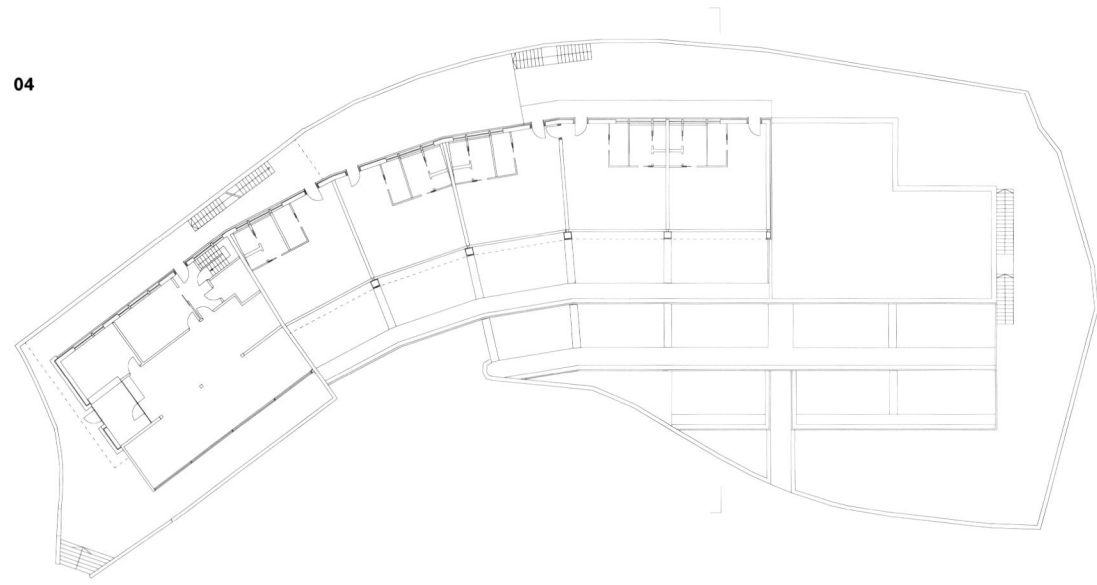

04

01 Detail façade **02** Exterior view with landscape **03** Entrance door **04** Ground floor plan **05** First floor plan **06** Living area and terrace **07** Inside-outside view

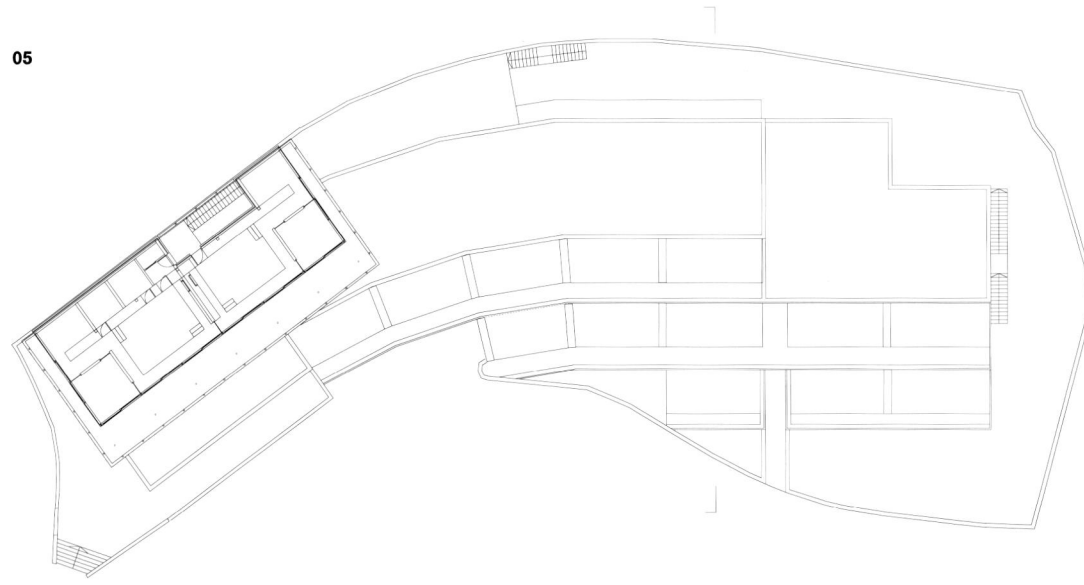

05

06

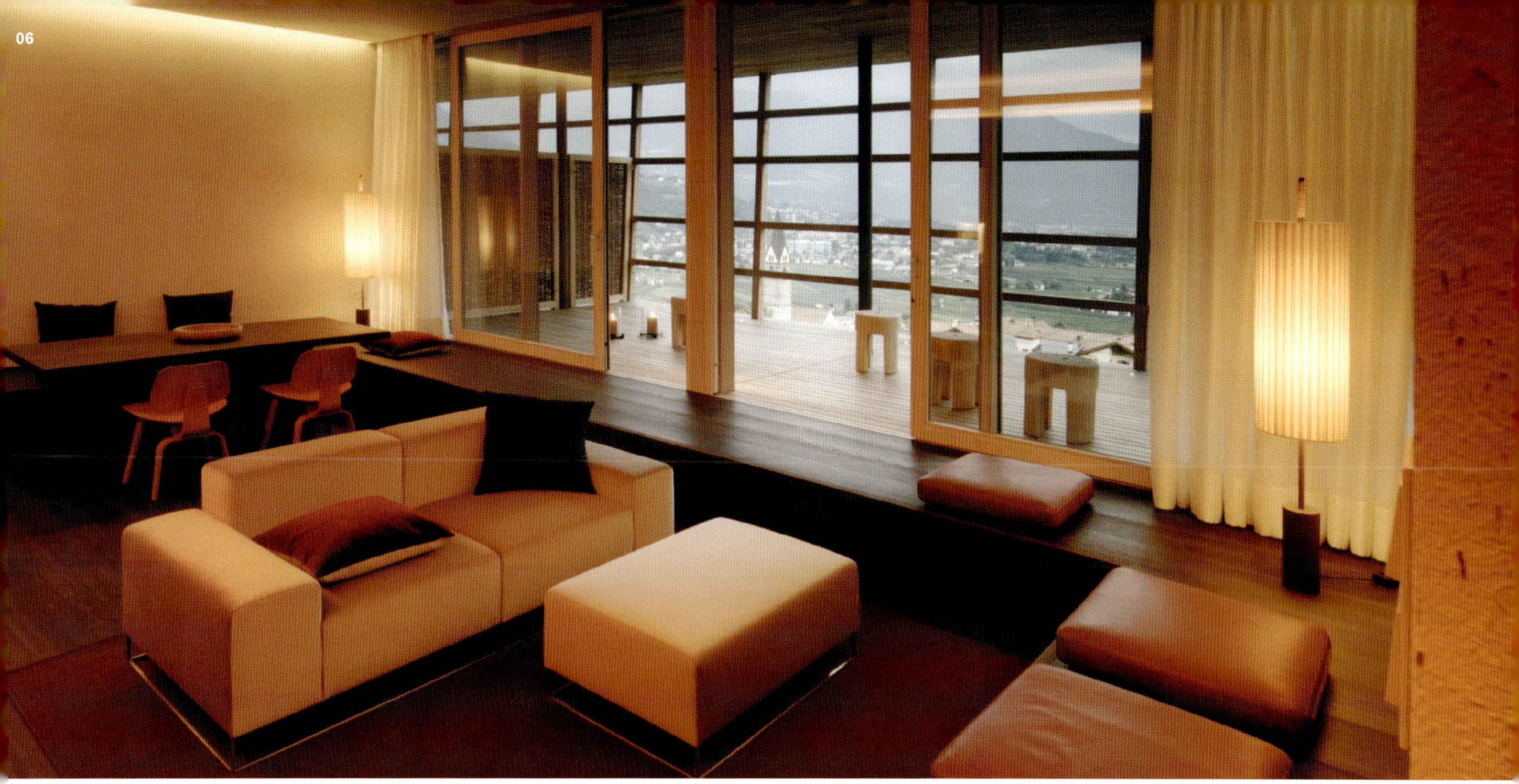

07

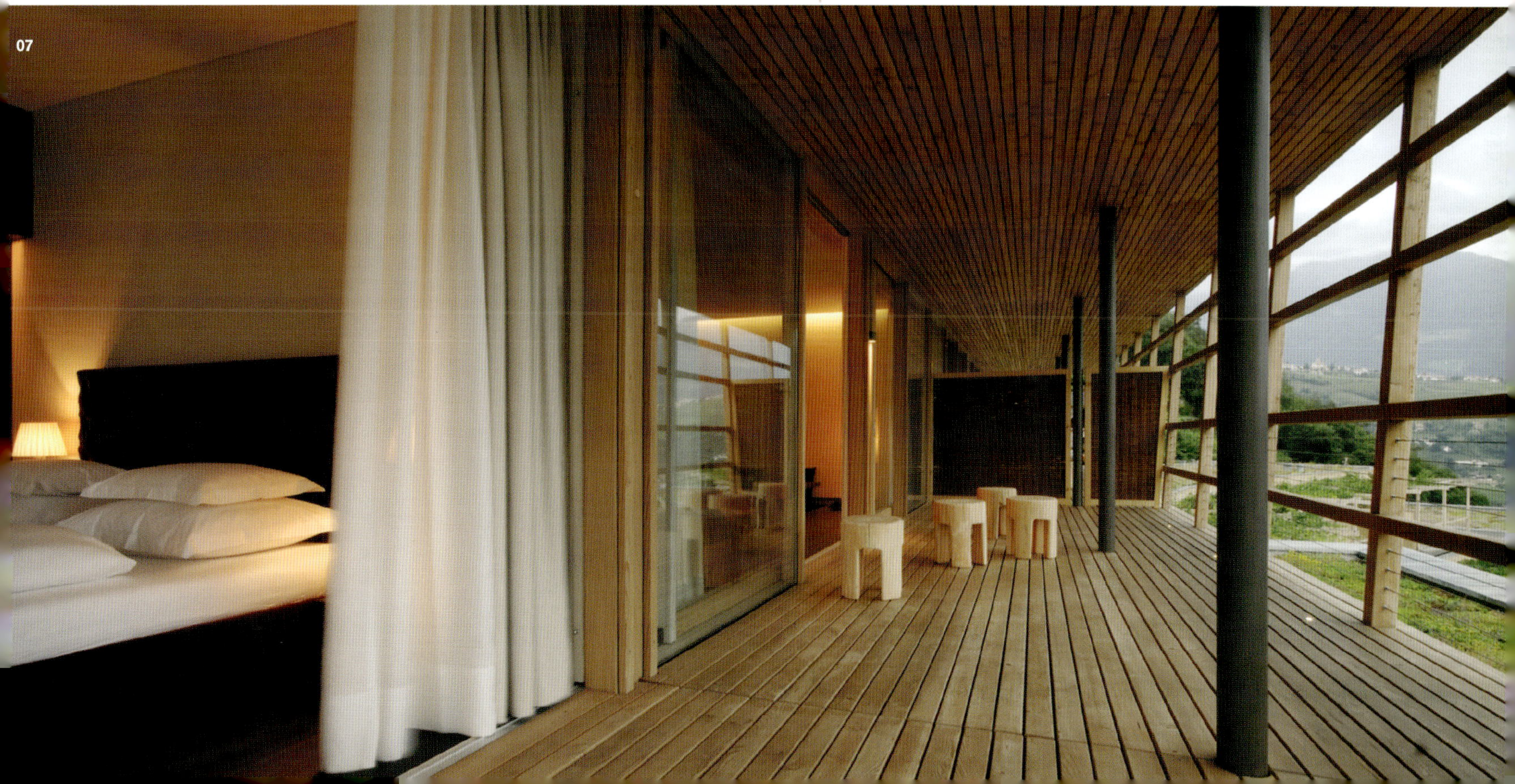

Berkhan House, 2006
Address: Schreinergasse 3, 72415 Grosselfingen,
Germany. **Client:** Julia Berkhan. **Gross floor area:**
154 m². **Materials:** wooden post-and-beam structure,
larchwood façade.

Wrapping the house

ARCHITECTS: Markus Fischer Architekt

This building is best understood as a three-dimensional
body, a kind of habitable sculpture. A simple, elongated
form was chosen in order to make optimal use of the
plot. Two elements were deployed to divide the space:
the staircase and two sanitation and technology units,
which were designed as built-in wardrobes that are colored on the inside to set them apart. These house the
bathroom on the upper floor, and the guest toilet and
cloakroom area on the ground floor. All of the service
functions, such as water heating, service connections
and plumbing fixtures are built into these niches. When
these boxes are closed, everything appears white; when
opened they reveal brilliant colors that change the ambience of the rooms. The overhanging roof above the
entrance area and veranda, and expansive glazing facing the garden, allow the interior and exterior spaces to
interconnect. A huge curtain suspended from the front
edge of the roof acts as a privacy and sun screen, while
also creating an interim zone; an intimate exterior area
and veranda.

01

04

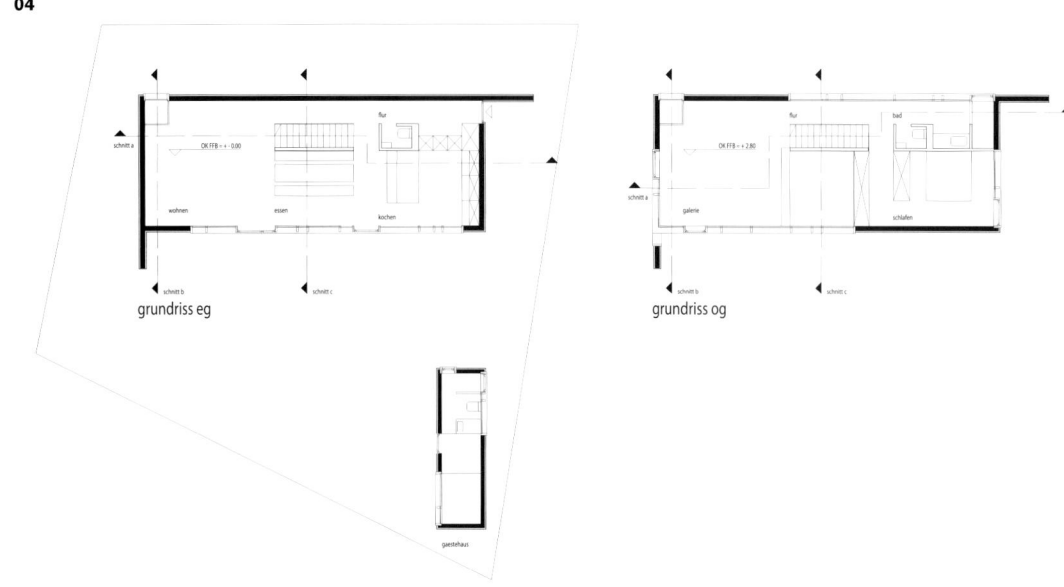

grundriss eg

grundriss og

05

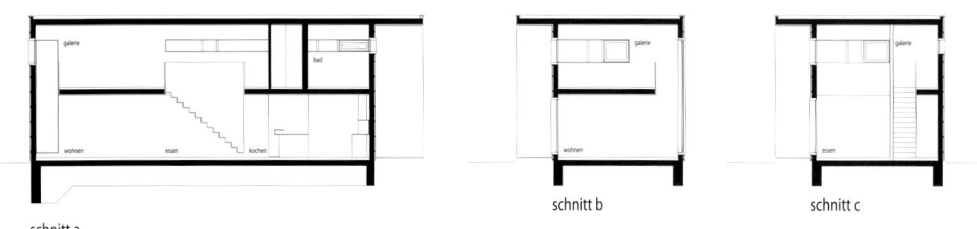

schnitt a

schnitt b

schnitt c

06

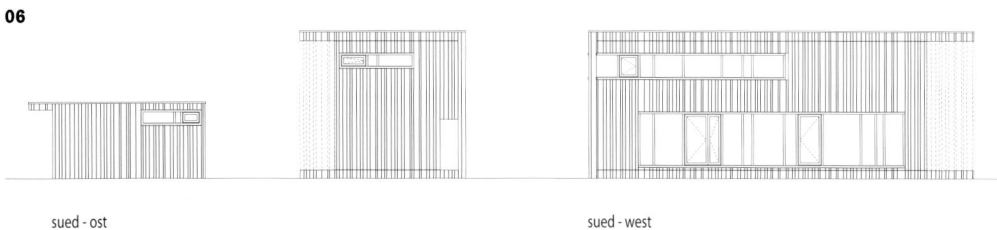

sued - ost

sued - west

Municipal forestry workshop, 2005
Address: 7107 Safien-Platz, Switzerland. **Client:** Municipality of Safien and Tenna. **Gross floor area:** 2,151 m². **Materials:** sawn timber, certified from native wood.

Native wood, locally processed

ARCHITECTS: Architekturbüro Robert Albertin

The Safien Valley is an idyllic yet remote region that is largely devoted to agriculture. The new forestry workshop was built exclusively with solid, FSC-certified timber. Furthermore, the workshop and surrounding buildings are heated by means of a modern wood chip furnace. Timber felled during essential forest maintenance can thus be processed locally, setting an example for the region and beyond. The building is located within a Class II danger zone for avalanches, leading the architects to take special precautions in the construction. The self-supporting hall is characterized by its V-shape supports, which are not only aesthetically appealing, but also serve a vital structural function. The interplay of two systems – the lattice-like support structure of the enclosing walls and the flat panel roof – helps to absorb high dynamic pressure caused by wind from an avalanche, and adds to the overall stability of the building. For fire safety reasons, the elevated basement and the silo for the wood chip furnace were built in reinforced concrete.

01 Inside-outside view **02** Detail
03 Exterior view from northeast **04**
Elevation façade **05** Floor plans **06**
Total view

04

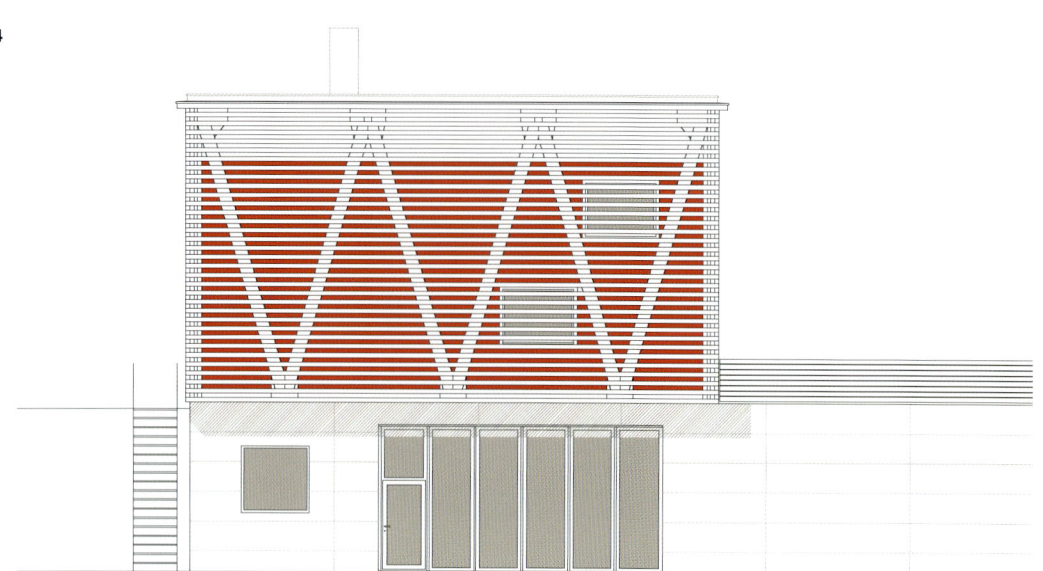

05

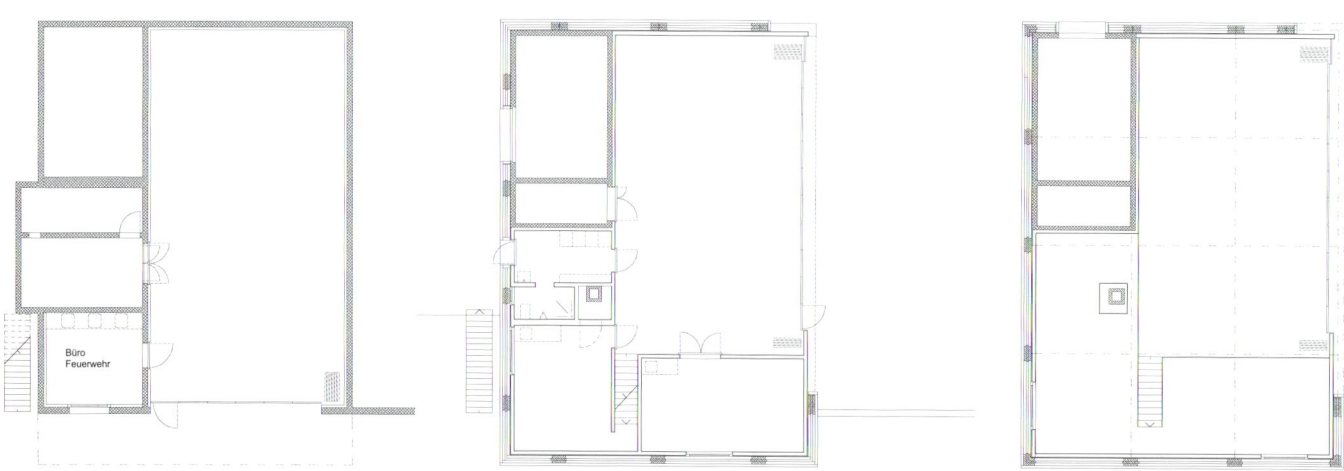

Büro
Feuerwehr

Samer Mösl Passive House, 2006
Address: Lerchenstraße 7–25, 5020 Salzburg,
Austria. **Project team:** Helga Huber-Hochradl, Simon
Speigner, Dirk Obracay. **Client:** Heimat Österreich.
Gross floor area: 6,111 m². **Materials:** timber-framed
wall / prefabricated construction.

In the crevices

ARCHITECTS: sps-architekten zt gmbh

The grounds of this building complex are rutted with furrows, running roughly on a north-south axis from the river to the marsh. The architect makes reference to these
furrows in the crevice-like and light-flooded access or
stairway zones. These act as through-ways that weave
through the entire complex at right angles to the elongated buildings. The recessed balconies within these
"crevices" also add to the rhythmic effect and break up
the rigid lines of the buildings. The balconies provide
11 m² of attractive, half sheltered, half exposed fresh-
air zones for these L-shaped apartments. Thanks to the
interlocking effect of these three-story angular blocks,
each of the three buildings extend at a different length
into the grounds. Since 2004, the city of Salzburg has
permitted public and residential buildings to be built entirely of wood to a height of four stories. Before then
the limit was three stories. The rough-sawn spruce façade of the Samer Mösl Passive House (self-sufficient
in terms of energy requirements) was given a silver-gray
varnish coat, which in the coming years will be gradually
supplanted by the natural gray patina of the spruce.

01 General view **02** Ground floor plan **03** Exterior view

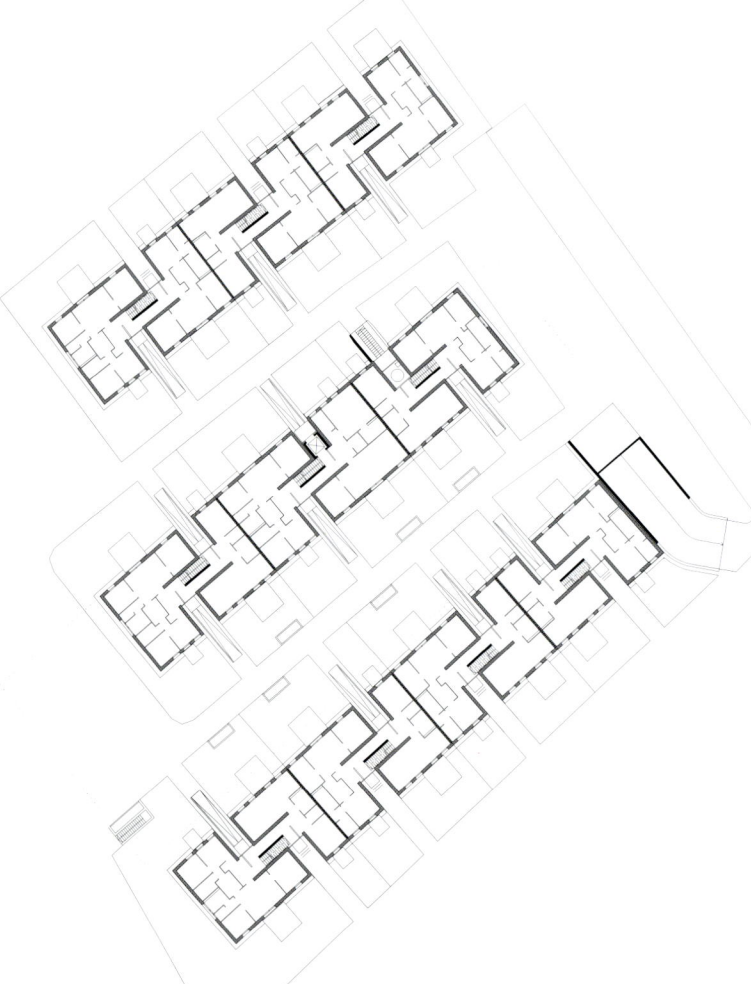

02

01

Youth and Community Center, 2004
Address: Donore Avenue, Dublin 8, Ireland. **Client:**
Dublin City Council. **Gross floor area:** 1,100 m².
Materials: mixed.

Double-functioned

ARCHITECTS: Henchion + Reuter Architects

The center facilitates two permanent user groups: a youth services center and a community drug team (CDT). Additionally, the larger rooms are available to other community groups. The expression of individual volumes and functions in the building is deliberately suppressed to emphasize the building as a single large house or villa. The interior design is flexible, so as to accommodate anticipated changes in usage. The space facing the street on the ground floor is occupied by a drop-in center for the local community. This also functions as the link between the two entrances; the main entrance and the CDT entrance. The largest volume in the building is the community hall. This is wrapped in beechwood on three sides with a clerestory three-story section connecting to a roof garden. Although the neighboring garden to the south belongs to the local church, it is hoped the side door will allow joint events and programs to spill out into this garden.

02

04

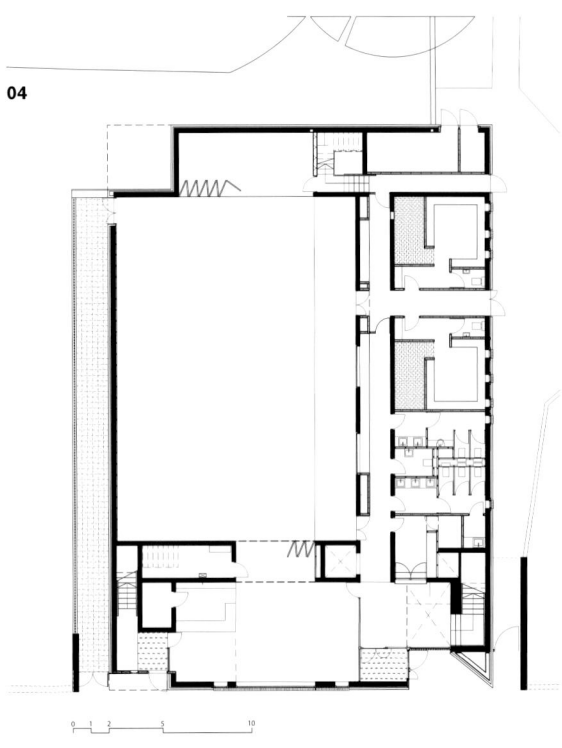

0 1 2   5   10

05

0 1 2   5   10

06

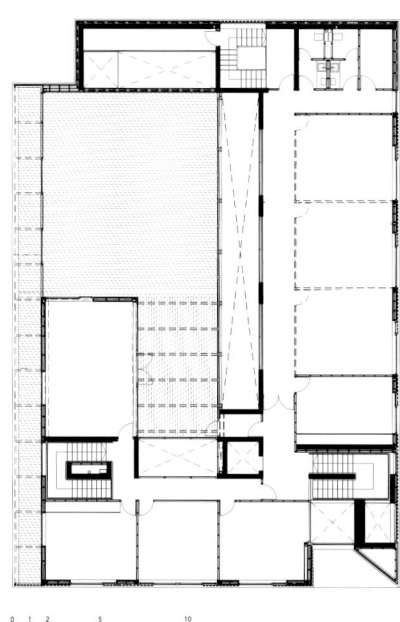

0 1 2   5   10

House for everybody, 2002
Address: Kusatsu-shi Shiga pref., Japan. **Client:** Shini-chiro Taguchi. **Gross floor area:** 98.89 m². **Materials:** wood, reinforced concrete and steel support structure.

A home to several generations
ARCHITECTS: KOHKI HIRANUMA /
Hs WorkShop-ASIA

The residents of this house are a family of six and are split into two households. The average height of the family members is 150 cm, thus the project focused on adapting the space to the particular human scale, on establishing a sense of variation. The site covers a rectangular area of eight-by-eleven meters, and there was a requirement to create a carport at the entrance on the south side of the site with six meters of street frontage. Reconciling the demands of the client with government regulations is often difficult in small projects. The gap in mentality between the different generations in the family triggered the idea to move the floor plan slightly to the right or left, and upward or downward within that small space.

03

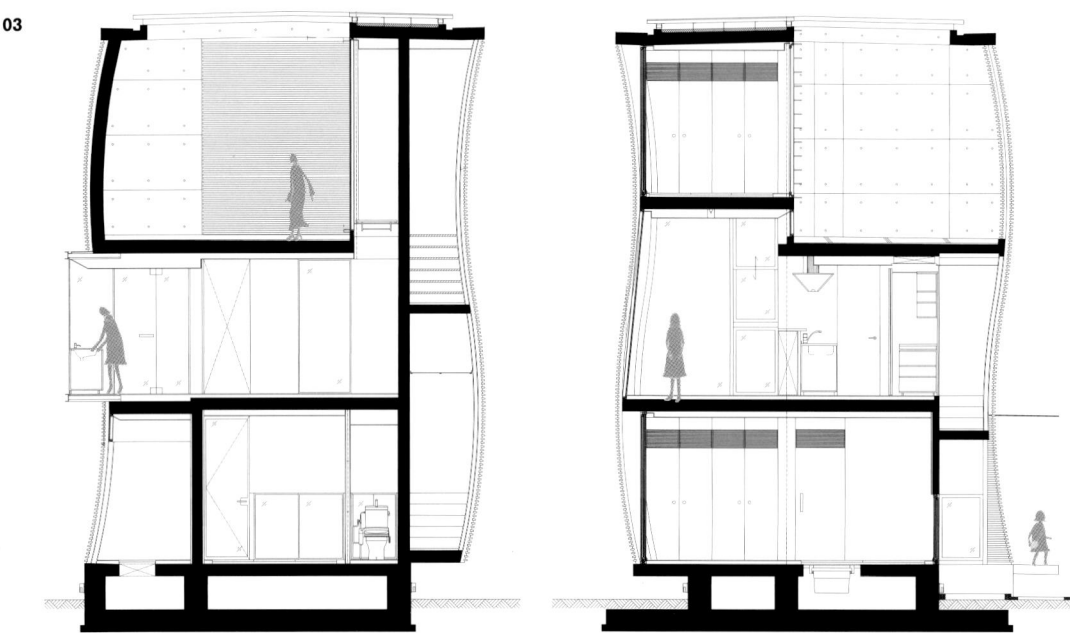

04

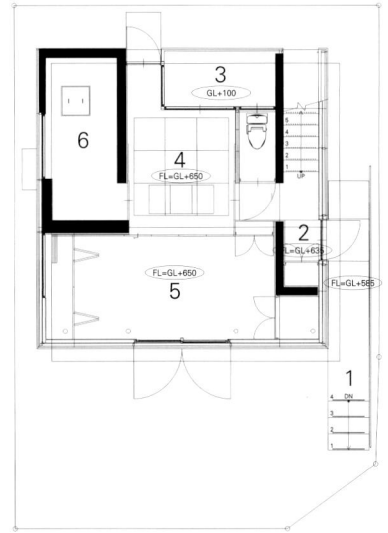

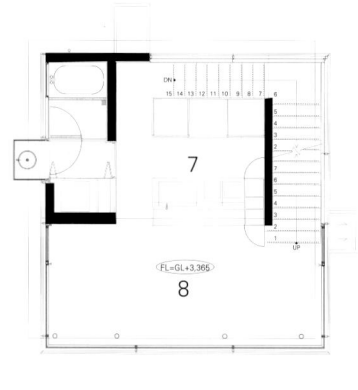

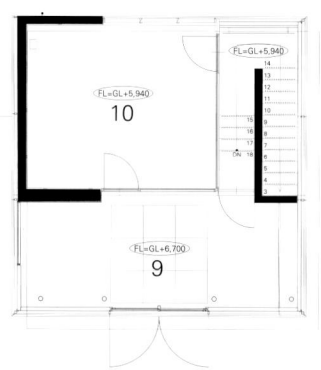

1.Walkway   6.Walk-in closet
2.Entrance   7.Kitchen
3.Courtyard   8.LDK
4.Space2   9.Space3
5.Space1   10.Terrace

Svartlamoen Housing, 2005
Address: Strandveien 37–39, 7042 Trondheim, Norway. **Client:** Svartlamoen Housing Trust. **Gross floor area:** 1,015 m². **Materials:** solid wood elements used for outer walls, partitioning walls, floors and roof.

Typically Norwegian

ARCHITECTS:

Brendeland & Kristoffersen arkitekter AS

Trondheim is a typical wooden city, yet the typology of the large wooden urban building largely disappeared during the last century. Almost all large new buildings have been constructed in steel and concrete. The Svartlamoen housing project departs from this trend, demonstrating the potential of new technology in timber construction, thanks to which it is no longer necessary to compromise on fire safety. A principal objective of this project was to create a sustainable building, and few materials meet this criterion better than wood, a renewable resource. The prismatic wooden buildings and their perpendicular volumes respond to a particular micro-context. The adjacent blocks belong to the nineteenth-century grid; partly residential, partly small-scale industries, they are today overgrown by weeds and bushes. Opposite Strandveien, beyond an industrial railway and on the sea front, sits a submarine bunker of massive proportions that was kindly left behind by the Germans and has resisted all attempts at demolition.

06

01 Side view **02** Exterior view **03** Rear view **04** Interior view, living space **05** Interior view, kitchen space **06** First floor plan **07** Top floor plan

07

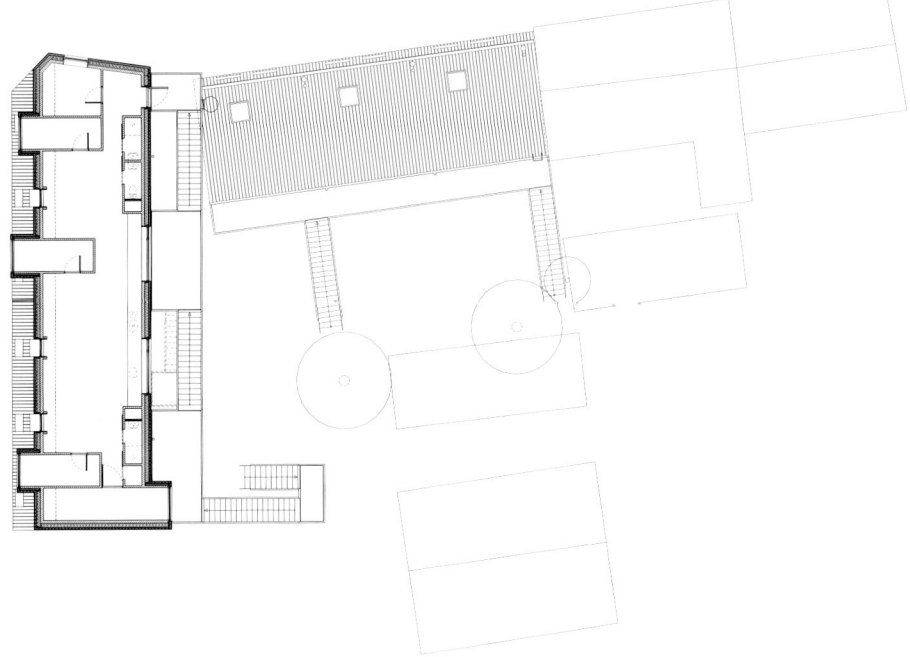

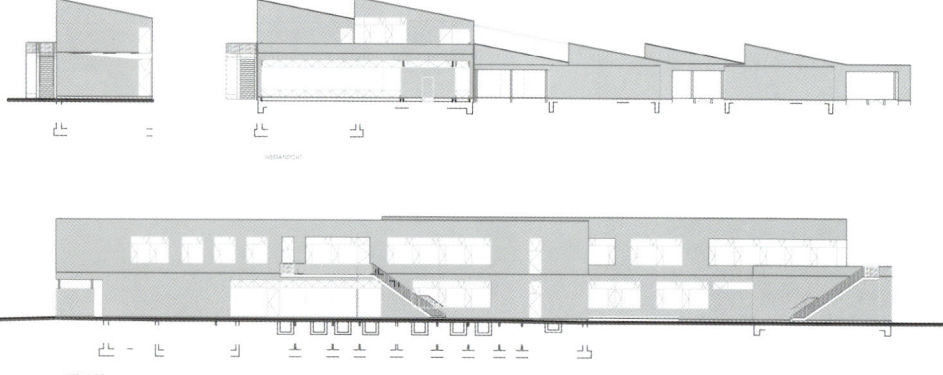

ILMASI School (special school for mentally disabled children), 2002
Address: Ludwigstraße 9, 30827 Garbsen-Berenbostel, Germany. **Client:** Region of Hanover. **Gross floor area:** 4,000 m². **Materials:** solid wood, shell construction, nail-laminated timber with "Thermoholz" (heat-treated wood) curtain wall.

A sensual building

ARCHITECTS: Despang Architekten

This school, which accommodates 100 mentally disabled children and 40 teachers, was designed as a patchwork of different components and forms. The result is an ensemble of attractive spaces and rooms. The distinguishing feature of this structure is the use of nail-laminated timber elements. The architects describe this as "a consistent texture that add a large measure of sensual stimulation to the building. The tectonics of the layered boards symbolize the effort to strengthen and support the individual pupil while maintaining a solidly united school community." This is a building that is best experienced with the senses; in addition to its changing moods of light and shadow, it can be felt, heard, smelt and – as resins bleed from the wood – even tasted. Wood features here in a wide variety of forms: in durable, white-pigmented, oiled spruce walls; in sturdy doors; in the floors of the upper level, in handrails and coatracks of fumed oak; and in the larchwood canopy above the classroom courtyard.

01 West and north elevation **02** Exterior view **03** Recreation court
04 Larchwood canopy above classroom courtyard

02

Palmwood House, 2007
Address: Battersea, London, United Kingdom. **Client:**
private. **Gross floor area:** approx. 100 m². **Materials:**
brick, recycled flooring, sustainable timber.

Building in difficult urban sites

ARCHITECTS: Undercurrent architects

This is a prototype building for problematic urban sites –
a small vacant lot severely constrained by height restric-
tions and poor planning history. The building works with
a gradation of spaces, views and daylight to achieve an
extensive living experience despite its restricted volume.
The site has a tight, triangular shape, at the end of a
terraced row in the riverside district of Battersea. The
development encompasses the equivalent of three terraced houses cut across their diagonal. The construction combines low energy and sustainable materials with
advanced building technologies that minimize energy
consumption. These included high-tech insulants, high
performance insulated glazing, reclaimed brickwork, recycled flooring and sustainable woods – including the
first use in Europe of palmwood, an ecologically-sound
plantation hardwood.

01 View of balcony and courtyard
02 Exterior view **03** Ground floor
plan **04** First floor plan **05** View
from the balcony into the house
06 View from the house onto the
balcony

03

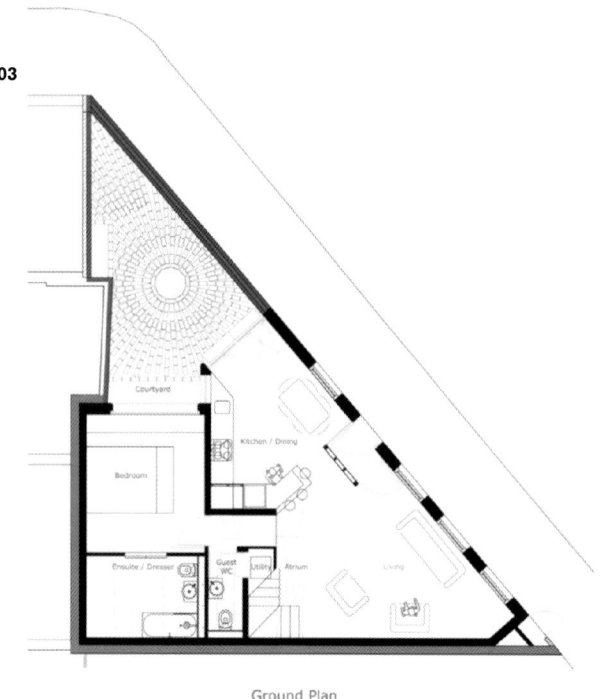

Ground Plan

04

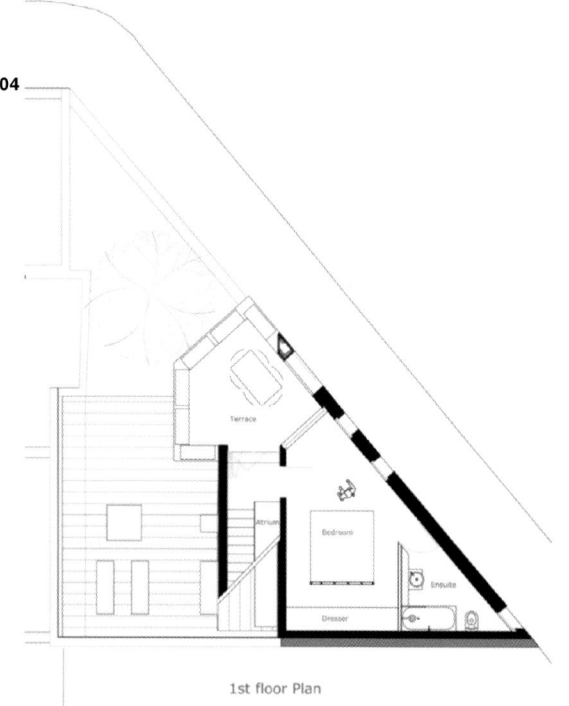

1st floor Plan

Flydalsjuvet – tourist route, 2006
Address: Flydalsjuvet, 6216 Geiranger, Norway.
Landscape architects: Smedsvig Landskapsarkitekter AS. **Client:** The Norwegian Public Routes Administration. **Gross floor area:** 3,000 m² (buildings: 170 m²).
Material: wood, glass, steel and concrete.

Wood on glass

ARCHITECTS: 3rw architects

This site, known as Flydalsjuvet, is located on the ridge of the steep mountain chain that rises from the Geiranger fjord. The timbered modules were collected from a local site and have been refurbished by traditional craftsmen. The house was part of an old farm and had fallen into disrepair. The roof was falling apart and some of the wood was rotten. This is a general problem in Norway: traditional farmhouses become ruinous symbols of a culture in the process of change from farming, hunting and fishing to tourism. Instead of reusing these buildings for new purposes, an aggressive building industry is facilitating tourism by using a traditional building system (cogging joint) but within an architectural framework that typically seems to refer to something between national romanticism and a post-modern Viking castle. In this project the old timber modules are mounted on a five-centimeter-thick glass base, which allows light to enter under the massive wooden walls. Thus an old local building tradition is preserved for the future, floating on a modern glass structure.

04

5m

05

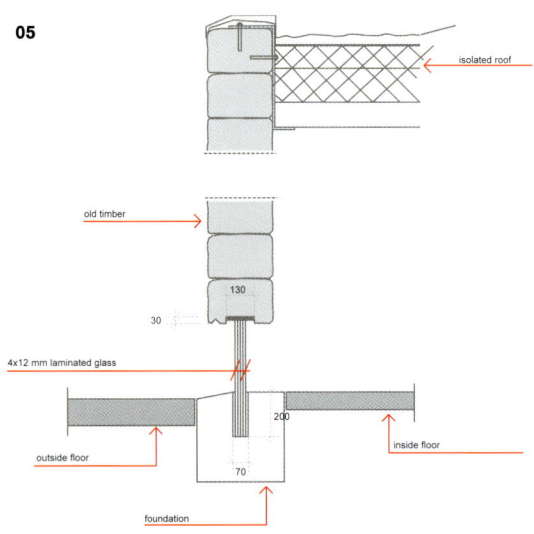

isolated roof

old timber

130

30

4x12 mm laminated glass

200

outside floor

inside floor

70

foundation

112

06

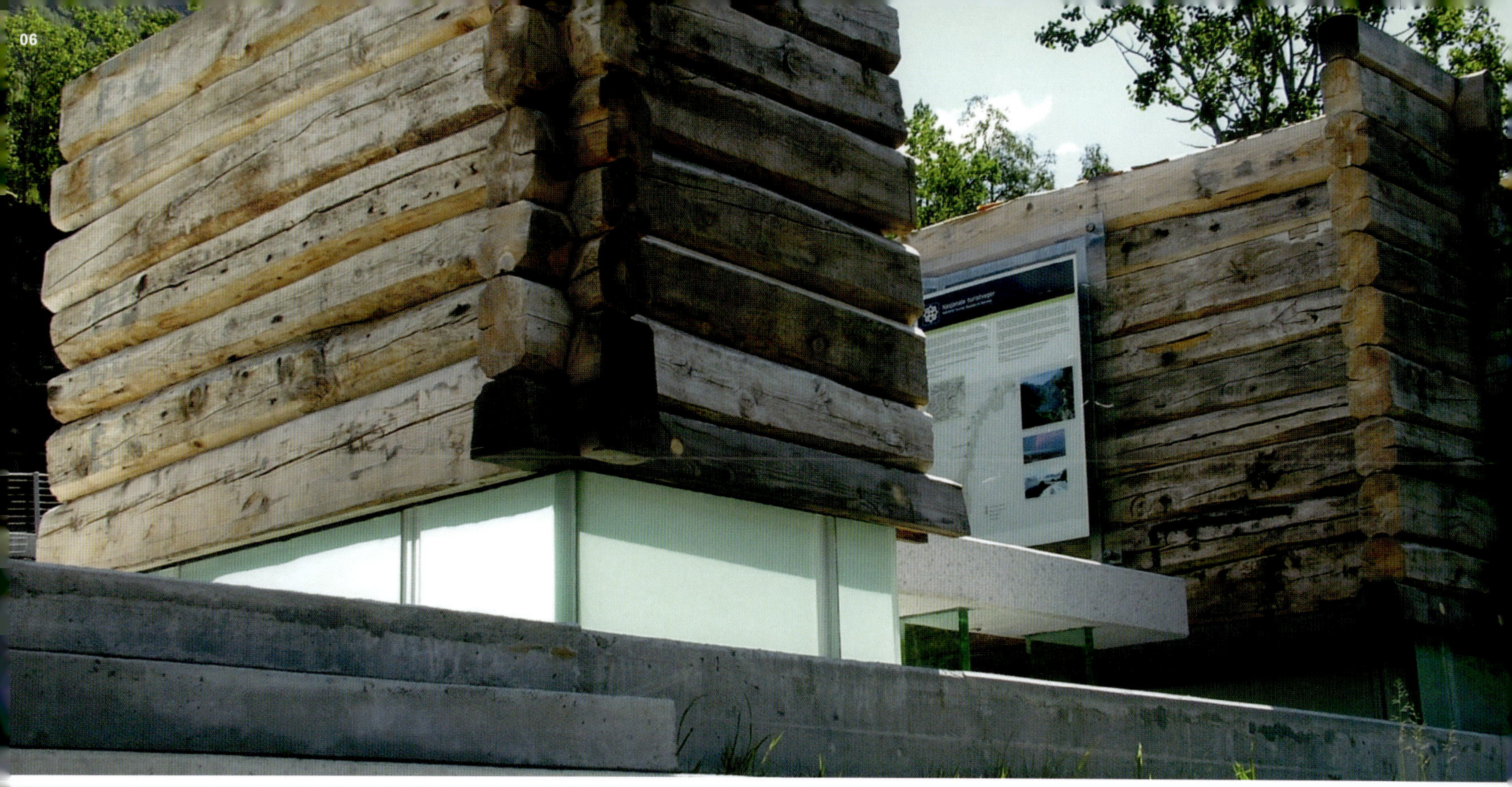

07

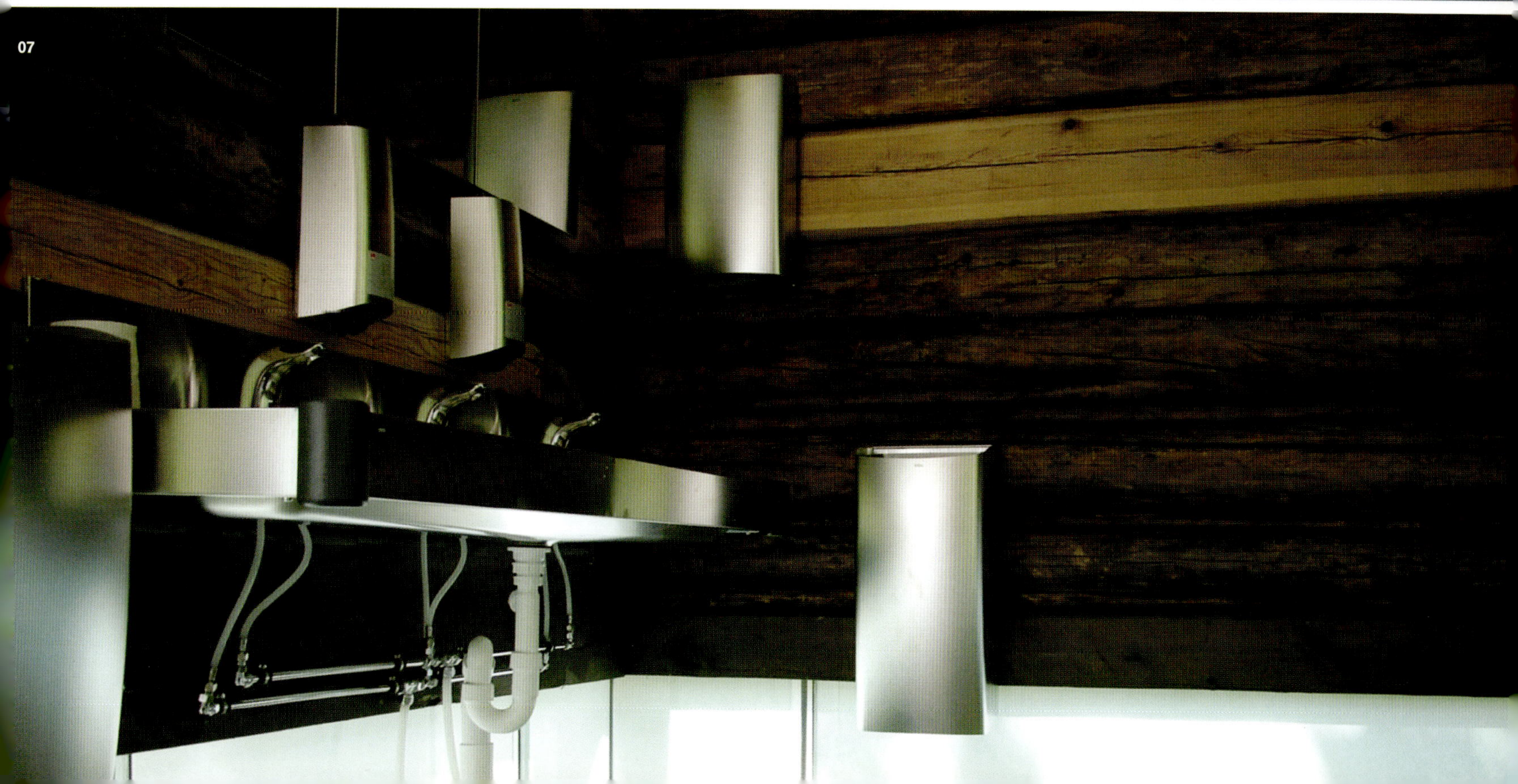

Conversion and extension of the Theodor-Heuss-Schule, 2007
Address: Gerberstraße 16, 27356 Rotenburg, Germany.
Client: City of Rotenburg. **Gross floor area:** 2625 m².
Materials: wood panel construction.

Touching up an old school

ARCHITECTS:

Dipl.-Ing. Architekt Jörg-Henner Gresbrand

An aging building from 1963 was extended to accommodate a student canteen, kitchen unit, library, computer rooms, Internet café, multimedia room, special needs teaching room, social / relaxation room, offices, assembly hall, staff area, etc. The existing ground floor was retained and an additional floor added. The new structures and extensions were created by means of classic wood panel construction. The assembly hall is surrounded by a gallery that provides both access to the hall and additional standing room for audiences. The roof is crowned by a 7 x 7 meter glass pyramid. A further interesting feature is the green roof. The canteen on the ground floor has a curved glass façade and the roof functions both as a terrace and, if necessary, as an emergency exit. All of the façades have been clad with horizontal larch battens. Thanks to a deliberate choice of materials and forms, this scattered, red-brick school complex has been given a confident new center that fulfills important school functions and ties the surrounding buildings together.

04

Sportplatz

Theodor–Heuss–Schule

Turnhalle

Parkplatz

Hausmeister / Trafo

05

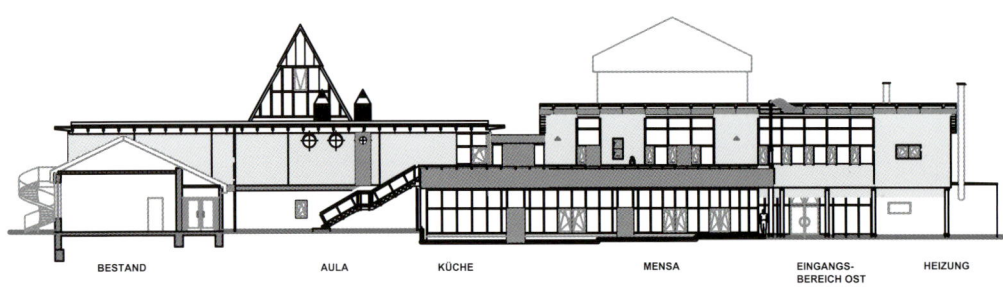

BESTAND AULA KÜCHE MENSA EINGANGS-BEREICH OST HEIZUNG

116

**Mimers Hus, cultural center and
upper secondary school, 2004
Address:** Trollhättevägen 4, 44234 Kungälv, Sweden.
Landscape architects: Landskapsgruppen. **Client:**
Kungälvs kommun / Sverigehuset. **Gross floor area:**
23,000 m². **Materials:** birch wood (interior)
and others.

Multifunctional

ARCHITECTS:

Wingårdh Arkitektkontor AB

This is a low-budget building. It called for a very plain
scheme for the general layout with façades generally
made of prefabricated concrete elements, but designed
with great attention to the most visible parts. It houses
a senior technical high school as well as a library and
an auditorium serving the entire community. It is located close to the center of the town of Kungälv, north
of Gothenburg. Vertical and horizontal lamellae act as
sunscreens and lend the building a graphic pattern,
endowing it with a distinct character in relation to the
surrounding urban space, while birch paneling gives the
interior a warm and sensitive atmosphere. Accessibility
for the disabled has been another prime concern, espe-
cially in the theatre.

04

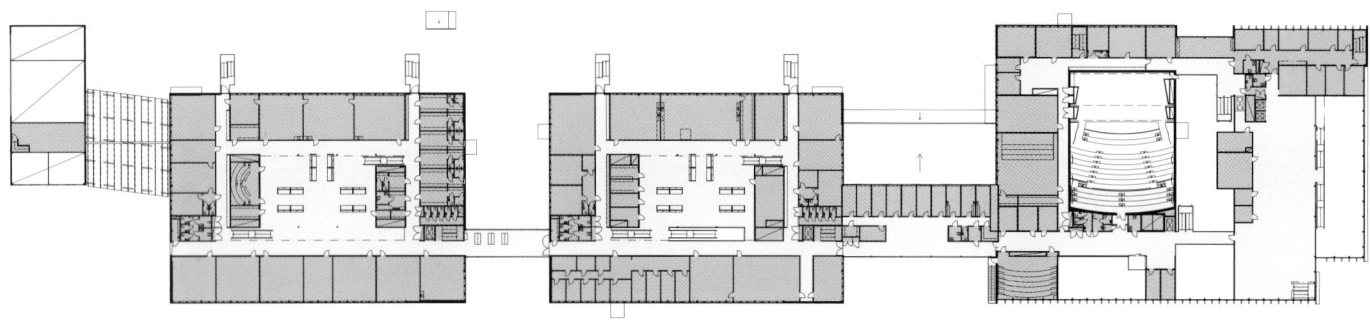

05

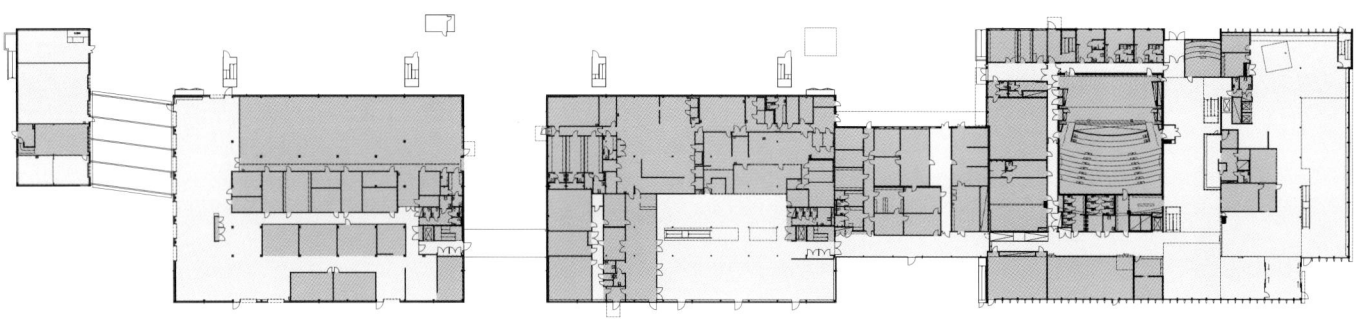

06

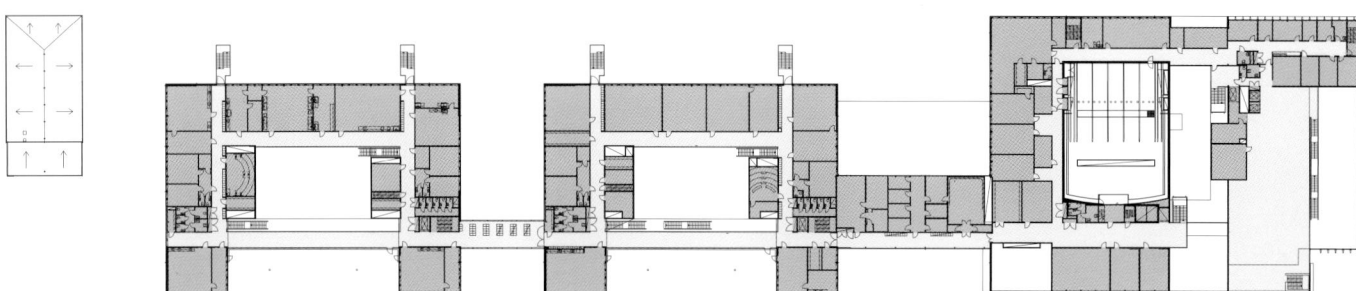

Ahomansikka Housing, 2004
Address: Nuppukuja 5–7, 00710 Helsinki, Finland.
Client: Skanska. **Gross floor area:** 3,750 m². **Materials:** timber, concrete.

Key material: wood!

ARCHITECTS:

Kirsti Sivén & Asko Takala Architects

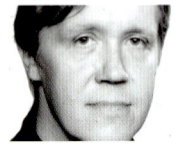 

The Ahomansikka residential development is located in the experimental ecological building area in Viikki. The terraced houses that were constructed during the competition phase have been converted to small-scale blocks of flats at the client's request, with terraced houses remained only at the ends. The balconies with a balustrade of slender slats and tall sliding glazing units are consistent with Ahomansikka's traditional timber architecture. Energy is conserved by passive means: orientation of dwellings, distribution of openings, and buffer zones of balconies and conservatories. The flats are pleasant and easily furnished. The perimeters of the yards are defined by communal sauna buildings, each of which is equipped with a timber-heated stove. The key material throughout this project is wood.

05

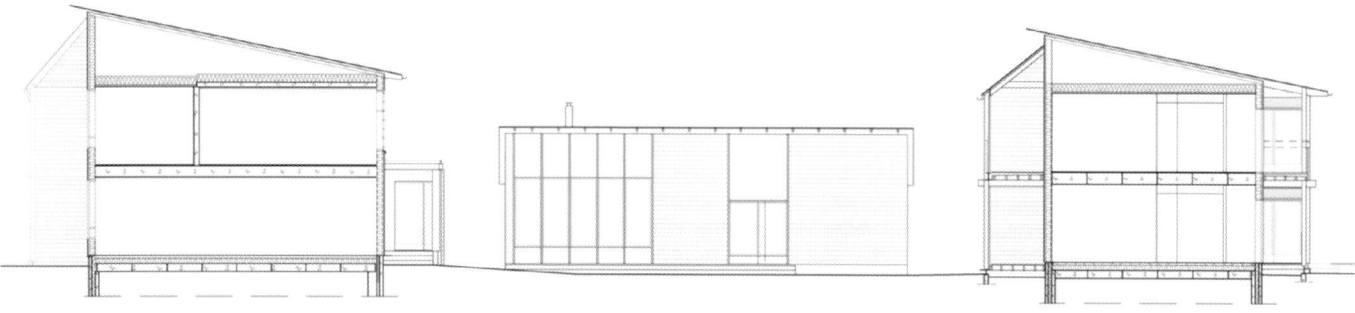

Casa Duplo, 2004
Address: Cureglia, Ticino, Switzerland. **Client:** Guerriero Sassi. **Gross floor area:** 227 m². **Material:** wood.

Simple beauty

ARCHITECTS: Stefano Tibiletti, Enrico Sassi

The project deals with the relationship between interior and exterior, between architectural space and environment. The visual and spatial continuity between day area and external space is expressed through the use of large, square, full-height windows and through the large transition space of the porch, which is covered but not enclosed. Walls and slabs are made of wood; the house was built using the prefabrication technique. The flooring is made from wood blocks, and the interior face of the slab is given a natural finish. Natural wood is used on all horizontal surfaces, while the vertical planes are characterized by the color white. The building's supporting structure (walls and slabs) is likewise made of wood. The outer surface is clad with untreated Nordic larch boards, disposed vertically. The boards' utmost height is six meters, their width nine centimeters.

03

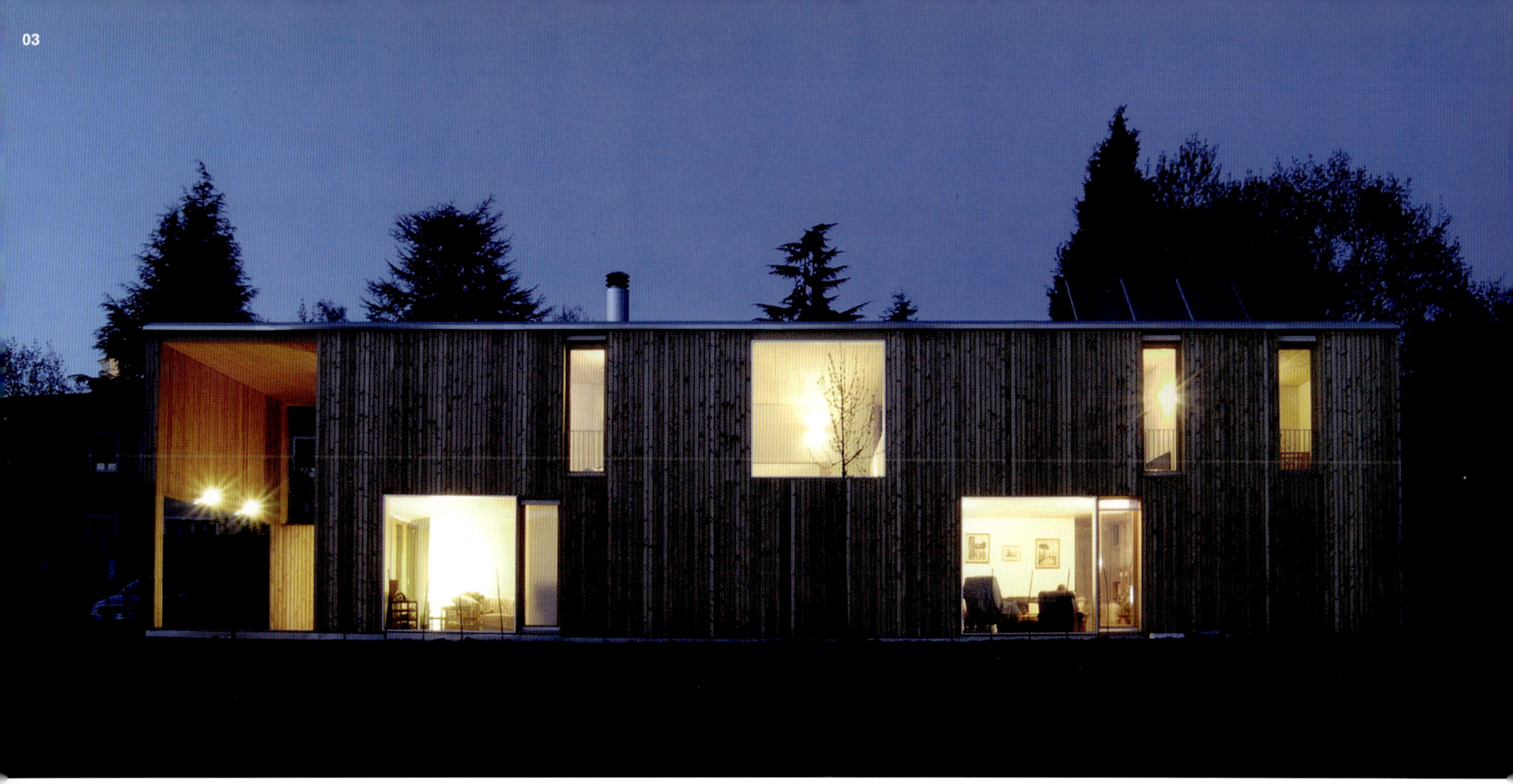

04

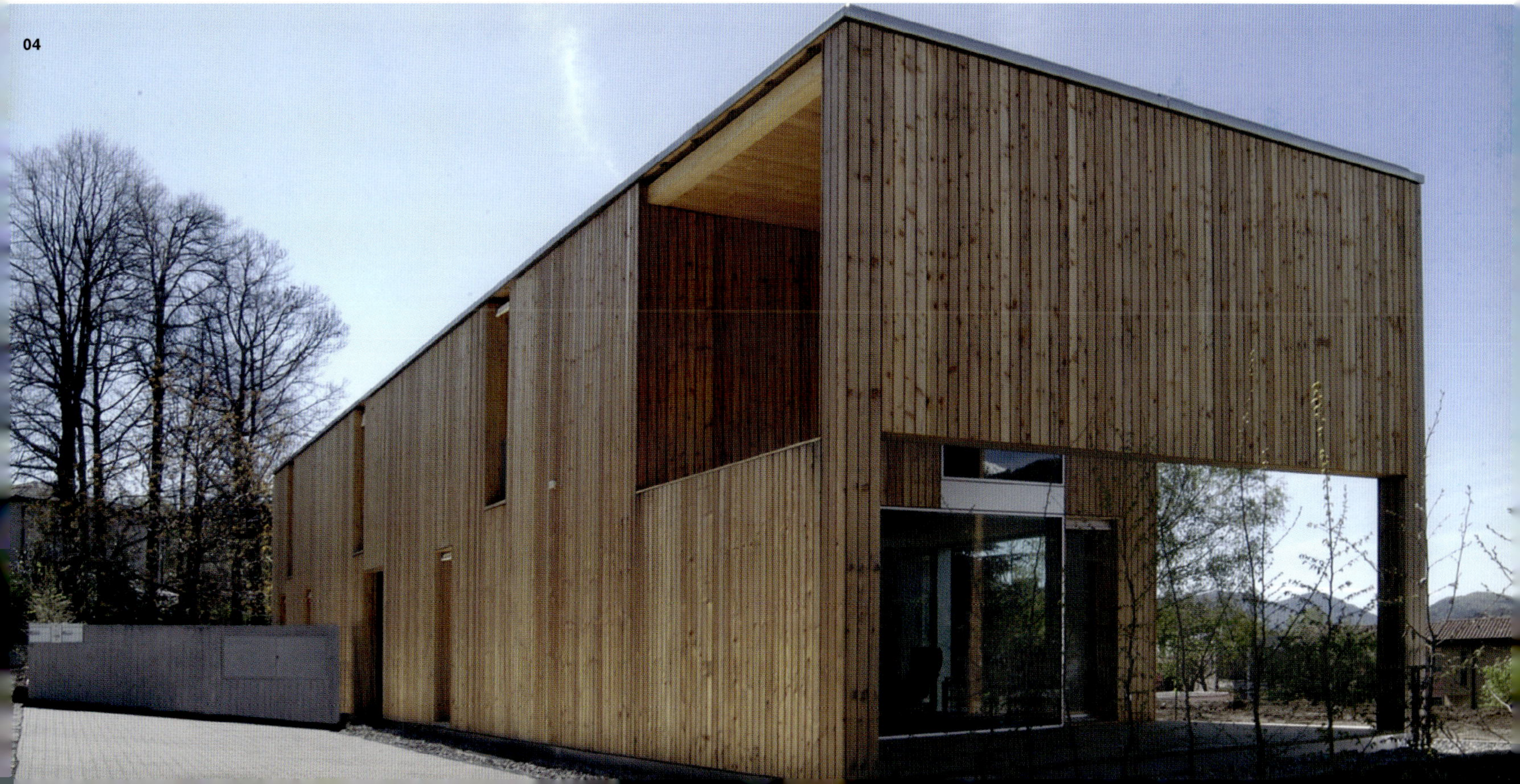

05

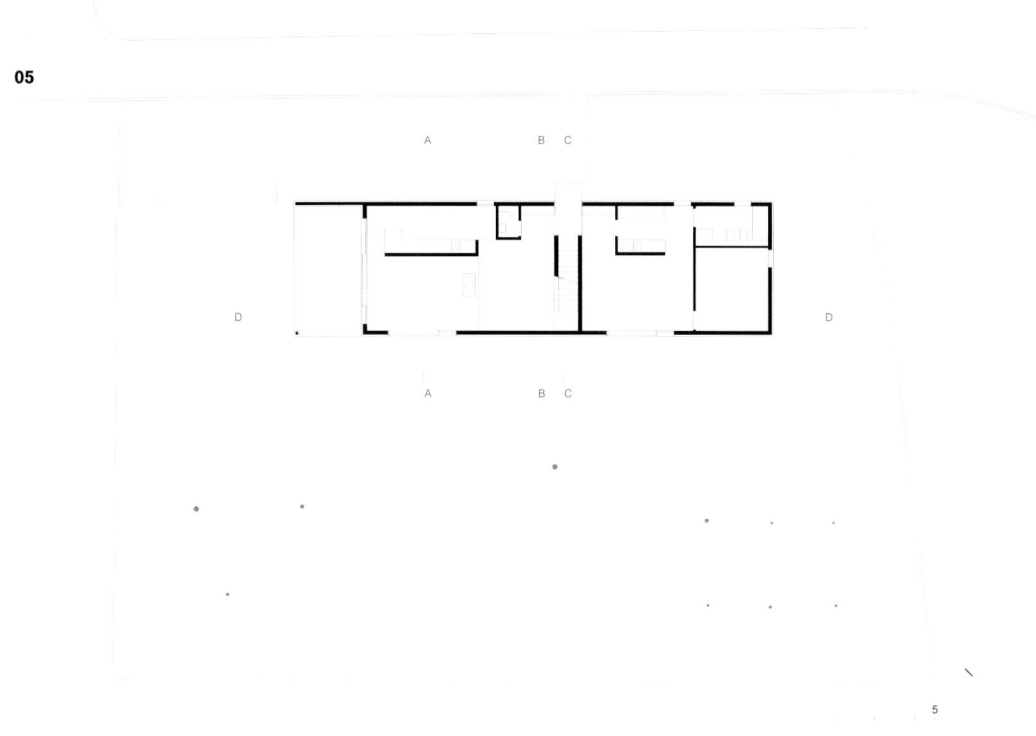

06

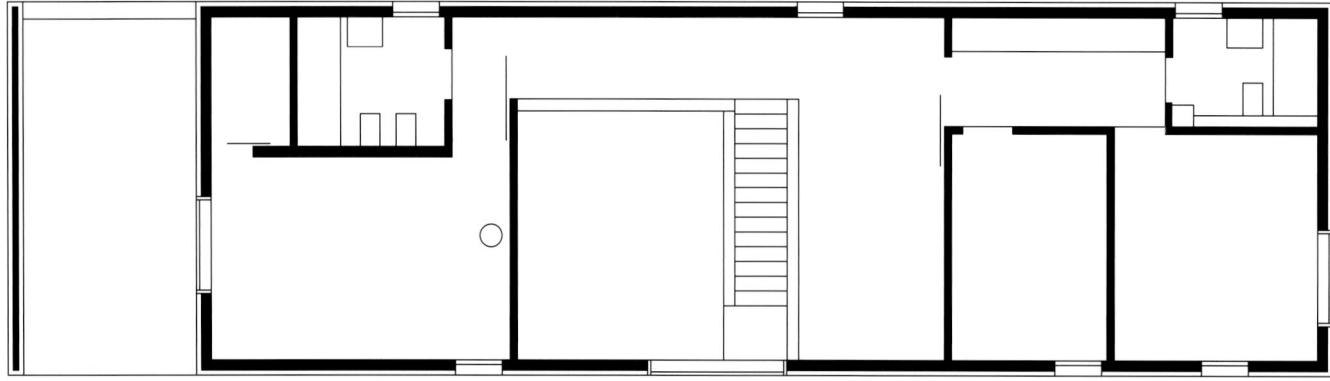

07

Fire department and cultural center, 2000
Address: Platz 501, 6952 Hittisau, Austria. **Client:**
Municipality of Hittisau. **Gross floor area:** 1,191 m².
Materials: solid, enclosed base underlying a two-story
wooden structure.

The space becomes a vessel

ARCHITECTS: cukrowicz nachbaur architekten
with Siegfried Wäger

The plot for the new fire station is located right next to
a forest on the site of a former gravel pit. This building's
unusual design was largely influenced by an equally unusual requirement, but one that makes perfect sense in
the context of a small village community – to combine
two very different functions within one building. While
the fire station opens onto lightly sloping terrain that
leads to the main street of the village, the cultural center
above the fire station opens to the village square via an
expansive glass front. The materials used for the fire
station were concrete, galvanized steel and glass. The
cultural center, meanwhile, in keeping with local building
traditions, used only untreated native silver fir for walls,
ceilings and floors. Due to the uniformity of materials
used in this section of the building, the space becomes
a vessel; it retreats into the background. The color, tem-
perature and smell of the wood creates a subtle pres-
ence – inducing a sense of slowness and calmness in
the visitor.

04

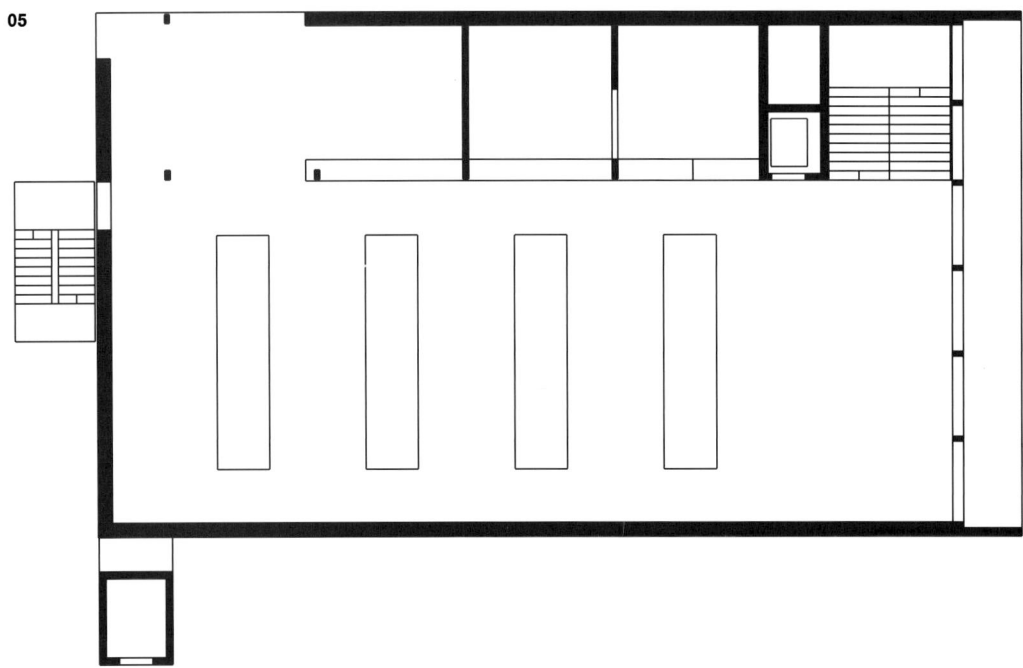

05

132

SLM Residence, 2006
Address: Finistère, Brittany, France. **Client:** private.
Gross floor area: 135 m². **Materials:** concrete floor
(with outside insulation), wooden platform framing,
(with 20 cm mineral wool insulation), chestnut siding,
aluminum openings, zinc roof, pillar in granite stone,
Scandinavian wooden stove.

Traditional Breton farmhouse

ARCHITECTS: Jean-Charles CASTRIC –
architecte D.P.L.G.

The site is a large meadow near an ancient hamlet and
its chapel. The simple volume of the chestnut-sided
house, its long façade oriented towards the sun, seems
to float above the grass. This house, like most traditional
farmhouses in Brittany, orients south-southeast, with the
southerly façade open to the meadow and the sun. Two
substantial "bookends", punctuated by strong horizontal window openings, frame a long wooden terrace that
naturally extends the living room and bedroom spaces.
The north façade on the opposite side is very different;
it is closed and protected against the elements. The attention to orientation and thermal qualities results in a
very energy-efficient building, heated by a single wood
stove. In this project, wood is used both as wall structure
and siding.

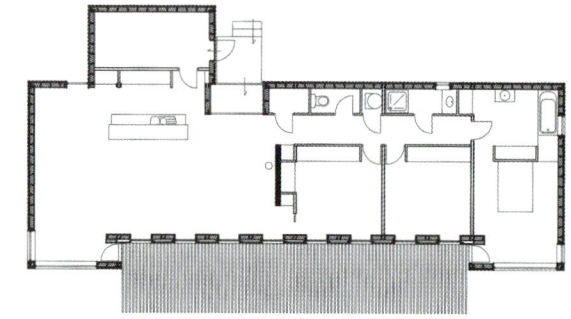

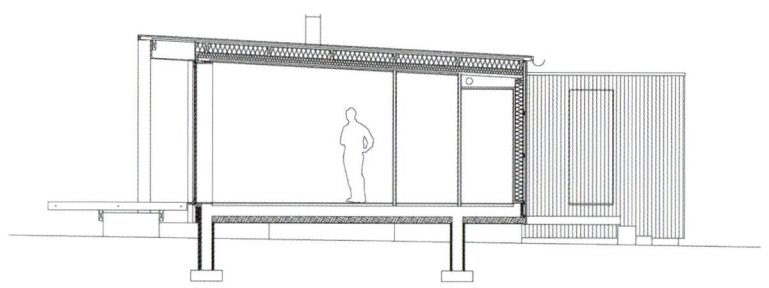

01 South terrace **02** Plan and cross section **03** View from southeast **04**
Wood stove in the living room

03

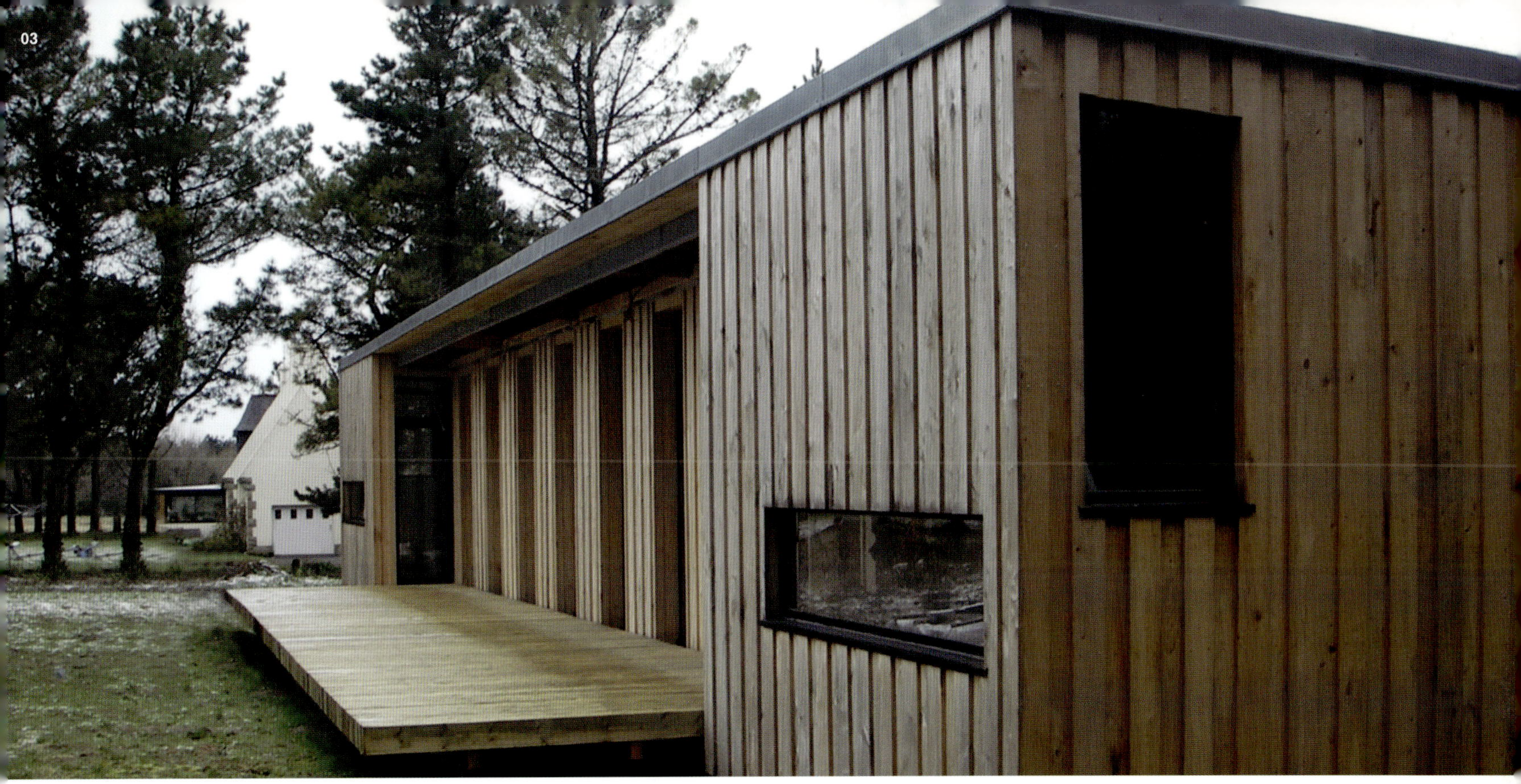

04

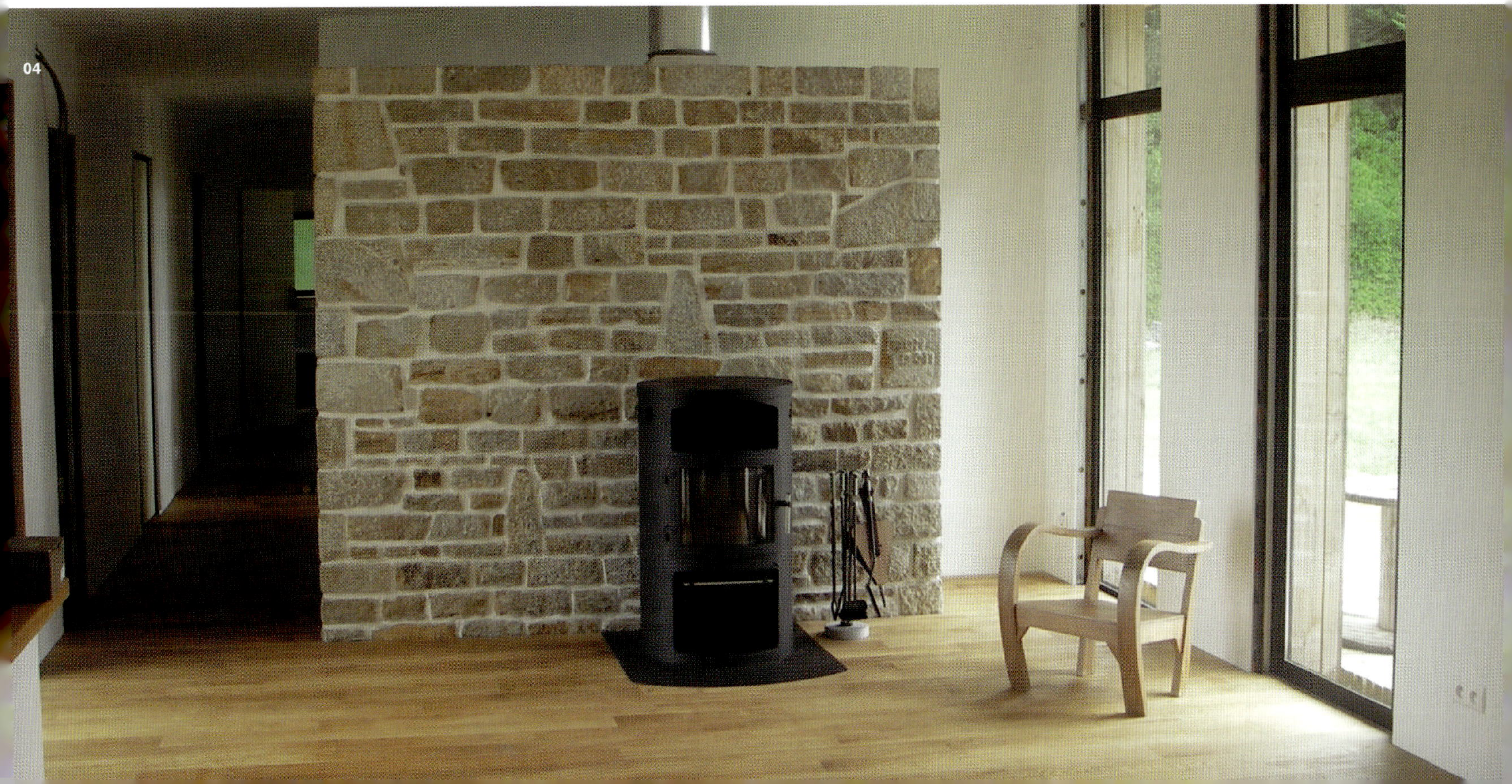

Apartment building, 2006
Address: Gebhartstrasse 15, 3097 Liebefeld, Switzerland. **Client:** Bächler-Haartje family, Arx-Bürgi family, Schürch-Stepper family. **Gross floor area:** 550 m².
Materials: timber-framed construction; cellar, stairway and bracing in reinforced concrete.

Wooden cooling ribs

ARCHITECTS: Halle 58 Architekten GmbH /
Peter Schürch

Seven garages were demolished to make way for this three-story building at an intersection between a 1950s housing estate and older townhouses. The boat-shaped ground plan of the new wooden house was determined by the shape of the property. The ground plan and elevation show the layout: Three apartments of equal size entirely built in wood, accessible via the concrete staircase, are perched slightly above the level of the site. The concentration of sanitation and technology services into a compact core, plus a load-bearing façade frees up the interior design of the apartments, permitting a loft-like spatial scheme. On each floor the façade is composed of a combination of wooden framework elements, glazing and entrance doors. What appears at first glance to be concrete cooling fins are in reality made of wood, derived timber sheets and Duripanel particle board.

02

03

04

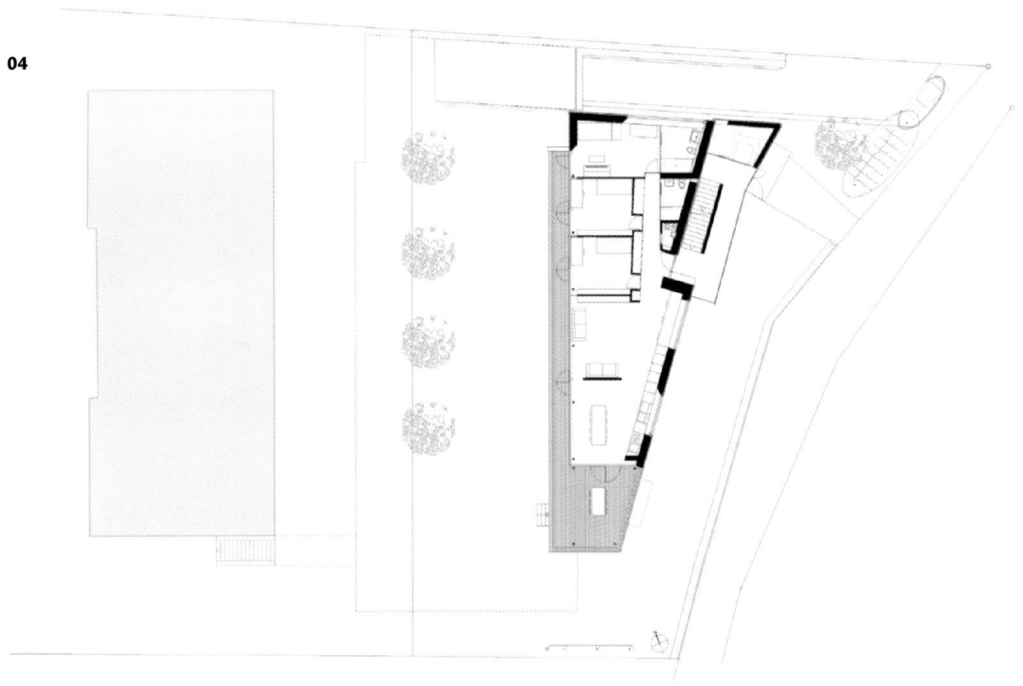

05

06

138

07

08

RURAL

Orazietti / Bernadi Residence, 2007
Address: Burnaby, British Columbia, Canada. **Client:** private. **Gross floor area:** 326 m². **Materials:** wood frame construction.

Western style

ARCHITECTS: BattersbyHowat

The site is located in a tranquil suburb of Vancouver with neighboring houses on both sides. The house facing the street and the garage on the back lane are positioned in such a way that they create a private courtyard-like garden space with a generous concrete terrace off the house. The three-story house (including the basement), which was built for a young family of four is organized conventionally. The main level has an open-plan kitchen, dining room and living room arrangement, with a small office next to the entrance. Service rooms are located to the side, separated by a central staircase. The staircase is constructed with a single central stringer and cantilevered treads. On the upper level the children's bedrooms are separated from the master bedroom by the bathroom, laundry area and adjacent stairs. The play room, a guest bedroom and a traditional cantina for wine-making (the client's family background is Italian) are located on the basement level.

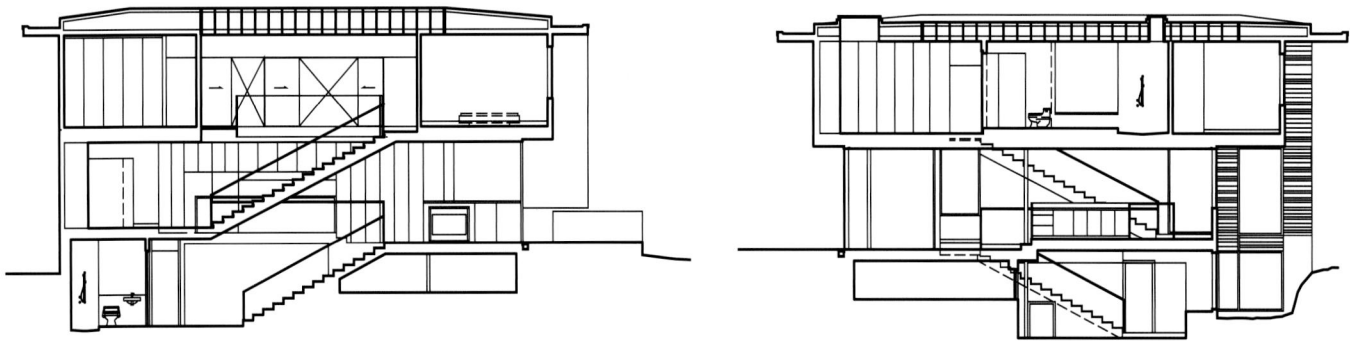

Museum of Modern Art – Bruno Gironcoli's sculpture house at Schloss Herberstein, 2004
Address: 8222 St. Johann bei Herberstein, Austria.
Client: Schloss Herberstein zoo and nature reserve.
Gross floor area: existing: 1,263 m², new structure: 920 m². **Materials:** Façade: Alufix® framing, translucent plastic façade elements with UV-reflecting coating; Roof truss: wood.

Old and new in harmony
ARCHITECTS: Dipl.-Ing. Hermann Eisenköck

This project consisted of two stages. The first involved restoring the old grain-threshing hall. The impressive wooden load-bearing structure beneath the old half-hipped roof needed only to be cleaned and in places touched up. The rafters were in excellent condition. These were integrated into the new insulation system, leaving the original wooden structure exposed. Secondly, a new gallery level was introduced at the roof truss. Roof dormers with openable slatted windows provide natural lighting and ventilation. The new structure with its modern glass, steel and plastic form represents a deliberate, clear and reserved use of form that allows the original building to retain its impact while also providing sufficient space for the sculptures.

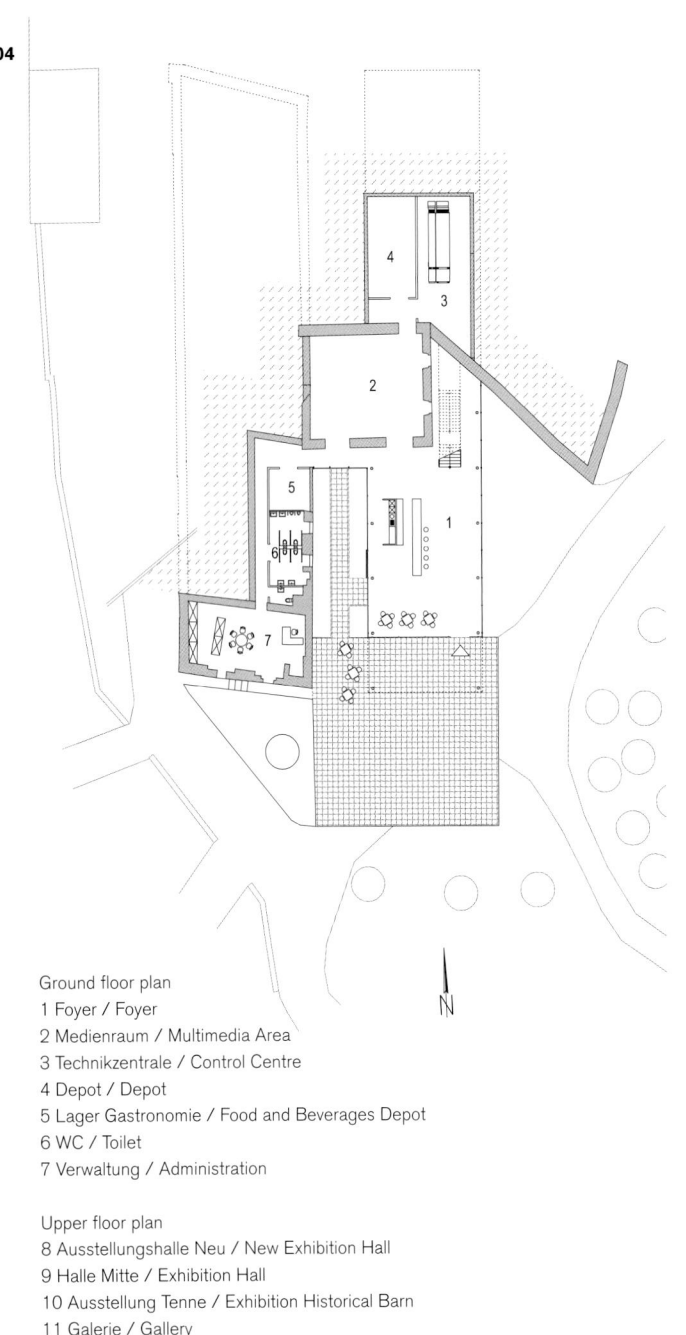

05

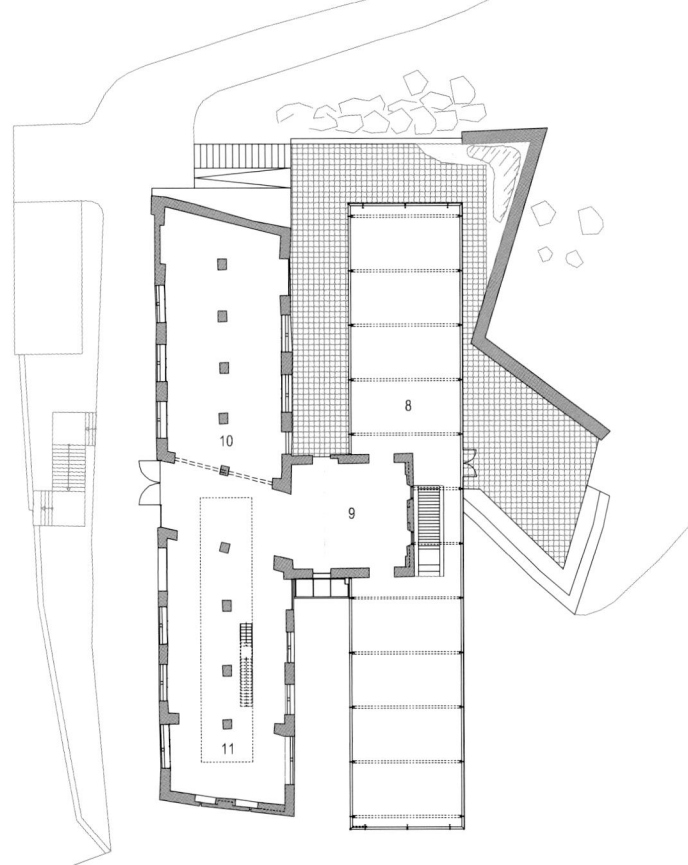

N

Ground floor plan
1 Foyer / Foyer
2 Medienraum / Multimedia Area
3 Technikzentrale / Control Centre
4 Depot / Depot
5 Lager Gastronomie / Food and Beverages Depot
6 WC / Toilet
7 Verwaltung / Administration

Upper floor plan
8 Ausstellungshalle Neu / New Exhibition Hall
9 Halle Mitte / Exhibition Hall
10 Ausstellung Tenne / Exhibition Historical Barn
11 Galerie / Gallery

01

Experimental House, since 1999
Address: Annaghmaconway, Cloone, County Leitrim, Ireland. **Client:** Dominic Stevens and Mari-Aymone Djeribi. **Structural engineers:** John Casey, Casey O'Rourke. **Gross floor area:** approx. 200 m² (fluctuating). **Materials:** frame fabricated on site in polytunnel workshop, wood.

Built with their own hands

ARCHITECTS:

Dominic Stevens, Mari-Aymone Djeribi

There are two different kinds of spaces in this home, drawing on different traditions and fulfillling different needs. The first sits within the timber frame. Two horizontal planes sail above the landscape. Between this floor and ceiling specific functions (cooking, eating and sleeping) are catered for. These rooms are four sided, the edges defined by walls or south-facing floor-to-ceiling glazing. The second kind of space is earth-bound. The floor runs with the landscape, the thick walls imply excavated space, the spaces formed are ambiguous — are you within the wall or beside it? These are places to withdraw from the world, to feel protected; it is as if you are enveloped within the landscape itself. This home was designed so that the owners / architects could build it themselves. It is built of local materials, using a constructional logic that combines the modern with the vernacular. This approach to technology has resulted in a per-square-meter building cost of less than € 600, including services, site works and all finishes.

02

N

Steger Residence, 2002
Address: Künighof 29, 39030 St. Jakob, Ahrntal, Italy.
Client: Walter Steger. **Gross floor area:** 335.79 m².
Materials: Kerto® wooden structure, glass façade.

House in a glass case

ARCHITECTS: Dr. Arch. Stefan Hitthaler

The aim of this project was to modernize a residential building while retaining the original structure. Thus the farmhouse, which dates from the 18th century, was enclosed within a glass shell. This insulates the building and protects it from wind without altering the structure of the walls or the size of the windows. The new living space that has been created between the old house and the glass façade is bright and extroverted. By contrast, the wood-paneled living room within the old interior provides a cozy retreat. This solution has ensured that a valuable architectural structure has been retained. Recycling was also a key consideration in the design of this extension: in the event that the owners choose to restore the original form of the building, the wood used in the extension can be reused or recycled. The wood used in the flooring, cladding and structural beams was felled in the client's own forest and finished locally.

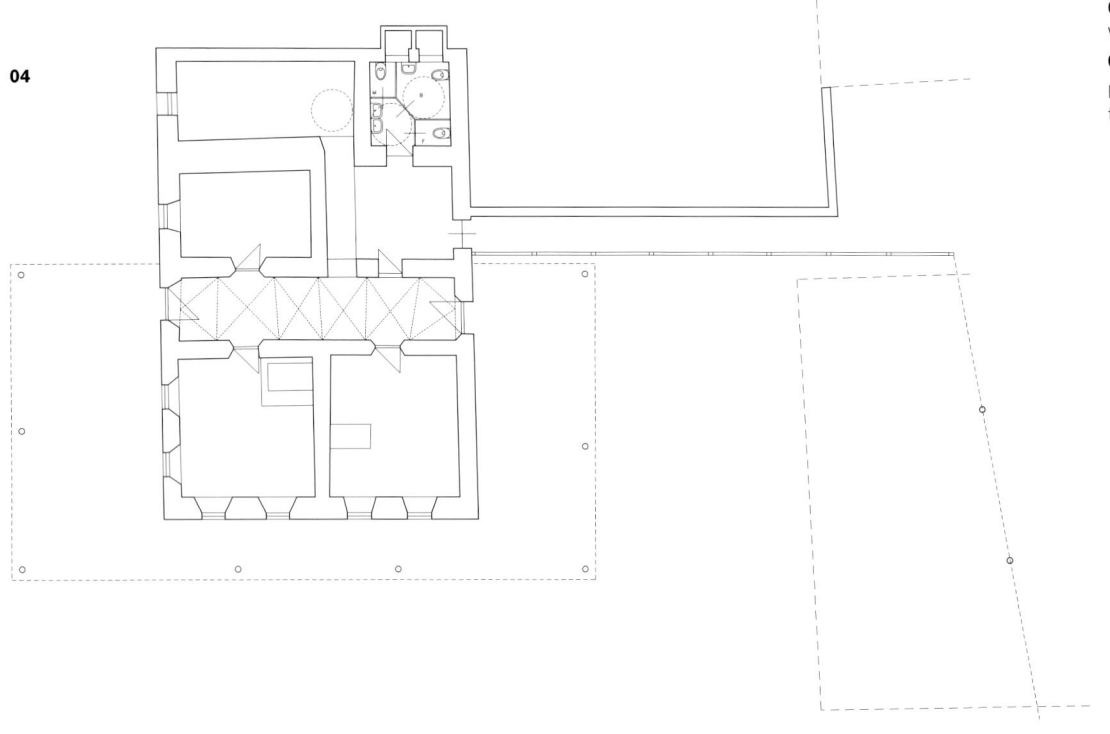

04

05

06

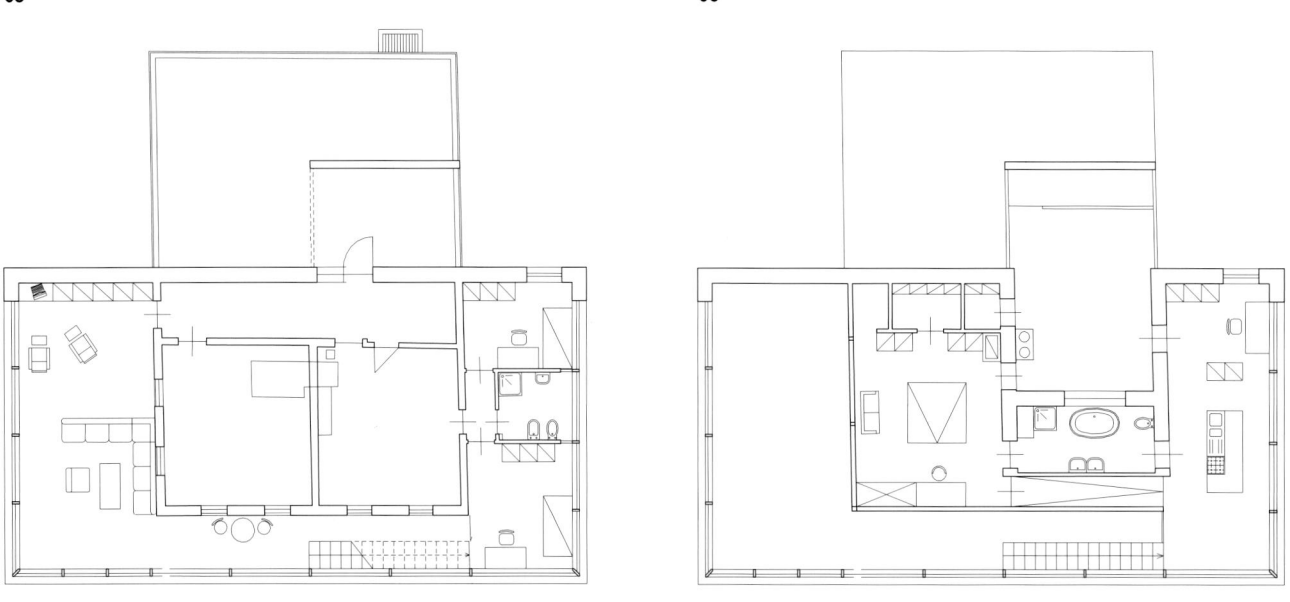

156

07

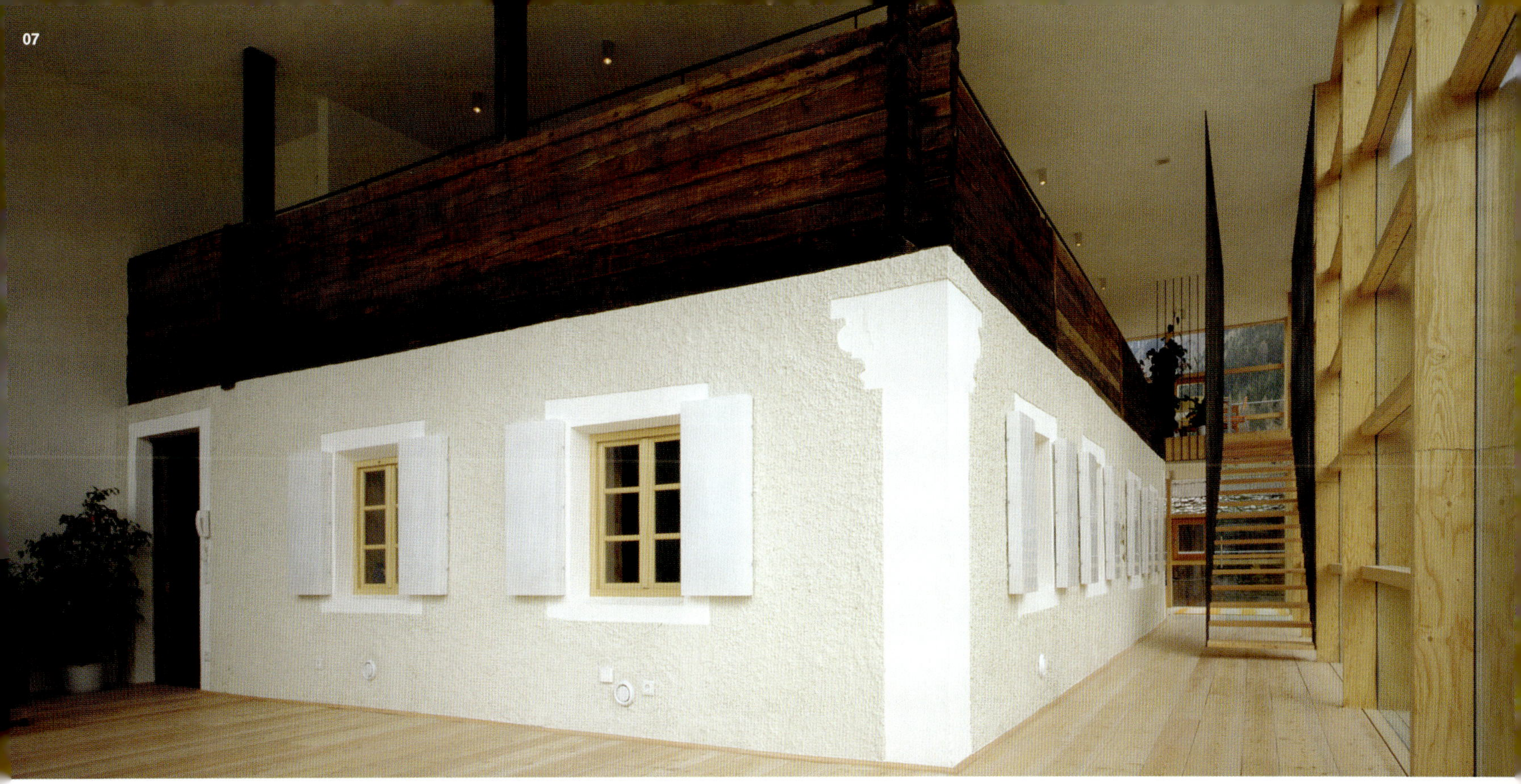

08

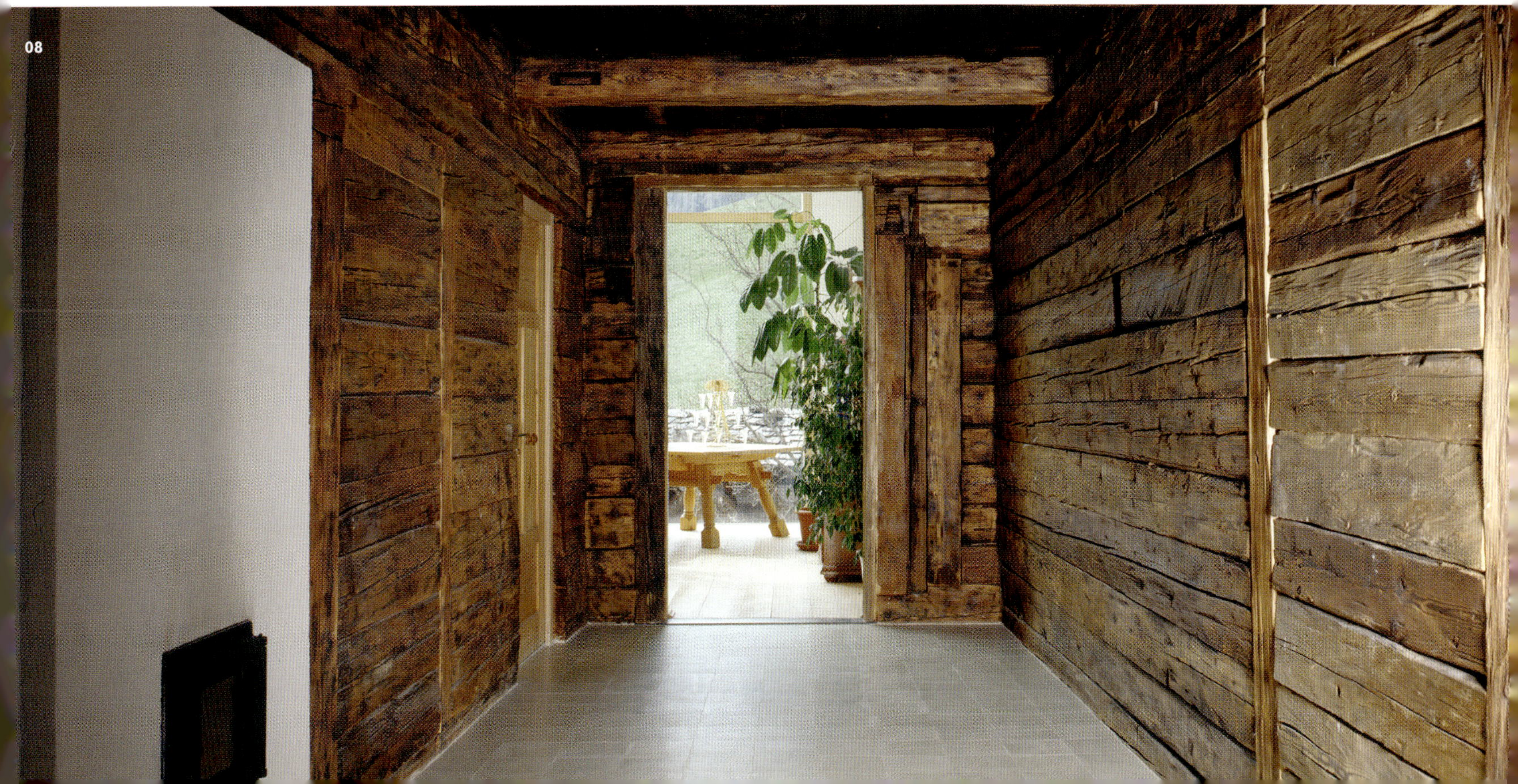

Private home in Wellingsbüttel, 2006
Address: Hochestieg 3, 22391 Hamburg, Germany.
Client: Dr. Katharina Waselowsky. **Gross floor area:**
new structure: 230 m². **Materials:** wood-frame structure with cladding of titanium-zinc borders and larchwood slats, solid base of Wittmund clinker brick.

Twin houses

ARCHITECTS: Stefan Waselowsky Architekt

In the exclusive Alster Valley suburb of Hamburg a classic pitched-roof house from the 1950s has been repli-
cated so that new and old twins now stand next to each
other. The extension consists of an elongated, gabled
structure with a pitched roof. The architects adopted the
characteristic gabled style of 1930s homes. This represents a reduction in the geometry of the original house,
producing a design akin to a house in a child's painting.
This effect is further underscored by the visual continuity of the roof line into the exterior walls through the
uniform materiality of a zinc plate border. The extension
is connected to the original building via the entrance
hallway of the old house. This connecting section is fully
glazed on the ground floor yet largely enclosed on the
upper level. The extension as a whole is a prefabricated
timber-framed structure resting on a base of Wittmund
clinker brick. The gable ends have a wooden façade
of tapered larch slats, with spaces between the
individual slats.

02

03

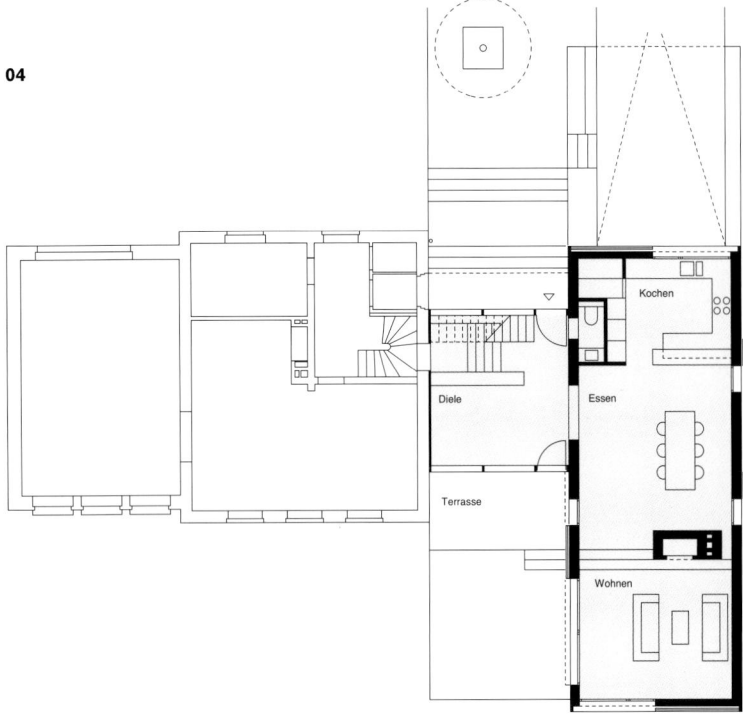

Kochen

Diele

Essen

Terrasse

Wohnen

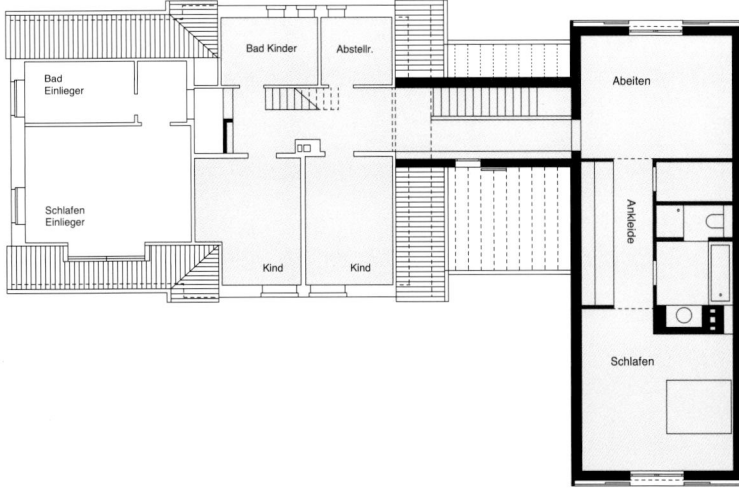

Bad Kinder

Abstellr.

Abeiten

Bad Einlieger

Schlafen Einlieger

Ankleide

Kind

Kind

Schlafen

06

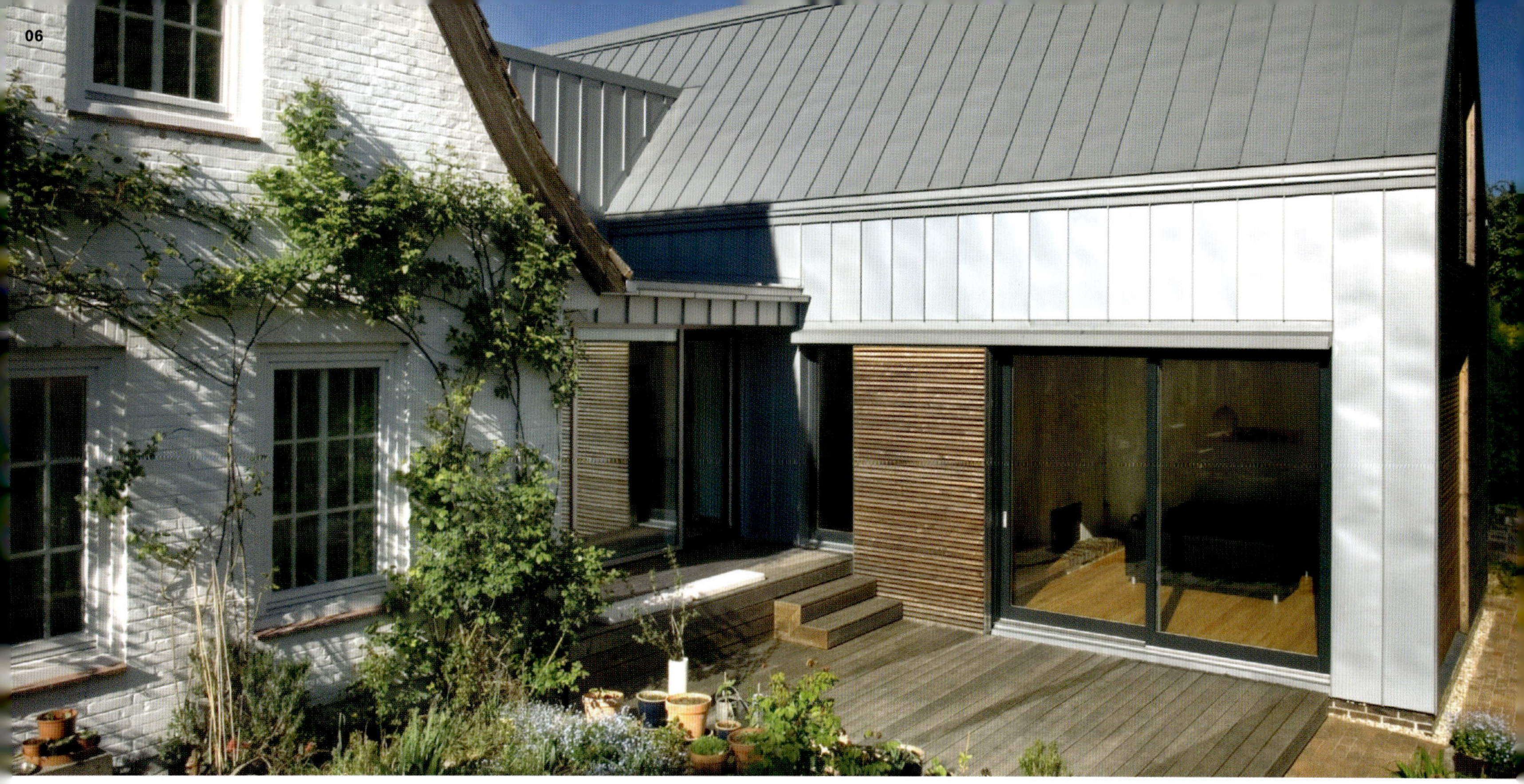

07

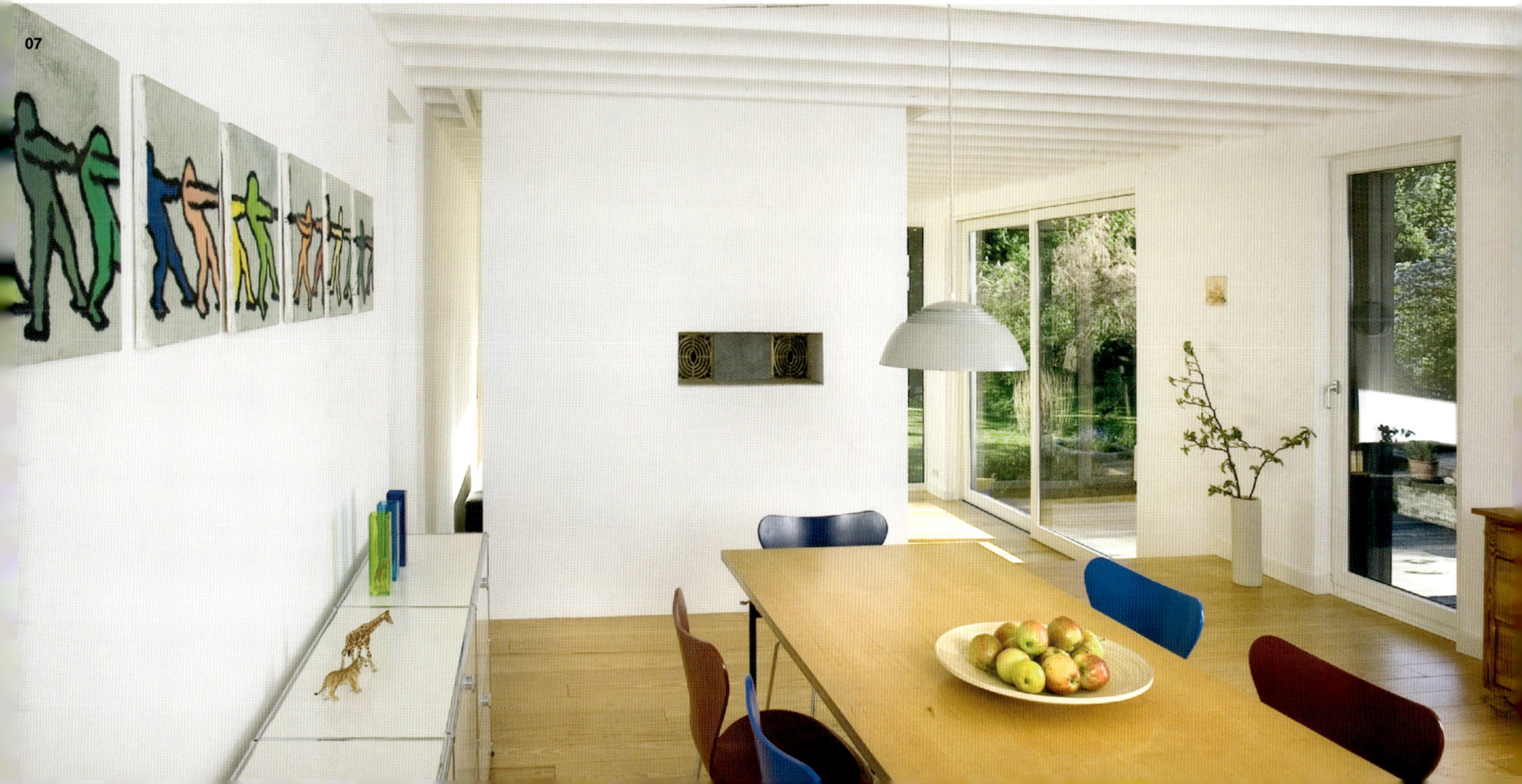

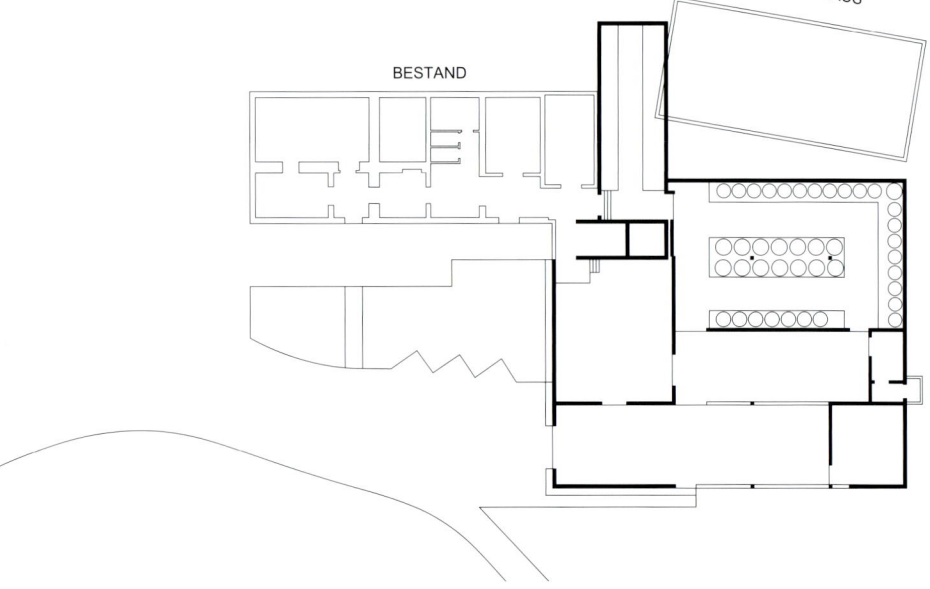

PRESSHAUS

BESTAND

Lackner-Tinnacher Winery, 2001
Address: Steinbach 12, Gamlitz, Austria. **Client:** Lack-ner-Tinnacher Winery. **Gross floor area:** 751.5 m².
Materials: larch laths, Nirosta® window panels, reinforced concrete.

Under a green roof

ARCHITECTS: Rolf Rauner

The new building consists of a plain yet powerful cube that optimally accommodates all of the winery's production processes and leaves room for future expansion. At its southern end the building burrows into the soil of the wine estate, while the slope runs into the green roof of the winery. The new structure is connected to the existing winery building at its northern and eastern ends. The untreated larchwood façade, which is the defining feature of this project, forms the climate-controlled shell of the ferro-concrete load-bearing structure at the north and west ends of the building. The natural patina of the larch attractively matches the color tones of the nearby vines.

01 Floor plan **02** Detail west façade **03** View from west **04** West façade

03

04

Amanogawa Bridge, 2007
Address: Tokachi Millennium Forest Minami-10, Hao-bi, Shimizu-cho, Kamikawa-gun, Hokkaido, Japan. **Art work:** Roger Holte, artist. **Client:** Tokaichi Millennium Forest, Tokaichi Mainichi newspaper. **Gross floor area:** 48 m². **Dimensions:** large bridge length 12.5 m x width 2.7 m x height 2.7 m; small bridge length 8 m x width 2.2 m x height 2.4 m. **Materials:** structures and surfaces wood, concrete and steel fundament, cast aluminum art work.

A childhood memory

ARCHITECTS: Sami Rintala

The natural landscape of Hokkaido is reminiscent of the Nordic countries. There are birch forests, one can hear cuckoos in the distance and smell the same fragrance of misty grass and wet forest after a chilly summer's night. The architect wanted visitors to this forest to notice the small forest creek, how the daylight plays on it and how its happy sound fills the constructed space. If one is still for a while, one may even see some of the small trout that live here. This atmosphere evoked in the architect a childhood memory of another forest far away on another continent, some thirty years ago. Amanogawa means "Milky Way" in Japanese, literally "river of the sky". Some indigenous people believe that time passes at different speeds in different places. The idea behind the Amanogawa Bridge was to create a small place where water and time move at a peaceful pace.

01

02

03

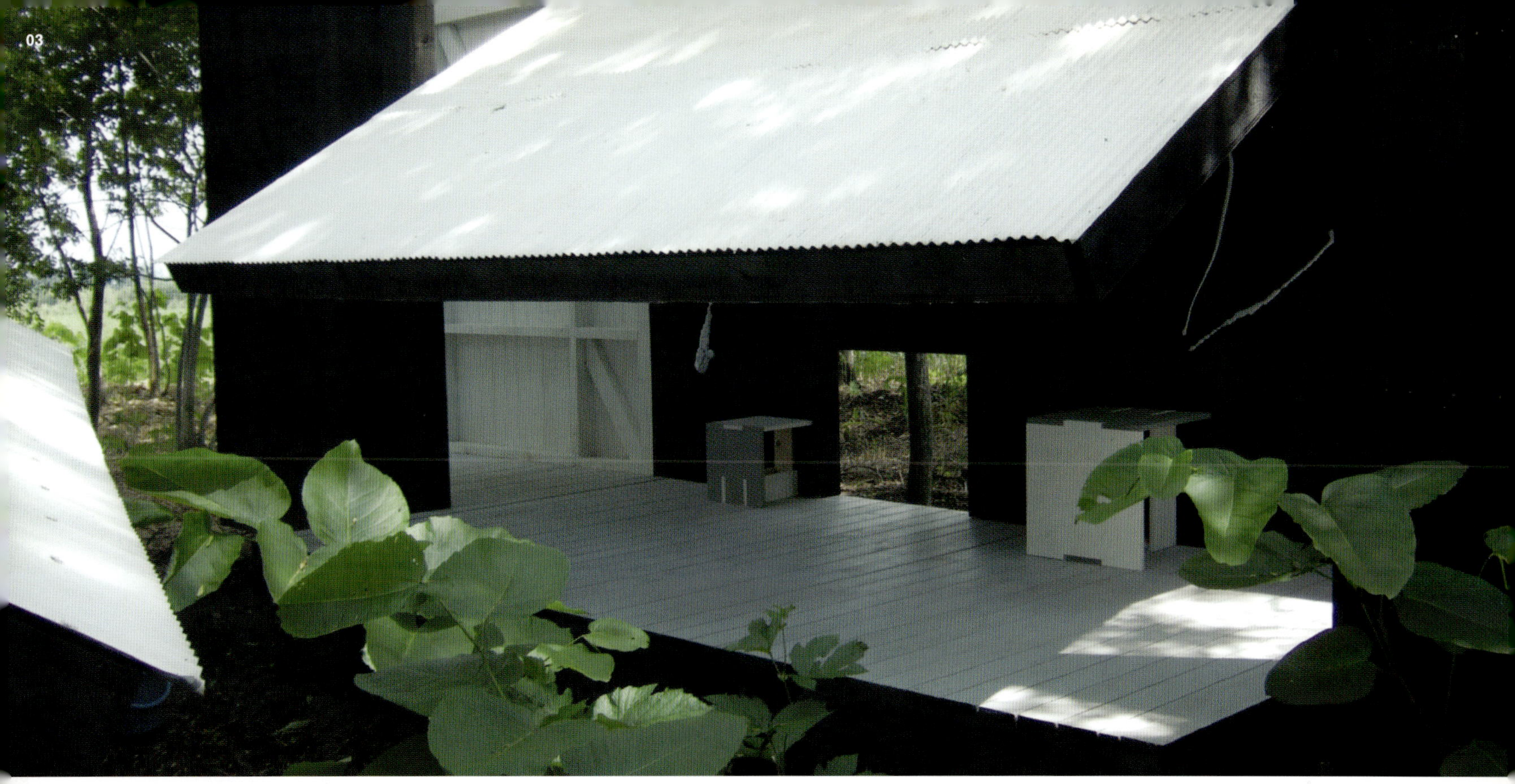

04

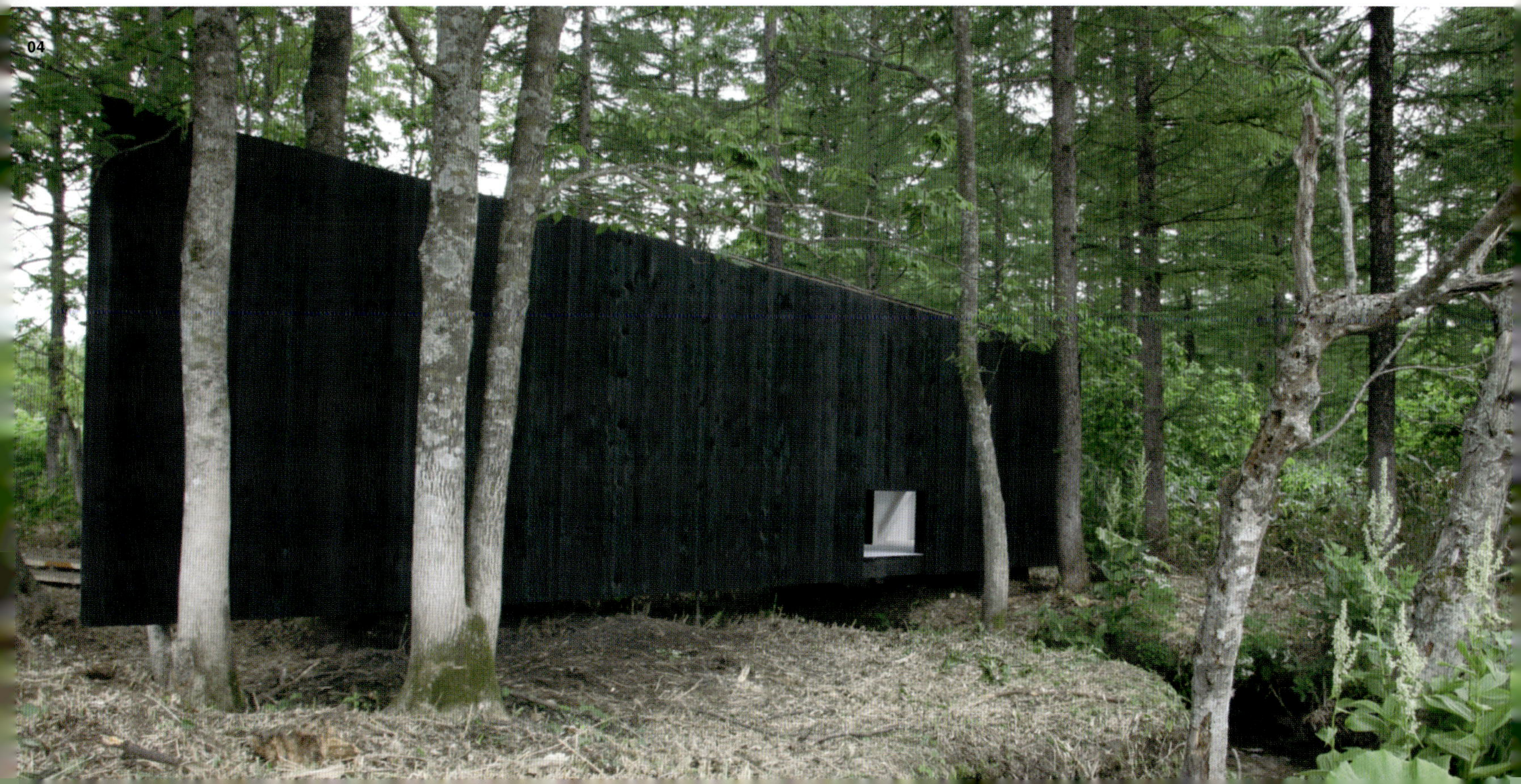

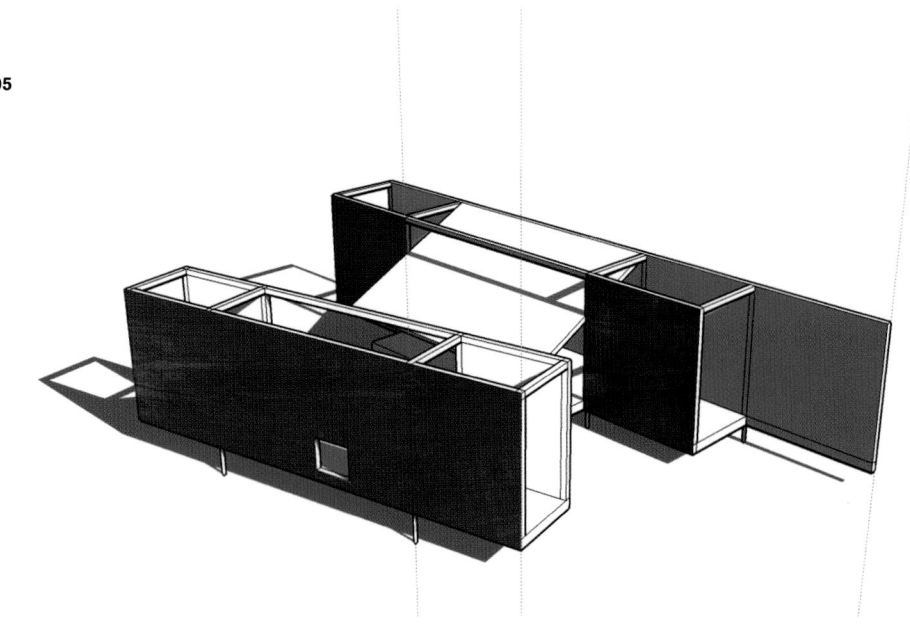

01 + **02** Detail **03** Front view **04** Rear view **05** Perspective **06** Perspective roof **07** View along the bridge **08** Bird's eye view

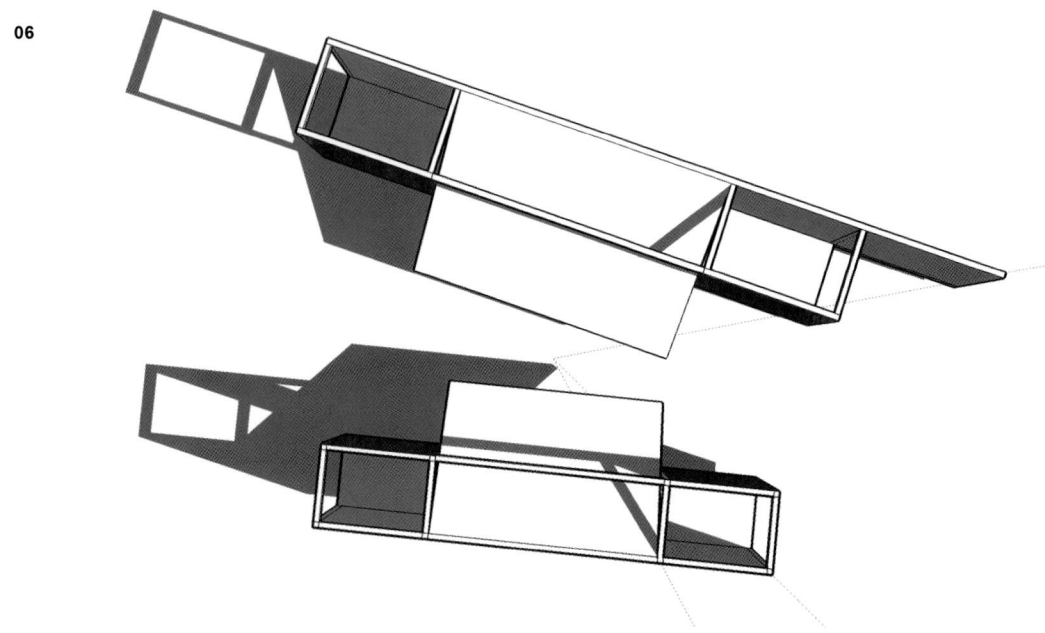

Haabakka extension, 2004
Address: 5472 Seimsfoss, Rosendal, Norway. **Client:**
Guddal family. **Gross floor area:** 24 m². **Materials:**
wood and glass.

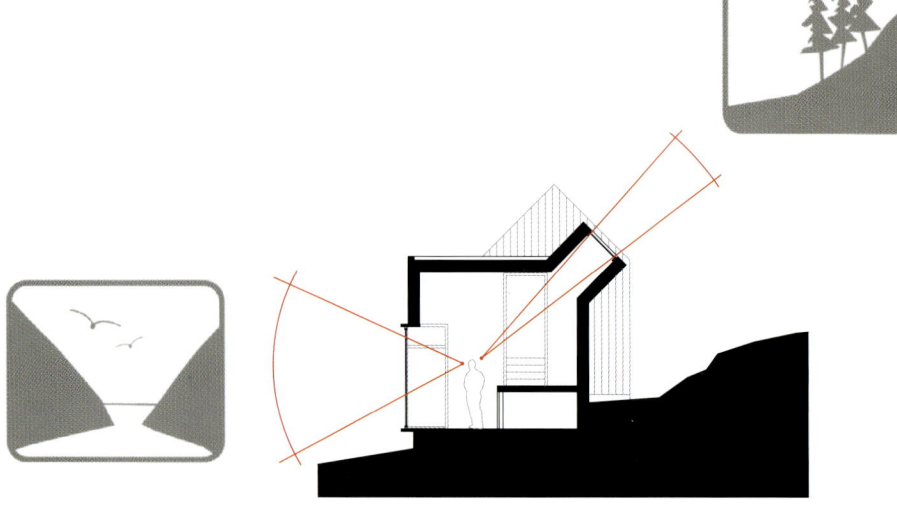

Multi-purpose linking structure

ARCHITECTS: 3rw architects

The Haabakka farm complex consists of five buildings
situated on a slope at the upper end of Guddal, near
the town of Rosendal. The buildings form a cluster, with
the housing units located at the center. The contemporary perception of the complex is rather static, but
this early Norwegian urban typology arose from a building tradition dominated by pragmatism and dynamics.
Some of the buildings at the Haabakka complex were
purchased elsewhere in the region when additional
structures were required. In this way the complex has
been an arena for constant change, depending on the
contemporary needs and resources of the inhabitants.
The infill-addition is built between the two housing units.
The adjacent housing units are extremely small with low
ceilings that allow very little daylight to enter. This generated an ambition to develop an open, multi-purpose
linking structure that enables the inhabitants to utilize
the two housing units in a more flexible way.

01 Section connecting the extension to the landscape **02** Front view,
extension **03** View of the front door

01

Wooden house, 2006
Address: Lieberichsweg 42, 53426 Schalkenbach, Germany. **Clients:** Cornelia Sternberg and Wolfgang Bauer. **Gross floor area:** 165 m². **Material:** timber-framed structure.

Éminence grise

ARCHITECTS:

architektur_raum bauer sternberg

Simplicity, modesty and archetypal design are the primary virtues of this house. It stands apart from the surrounding landscape thanks to its sharp, clear edges; yet the extensive use of wood reconciles it with its natural environment. Large window openings allow light to stream in and reveal spectacular panoramic views. The compact structure serves to minimize heat loss. Yet the ecological features do not end there: by making use of solar cells, a warm air pump and rainwater this house actively boosts its own energy budget. Wood is the defining element in this building. On the outside larchwood sheathing, which quickly assumed the desired gray patina, was used on the façade and roof. In the interior wood is mainly evident in the windows and flooring.

02

05

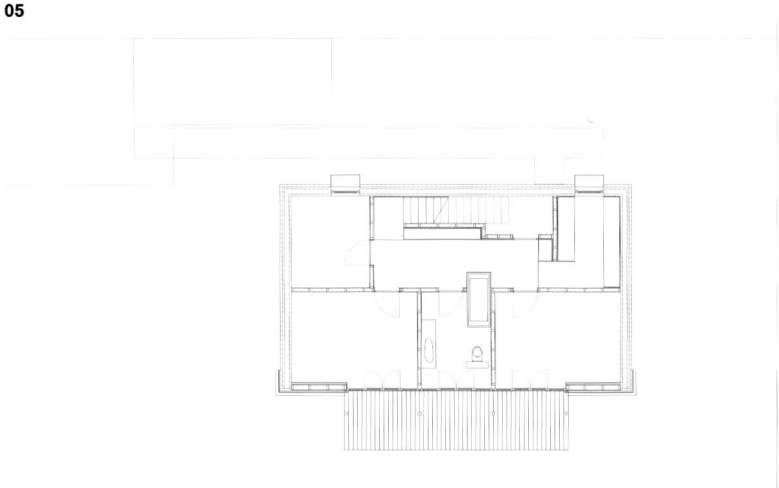

06

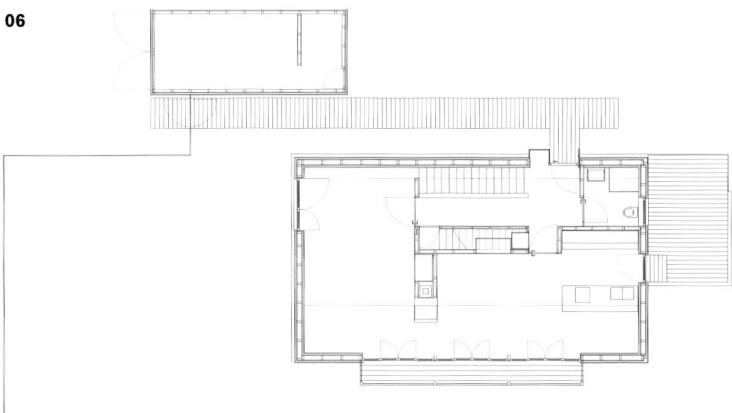

07

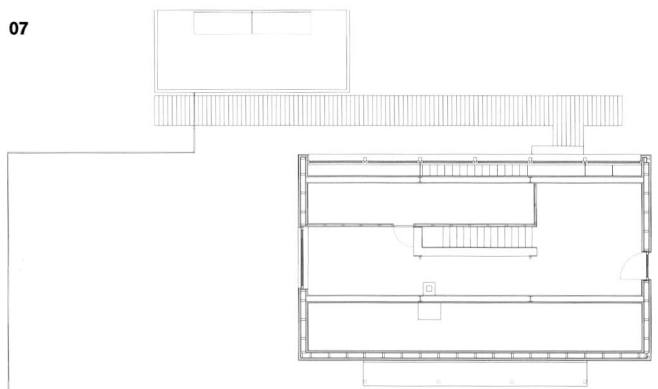

Black Dog House, 2004
Address: Karuizawa, Nagano, Japan. **Client:** private.
Gross floor area: 145.8 m². **Material:** wood.

Sylvan living

ARCHITECTS: Atelier Bow-Wow

A humble exterior, tightly contained; an interior of large and high spaces, expansive walls hung with art, and filled with natural light. In order to fulfill these seemingly contradictory requirements of the client, the architects made use of a variety of architectural "slippage tricks". First, they designed eaves, three meters above ground level, to run around the perimeter, visually dividing the building into upper and lower parts. The lower part, clad with larch boards stained black-green, forms a coagulation of shadows; while the upper section, an indented volume with clad with metal panels in silver and white, is a congregation of light. The low volume, set amidst a copse of 15-meter-high trees, stresses horizontality. These exterior impressions contrast with the verticality of the interior. A white wall, 3.7 meters high and with a total length of 65 meters, follows a convoluted path enfolding a set of indented spaces. Here, the axes of the convolutions are offset – "slipped" – in such a way that the indented spaces are interlinked at their corners.

01

02

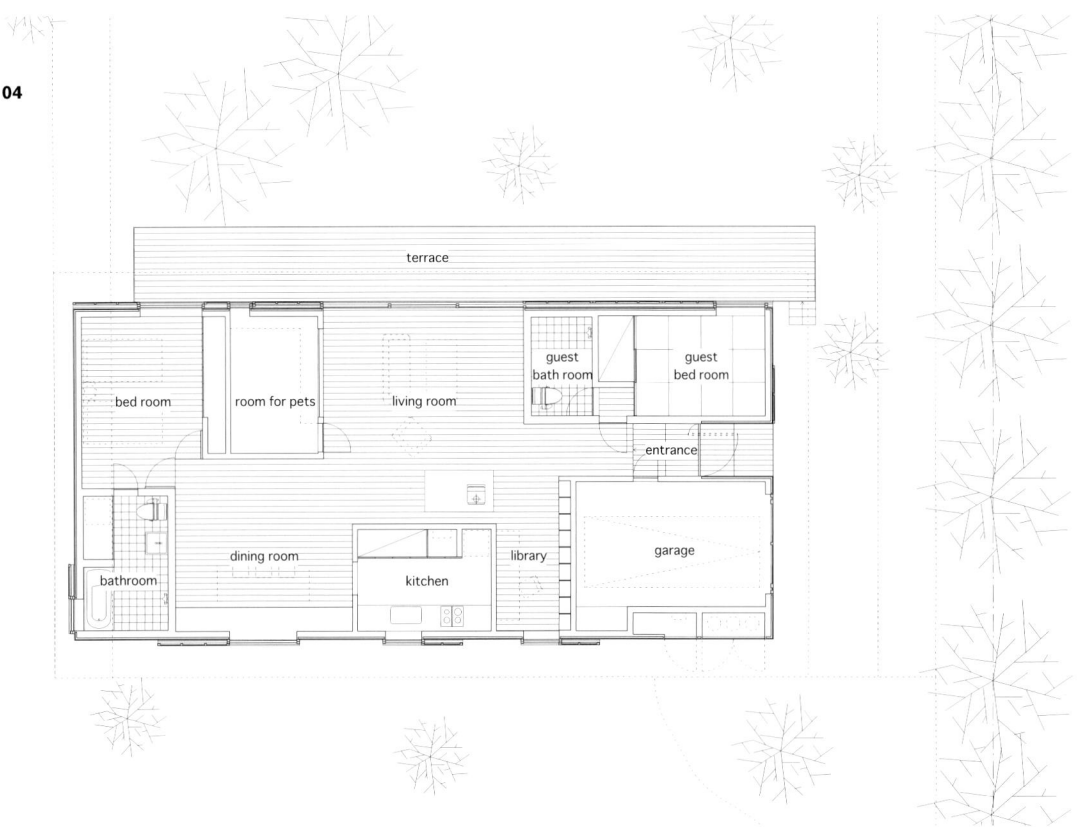

terrace

bed room

room for pets

living room

guest bath room

guest bed room

entrance

bathroom

dining room

kitchen

library

garage

05

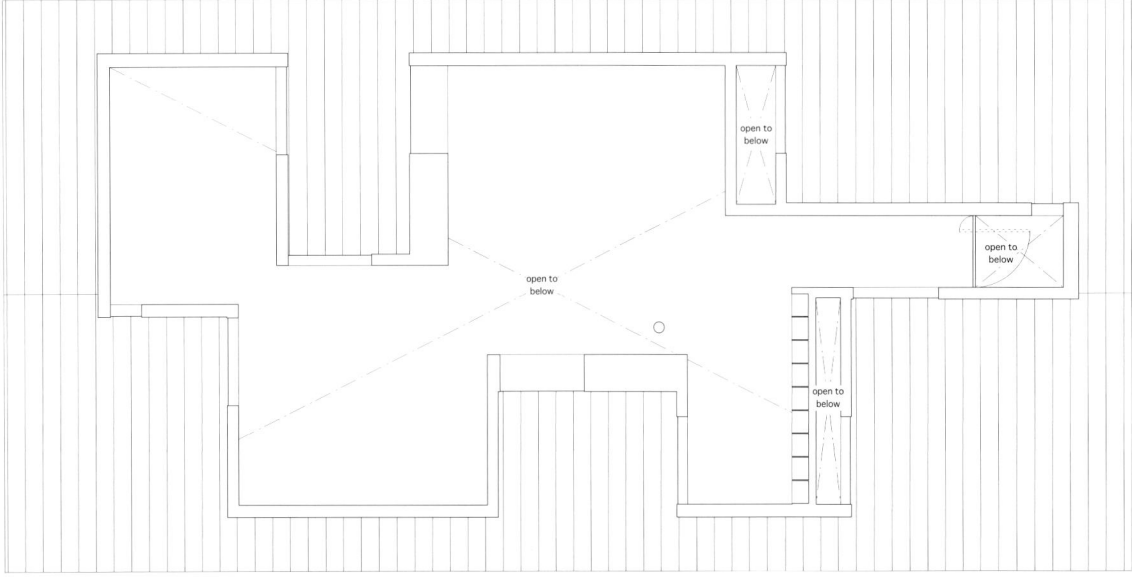

open to below

open to below

open to below

open to below

Flower Valley Edu-Care Center, 2003
Address: Flower Valley Farm near Gansbaai, South
Western Cape Province, South Africa. **Client:** Flower
Valley Conservation Trust. **Gross floor area:** interior:
65 m²; veranda: 16 m². **Materials:** cob (clay, sand,
straw), stone, timber.

With locally harvested poles

ARCHITECTS:

Eco Design Architects and Consultants

The brief was to create a multi-purpose edu-care center on a indigenous flower farm near Gansbaai in the
Western Cape Province of South Africa that showcased
an environmental approach to construction. The center
functions as a pre-school for the local farming community as well as a venue for social occasions. The concept was to create an L-shaped floor plan and roof form,
thereby also creating a wind-sheltered zone for outdoor
teaching. By using local, natural and recycled materials, the project helped to maximize the involvement and
education of local farm laborers in the construction
process. The building was designed as a timber-framed
structure, in-filled with a mixture of cob and timber paneling. Locally harvested timber poles were used as supports with stone piers used to provide additional bracing. Timber poles were used for the roof structure, and
are visible in the interior. Poles are structurally superior
to cut timber, and result in a very lightweight structure.
The poles were locally harvested and treated on-site
with boron, a non-toxic treatment method.

01 Sketch **02** View from northeast **03** View from northwest **04** View
from east

03

04

Bonetti Residence, 2005
Address: West Vancouver, British Columbia, Canada.
Client: Melissa & Ross Bonetti. **Gross floor area:**
433.6 m². **Materials:** wood frame construction.

Enigmatic sloping shell

ARCHITECTS: BattersbyHowat

The Bonetti house is sited on a heavily wooded hillside
in a suburb of Vancouver. The house generates its own
territory within a traditional L-shaped courtyard, two stories high on its long leg, and only one on its short end.
The house is two-sided: an enigmatic sloping stucco
shell from the streetfront side paired with a detailed
wood-slatted inner courtyard configured for outdoor
entertaining. The walls around the courtyard slope out-
wards, giving some rooms a triangular feel. The relationship between the pool area and the interior space of
the house is a reflection of the client's "social nature".
On the main floor polished concrete flooring is used inside and out, linking the interior with the exterior spaces.
The walls facing the courtyard are clad in custom-milled
cedar drop siding. There are vertical aluminum reveals
between the panels. This detailing allows for the use of
shorter, less expensive timber pieces, and at the same
time ensures a sharp and modern appearance.

03

04

05

06

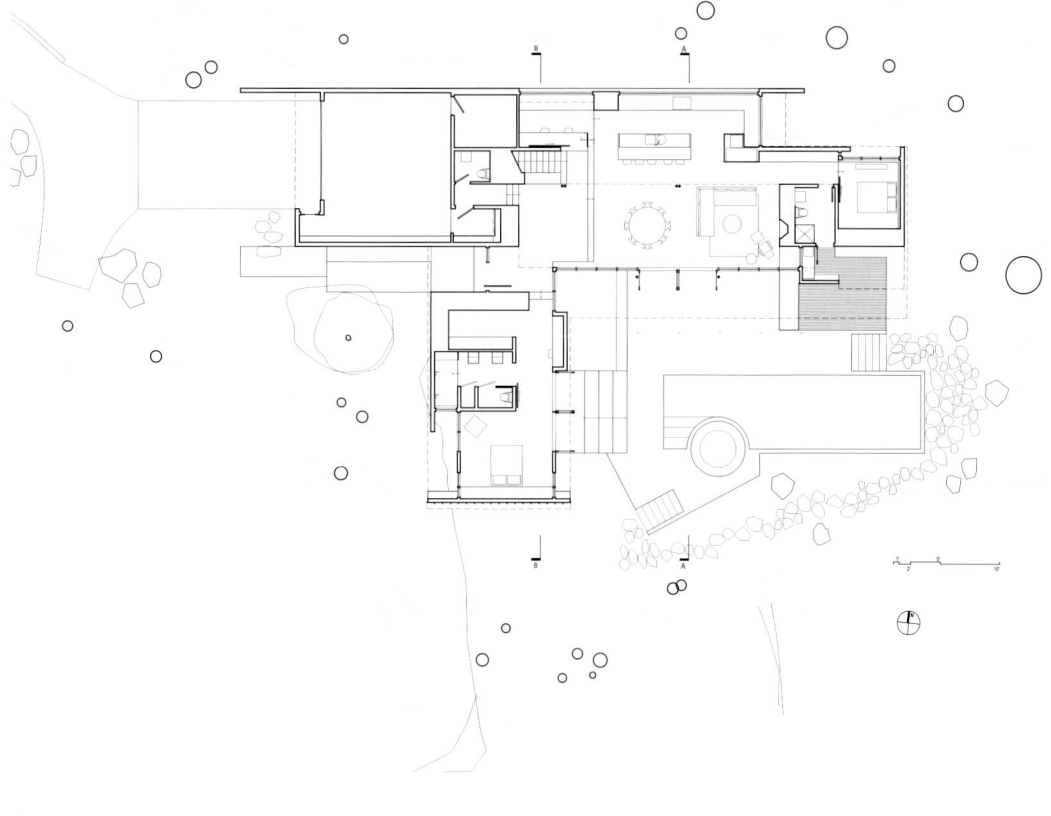

01 Pool 02 Courtyard and pool 03 Kitchen island 04 Tiled entry looking out 05 Dressing room 06 Main floor plan 07 Upper floor plan

07

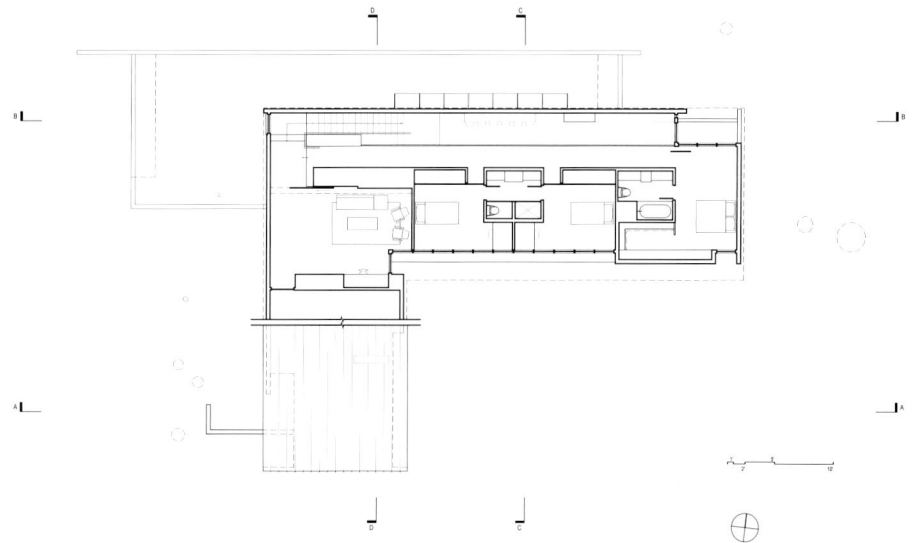

Wolfgang-Meier-House, 2001
Address: Pfarrer-Bichlmeier-Weg 5, 84405 Dorfen /
Schwindkirchen, Germany. **Client:** Parish of the As-
sumption, Archiepiscopal Building Office – George
Resenberg. **Gross floor area:** 1,085 m². **Materials:**
Existing building: brick masonry, whitewashed on the
inside and plastered on the outside; New building:
wood panel structure, wood and concrete composite
ceiling slab.

Simple skin

ARCHITECTS: Arc Architekten

(Horst Biesterfeld, Manfred Brennecke,

Christof Illig, Thomas Richter)

An unusual location for a new parish center: within a
former barn belonging to the parish church. This "house
within a house" embodies sustainability (though material recycling), respect for history and reference to the
surrounding region. The defining feature of this building
is, of course, its double exterior. The external shell and
structure of the old building acts as a shield, while the
space between the exterior walls and the inner building
functions as a buffer, much like a conservatory. Because
its external walls are not subject to the usual weather
conditions and insulation requirements all of the details
in this new parish center – right down to the window
frames – could be kept simple.

01 Buffer zone 02 Inner building
03 Longitudinal section 04 Energy
concept, summer 05 Energy concept, winter 06 Interior view, new
building

03

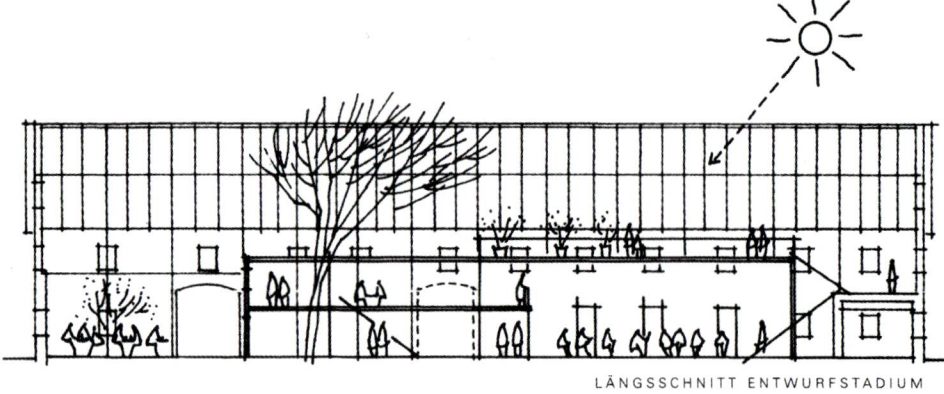

LÄNGSSCHNITT ENTWURFSTADIUM

04 **05**

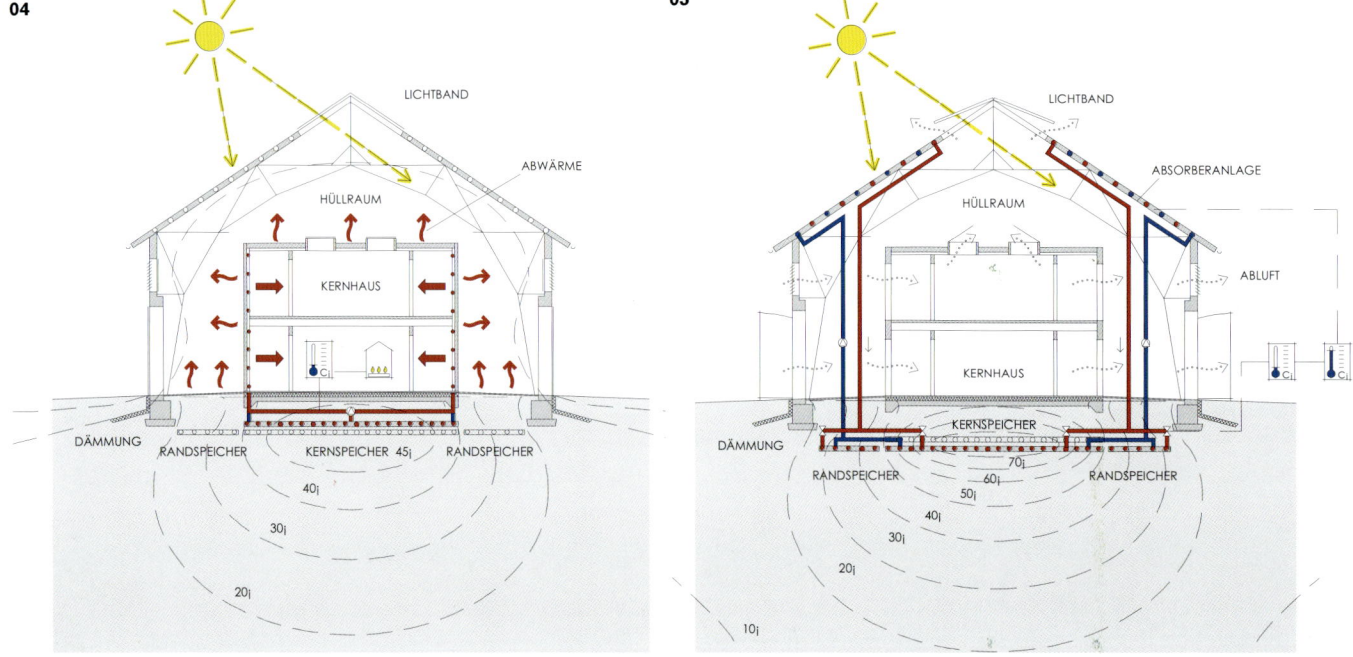

186

SCULPTURE

01

Finnforest Modular Office (FMO), 2005
Address: Tuulikuja 2, 02100 Espoo, Finland. **Architects wooden building parts etc.:** Finnforest Corporation. **Client:** FMO Tapiola Real Estate Company. **Gross floor area:** 13,048 m². **Materials:** coniferous wood, prefabricated wooden elements assembled on site, 1,200 wooden elements and a total of 17,000 individually worked wooden parts.

The tallest timber office

ARCHITECTS: Helin & Co Architects –
Pekka Helin, Peter Verhe and others

To showcase new ways of working with timber, in 2003 Finnforest organized the Modular Office architectural competition. "Sydänpuu – Heartwood" was awarded first prize. This building is now the tallest timber office structure in Europe. The prefabricated, modular frame, wall and cladding units are ideal for constructing timber office buildings in individual forms. The system is based on a series of simple rectangular modules, to which curved special modules may be added. The lifespan of the basic structural elements is over a hundred years, and costs per square meter match the average level for office buildings. The main section of the building consists of rectangular modules, reminiscent of a stack of sawn timber. The south-facing façade employs a conical module that is reminiscent of typical forms in woodworking. The workspaces are interspersed within the different modules in such a manner that all units enjoy different views, framed by timber structures, of Tapiola and its surroundings.

02

01 East façade 02 Detail balcony
03 South façade 04 Inner courtyard 05 Atrium, exterior view 06
Atrium, interior view 07 Section in
perspective

Nussraum (nut room), 2007
Address: Düsseldorf, Germany. **Client:** private. **Gross floor area:** cabin 8 m², terrace 10 m². **Materials:** wood, stainless steel.

Living in the trees

ARCHITECTS: baumraum / Andreas Wenning

Visitors to this tree house first climb a ladder to a terrace located slightly below, and from there access the "Nussraum" tree house via a narrow stairway. The tree house is supported by eight asymmetrical and tilted steel poles, which are set in concrete. The small terrace is suspended from the walnut tree by steel cables and heavy-duty belts, without damaging the tree in any way. The curved walls of the tree house, that imitate the shape of a walnut, have been constructed as frame supports and reinforced with additional steel frames. On the inside untreated oak shuttering, mineral wool insulation and windproof foil sheeting were used, while the exterior walls are clad with ventilated, horizontally laid oak laths treated with dark varnish. The interior furnishings consist of a spacious reclining area at one end of the "nutshell" and a bench at the opposite end. Both the reclining area and the bench incorporate sliding drawers and are covered with wool felt.

01 Entrance **02** View from below
03 Total view **04** Concept **05** Front
elevation **06** Interior view **07** Exterior view by night

04

nuss...............=...............raum

05

06

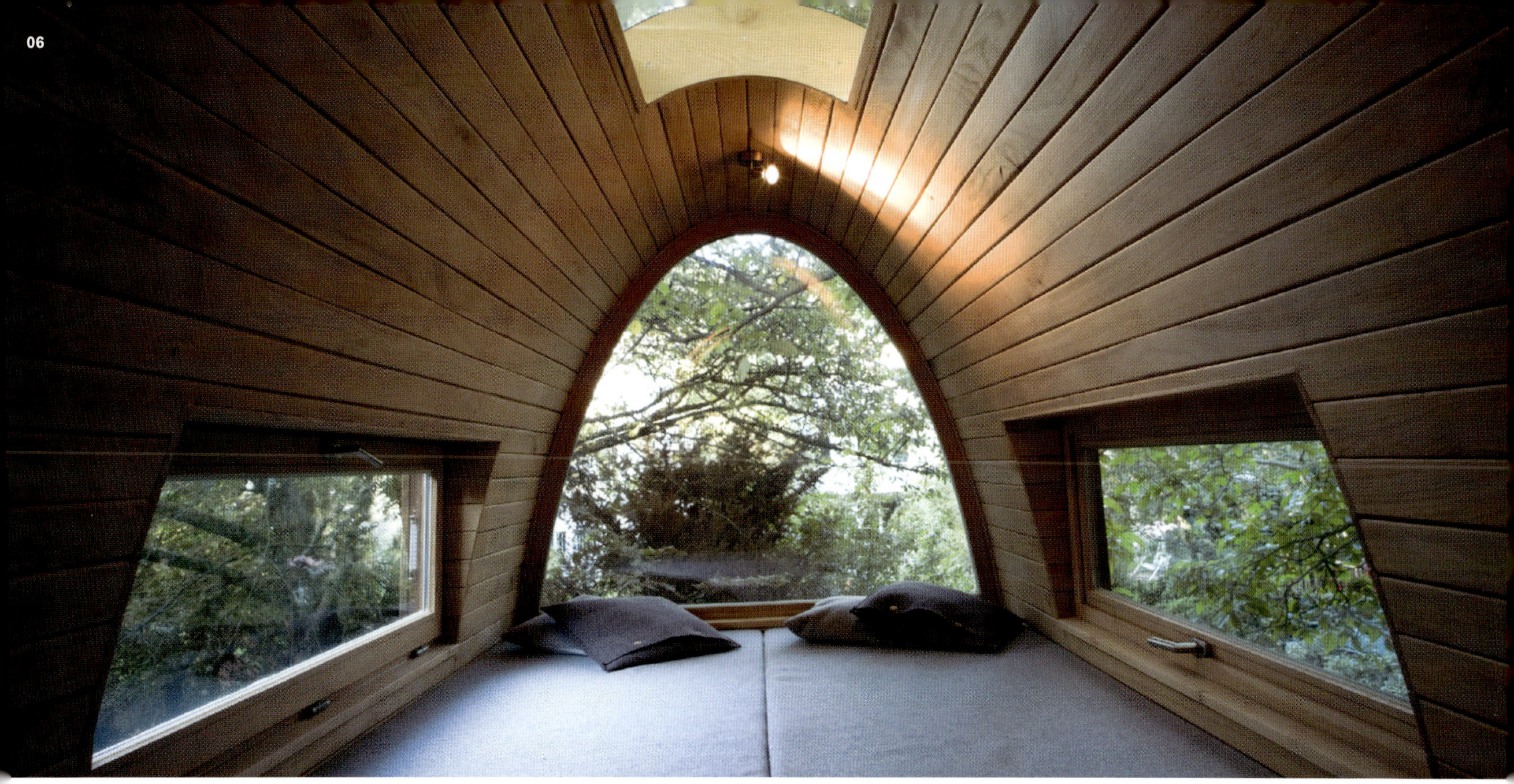

07

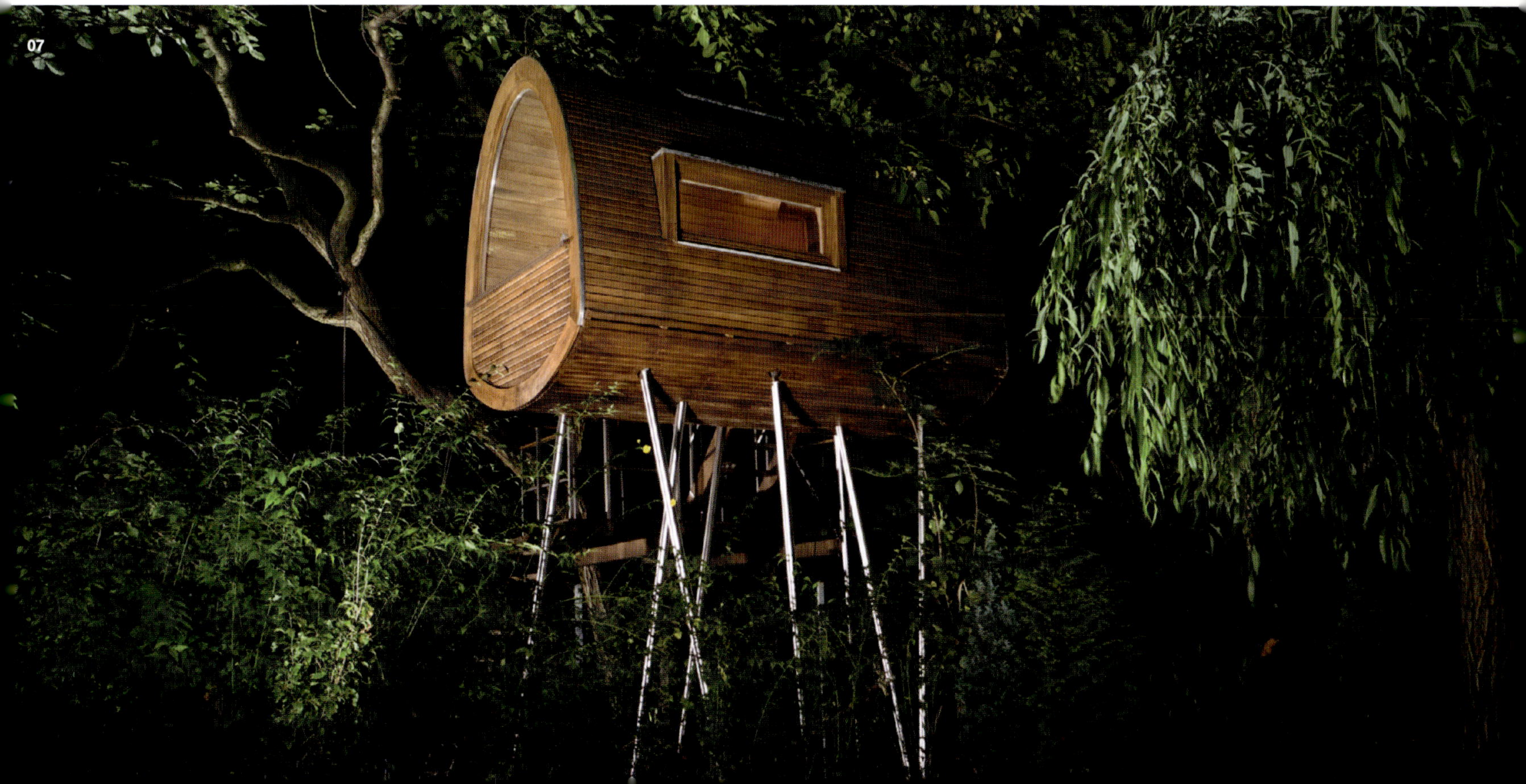

T-Bone House, 2006
Address: Holzweg 38, 71334 Waiblingen, Germany.
Client: private. **Gross floor area:** 151 m².
Materials: Façade: solid ventilated wood – native
larch; Ground floor: floors in Jura oil shale;
Basement: Ardex-Pandomo® mineral coating;
Loft: oiled oak parquet floors.

A house in the country

ARCHITECTS: COAST GbR

Alexander Wendlik, Zlatko Antolovic

This distinctive monolithic T-form was the combined result of building regulations and the spatial design of the
architect. This produced an exciting mixture of introverted and extroverted forms – rooms that are either largely
open or closed – all under one roof. The special feature
of this building is that it accommodates both man and
automobile: next to the "room with a view" is the "garage
with view". Brown oil shale, underfloor heating and built-
in closets set the tone in this snug multipurpose space.
A long, submerged box forms the base of the T-Bone.
Because the house is cleverly positioned at the edge of
a slope, there is a perfect transition from the house to
the sheltered courtyard garden and the mature orchard.
The basement level contains storage and utility rooms,
a reading area, as well as the cooking and dining areas.
The family's private rooms are located on the far more
enclosed loft level. The horizontally laid wooden façade
(Siberian larch), which continues on the roof and interior, hugs this building like a well-fitting dress.

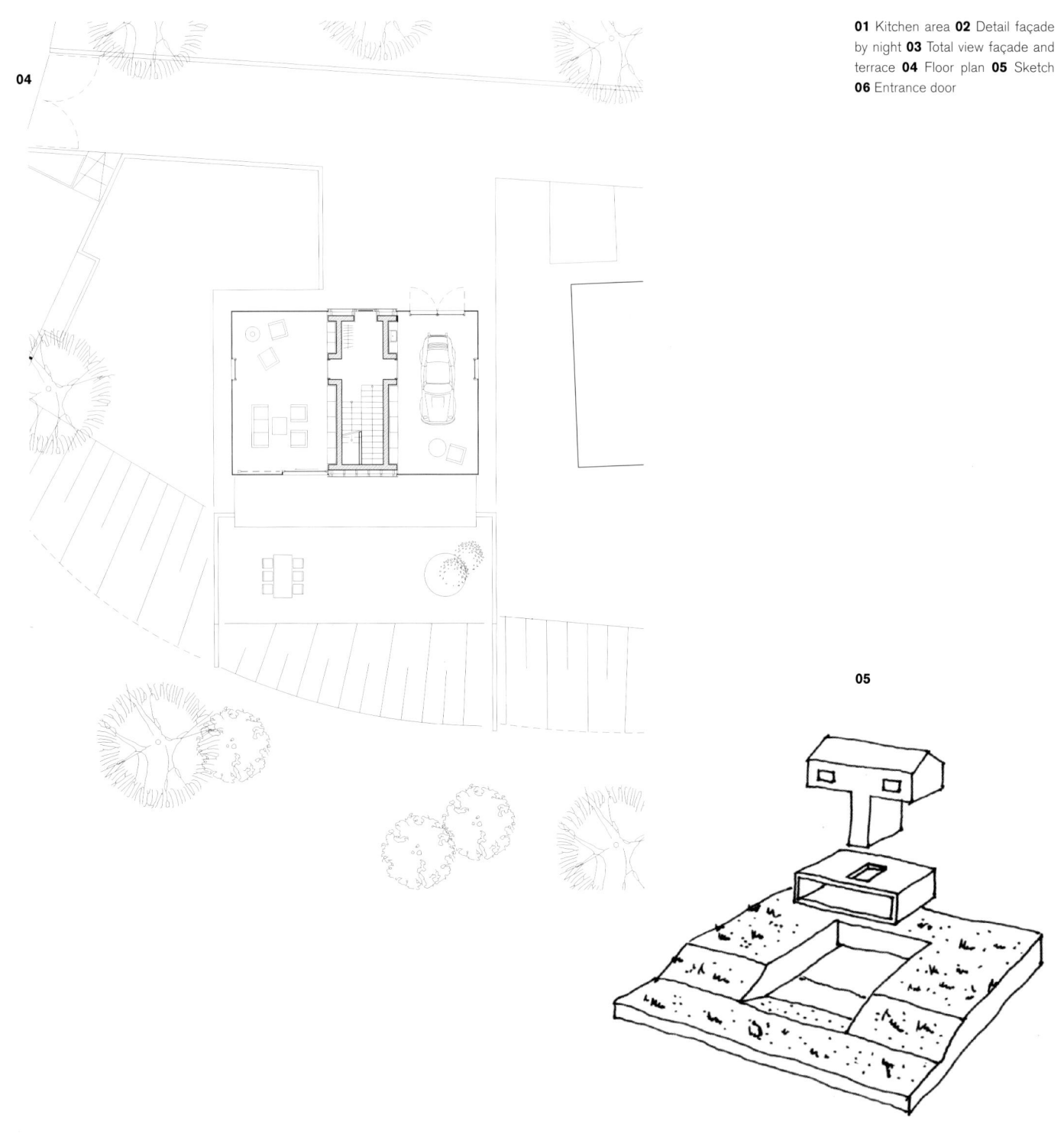

04

05

01

Müritzeum science and visitor center, 2007
Address: Zur Steinmole 1, 17192 Waren (Müritz),
Germany. **Landscape architects:** NOD. **Local plan-
ning partner:** DGI Bauwerk. **Client:** Rural District of
Müritz. **Gross floor area:** 3,137 m². **Materials:** princi-
pally timber.

Floating feature

ARCHITECTS: Wingårdh Arkitektkontor AB

The town of Waren in the scenic Mecklenburg Lake
District wanted a building that could serve as a visitor center for the old town as well as for the wildlife
of nearby Müritz lake. This 2,985 m² complex contains
areas for temporary exhibitions, an aquarium, a multimedia theatre and a restaurant. Two cones slightly shifted
in plan define the building. The circular form is opened
up by sharp incisions, the most prominent of which is
located at the main entrance. A thin glass shield stands
between two different kinds of wood paneling: burned,
black paneling on the façade and smooth light-colored
paneling in the interior. The "floating" feature of the
building matches its lakeside setting, and the rounded
form gives rise to unique spatial qualities in the interior.
Another unique feature is the exterior façade composed
only of solid wood elements in sufficient thickness for
full u-value, load bearing and burned in situ with a gasol
flame to the desired charcoal level.

02

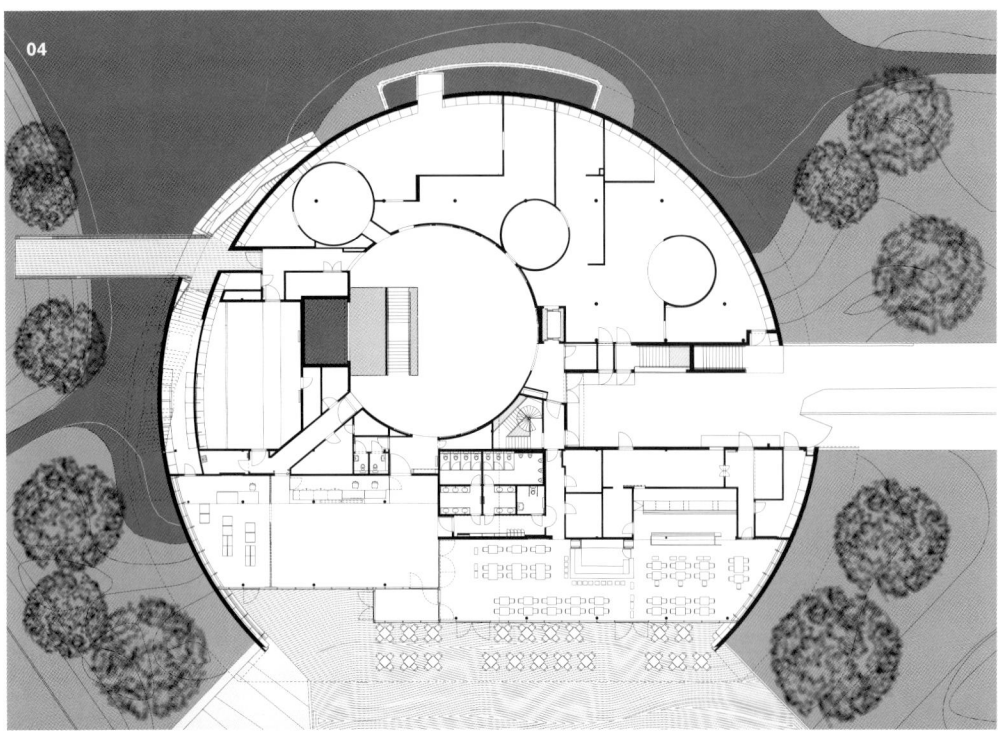

01 Entrance at night **02** Exhibition on the buildings sloping wall **03** Entrance towards the town **04** Ground floor plan **05** First floor plan **06** Façade of burned wood **07** Flight of stairs towards the roof

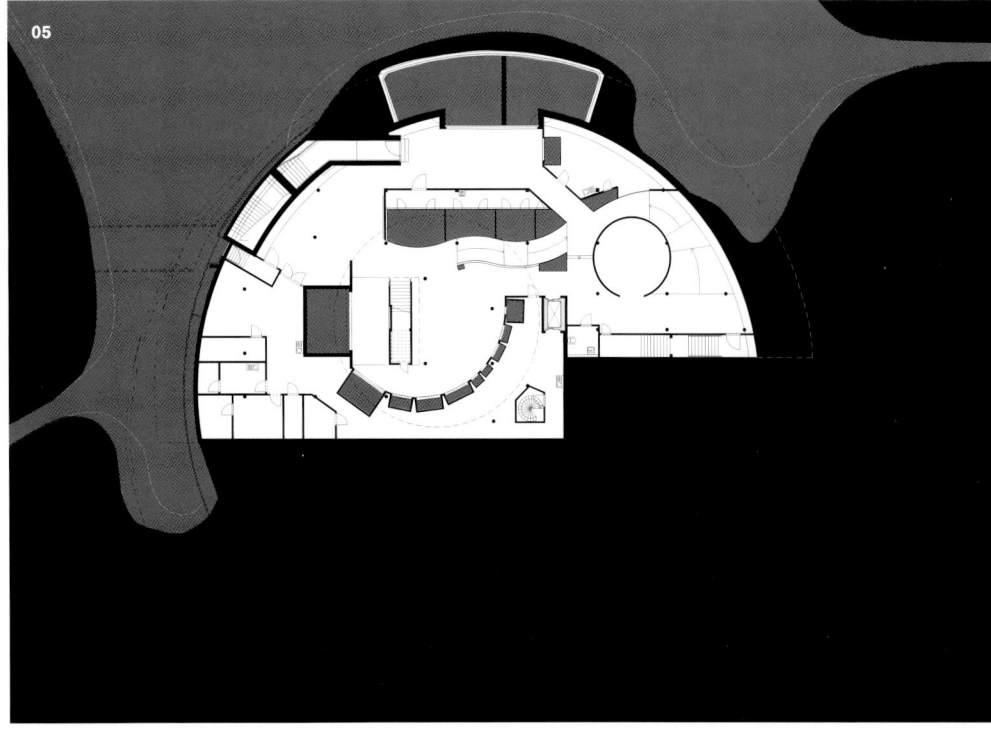

Graphite Apartments, 2008
Address: Murray Grove, Hackney, London, United Kingdom. **Client:** Telford Homes. **Gross floor area:** 2,750 m². **Materials:** KLH timber panel system.

Inspired by Gerhard Richter

ARCHITECTS: Waugh Thistleton Architects, KLH UK, Techniker Ltd.

To be constructed entirely in timber, this nine-story high-rise, when completed, is set to be the tallest residential timber building in the world. Murray Grove will comprise twenty-nine apartments, each with its own balcony. The concept for the façade was inspired by the work of the German artist Gerhard Richter. Recording the changing light and shadows formed on the vacant site by the surrounding buildings and trees, the pattern was captured through a sun-path animation technique. The resulting image was pixilated and blurred, then picked up and wrapped around the building. Each of the twenty-nine apartments will have their own internal balcony, and together with the deep-set windows these will form the "missing pieces" on the façade; an additional punctuated rhythm over the abstract image of the façade. The building has been designed using a cross-laminated timber panel system. The system was pioneered by manufacturers KLH of Austria and is akin to jumbo plywood, arriving on site in panels up to nine meters in length. Each of the panels is fabricated, and includes cut-outs for windows and doors.

01 View from the street **02** Floor plan **03** Exterior view

01

02

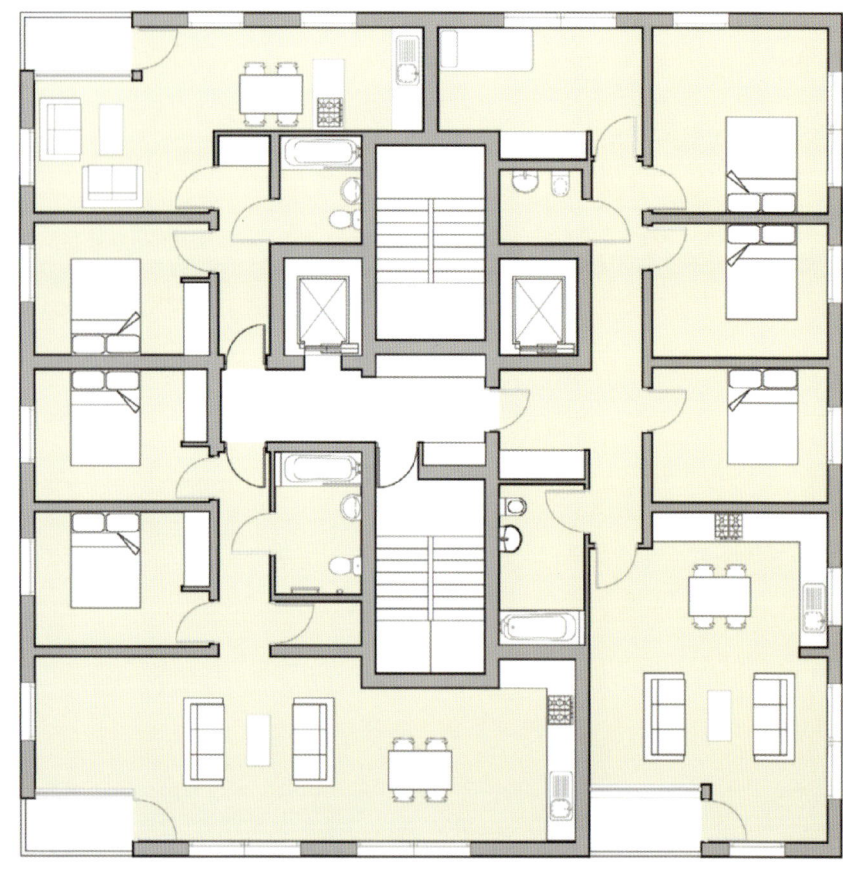

Element House, 2006
Address: Anyang Park, Anyang, Seoul, South Korea.
Client: Anyang Public Art Project. **Gross floor area:**
72 m². **Dimensions:** main space 6 x 6 x 6 m,
smaller rooms 3 x 3 x 3 m. **Materials:** steel, wood,
concrete, gravel, glass.

Water, soil, air
ARCHITECTS: Sami Rintala

This building stands on top of a small forest hill, along
an outdoor path that leads to the mountains at the far
end of the park. The main space is a large steel cube.
Four smaller wooden rooms are connected to this
space at different levels. In each of these small rooms
one natural element is present: in the cellar water; in the
courtyard soil; on the first floor fire; and in the loft air. On
a practical level, the idea behind this building is to provide a simple shelter where hikers can rest, enjoy their
lunch, enjoy a view over the mountains or burn a stick of
incense. Norwegian artist John Roger Holte has crafted
a platform and storage container in colored concrete
for the incense. This feature refers to the history of the
valley as an important Buddhist retreat. There used to
be many temples situated in this mountain region, only a
few of which survive today. The main building materials
used here are steel and wood. Concrete has been used
in the cellar and foundations. Openings are covered
with safety glass, floors with jade and marble gravel,
and different types and colors of stone are used in each
space.

01 View of the cubes **02** Inner courtyard **03** Exterior view **04** Sketch – fire safeties **05** Sketch – cellar **06** Inner courtyard **07** Interior view of the cube

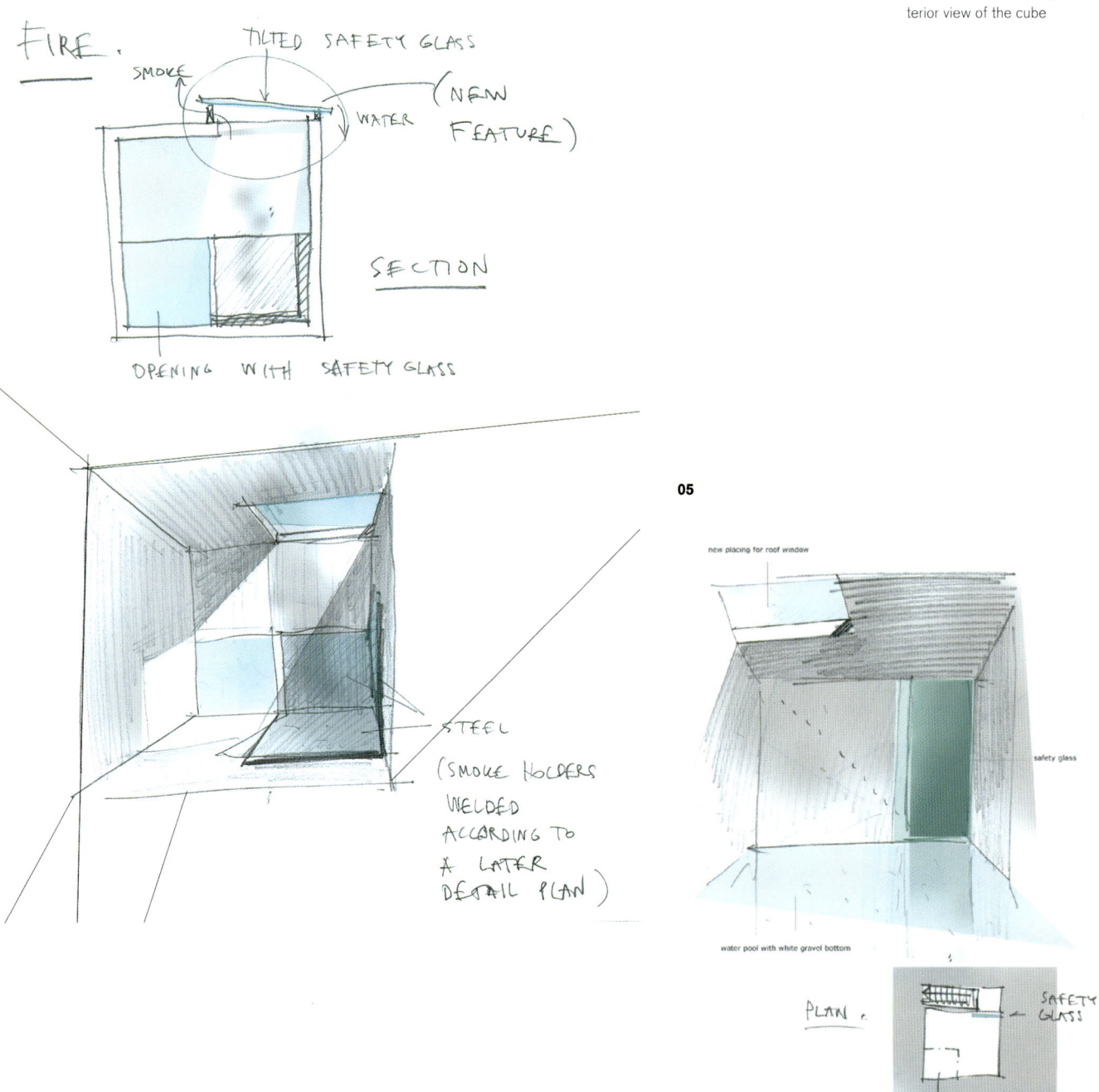

FIRE.

SMOKE

TILTED SAFETY GLASS

(NEW FEATURE)

WATER

SECTION

OPENING WITH SAFETY GLASS

STEEL

(SMOKE HOLDERS WELDED ACCORDING TO A LATER DETAIL PLAN)

05

new placing for roof window

safety glass

water pool with white gravel bottom

PLAN.

SAFETY GLASS

ROOF OPENING

Wine Estate of Erwin Sabathi, 2004
Address: Pössnitz 48, 8463 Leutschach, Austria.
Client: Erwin Sabathi Winery GmbH. **Gross floor
area:** approx. 2,000 m². **Materials:** concrete, stainless
steel, wood.

Shortcuts

ARCHITECTS: Wemmers Skacel architects

The fundamental idea behind this design was to put a "philosophy of shortcuts" into effect. Applied to wine production this meant that the grapes reach the presses and even the fermentation and must tanks by a process of "free fall". Likewise, customers have a short journey to the salesroom, which is located right next to the road. From the salesroom a concealed stairway leads directly to the vineyard, where grape varieties such as Sauvignon and Morillon await the visiting wine connoisseur. The complex is constructed of pre-cast concrete sections and built almost entirely into the steep hillside. The only section visible from the exterior is the south-facing salesroom. Glass and wood are the defining elements in this façade. These materials not only allude to the sunlight and oak casks that are essential in the production of fine wines, but also blend snugly and unobtrusively into the landscape.

02

03

04

05

01 Detail façade **02** Degustation room **03** Wooden façade **04** Sales area in the evening **05** Sections **06** Site plan **07 + 08** Exterior view

06

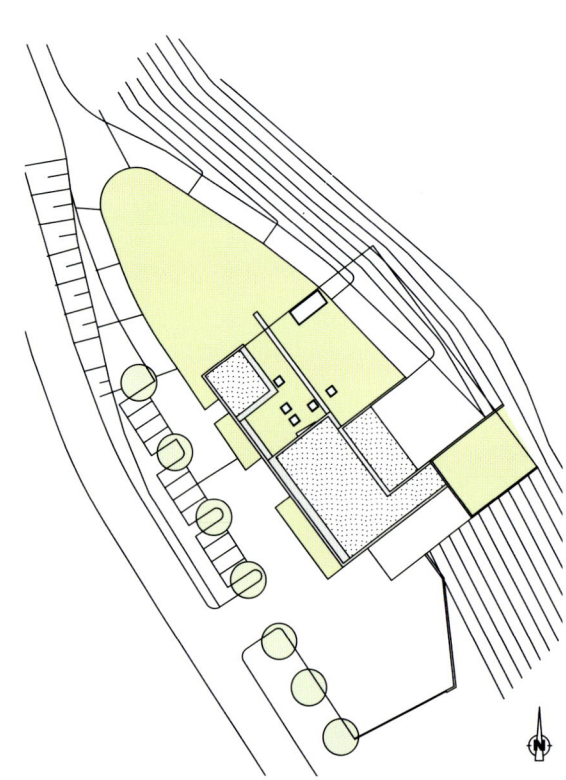

214

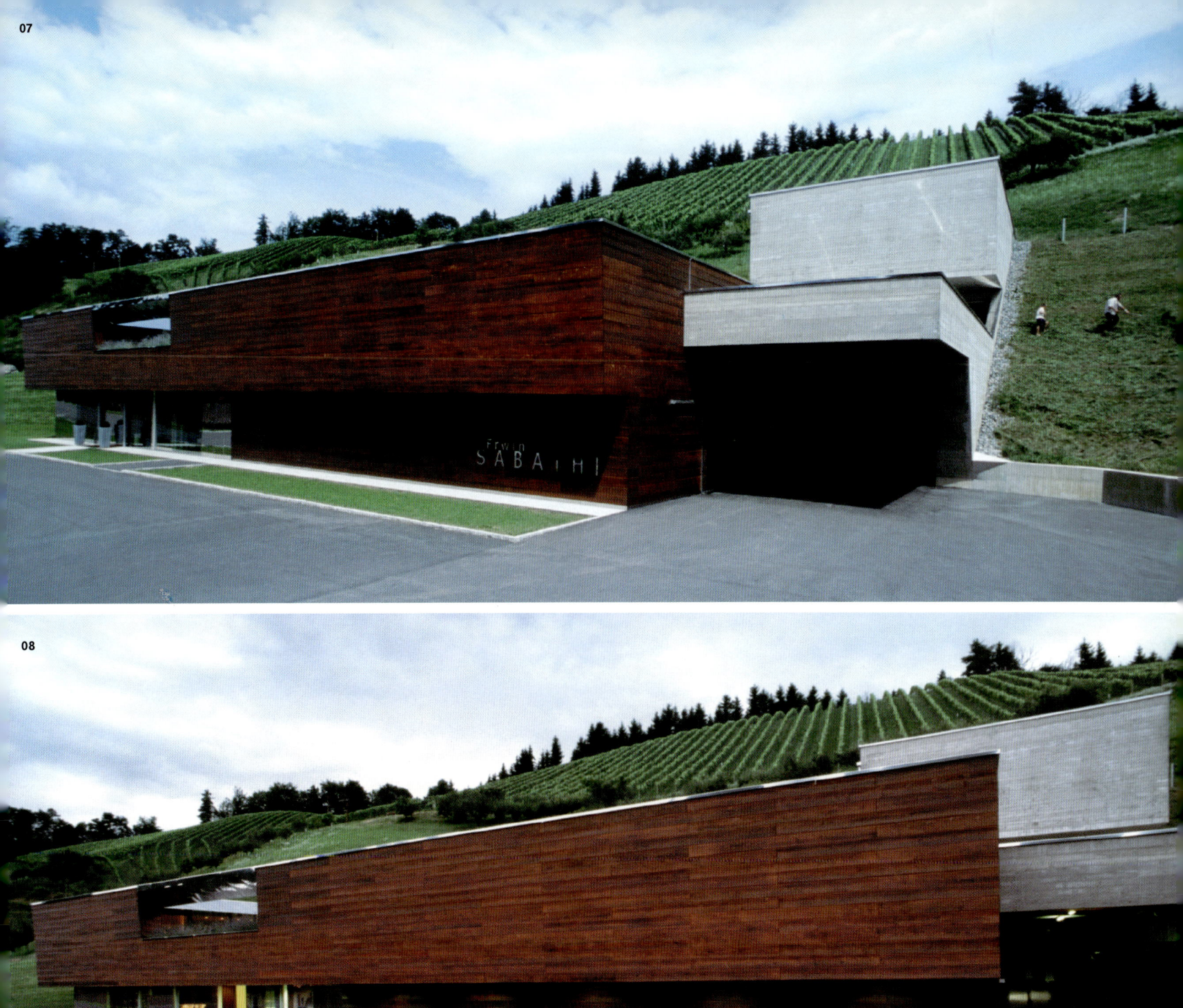

Tree house, 2005
Address: Schlössesweg 7, 71640 Ludwigsburg, Germany. **Client:** Christa Fentzloff, Ludwigsburg. **Gross floor area / gross cubic content:** 68 m² / 175 m³. **Materials:** wooden structure with copper cladding.

A window to the garden
ARCHITECTS: ARCHITEKTUR 109

The various spaces within this home are clearly designated: The ground floor of the original house is intended for the entire family, the second floor is for the children, while the new extension is for the parents. The lower, sloping garden level presented a certain problem: it is difficult to access from the house, and subject to noise pollution from the street. The architects thus grappled with the question of how to turn a negative feature into a positive one. The "tree house" solves this by allowing the family to live directly above the garden, and incorporating the trees and garden landscape into the living quarters. The distinguishing feature of this new building is its view of the garden and the top of the walnut tree. It creates a window to nature, opening up a resplendent panorama of the Neckar Valley and allowing an entirely new view of the surrounding countryside. A vital consideration in designing the extension was to open up a new dimension for experiencing the garden and the walnut tree.

04

05

06

07

08

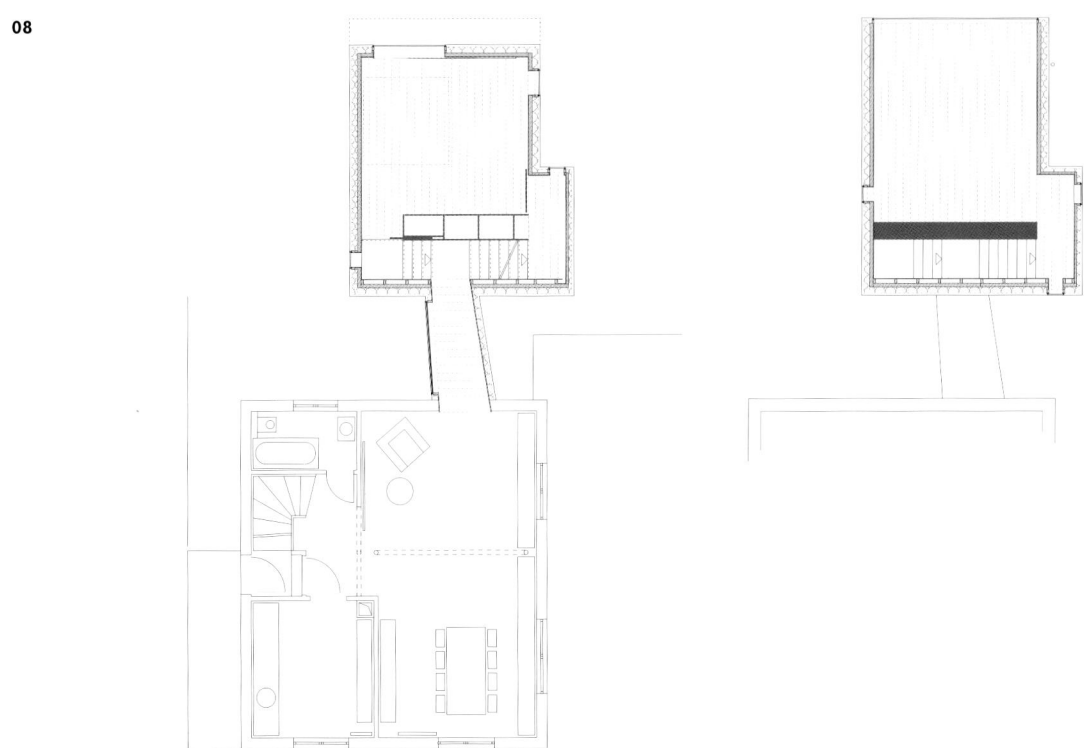

Y-Cabin, 2003
Address: Eastern Japan. **Total floor area:** 91 m².
Structural system: timber. **Materials:** galvanized steel, pinewood (vertical siding), cemented excelsior board, coniferous plywood.

A forest cabin

ARCHITECTS: Kengo Kuma & Associates

A quadrilateral plan drawn on a perpendicular Cartesian coordinate system would restrict the direction and appear too artificial and constructive in the natural forest. The panels, functioning as both roof and wall, are held by wooden ribs at a 300 mm pitch, and these ribs give an effect of diffusing light just like the branches and leaves of a tree. The slanted panels come together in a tree-like manner, giving an impression of top branches of trees tied together. This effect demonstrates why Frank Lloyd Wright and Buckminster Fuller preferred the triangular to the rectangular form for its quality of resembling nature. The plan becomes a hexagon, and once different elements (dining suite, fireplace, piano, kitchen counter, bed, writing table) are added to each section, the elements interact at obtuse angles and create a loosely partitioned room. This cabin, whose design aims to meet the criterion of "close to nature", somehow resembles Laugier's "Primitive Hut" and ancient pit dwellings.

04

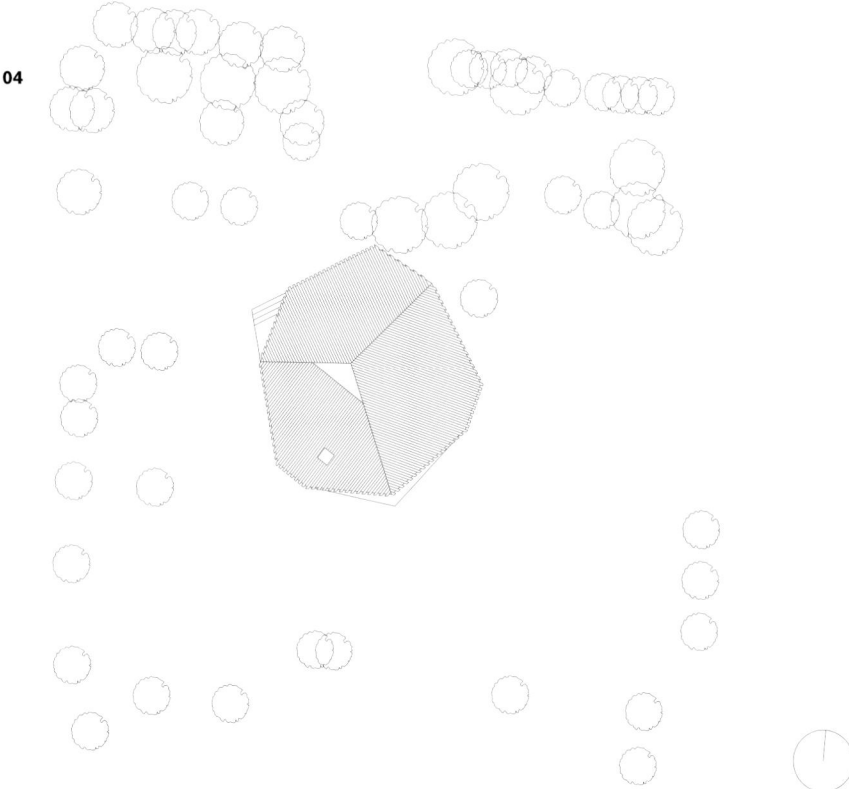

01 Front view **02** Total view **03** View into the house **04** Roof elevation **05** Floor plans **06** Interior view with gallery **07** Interior view with glass front

05

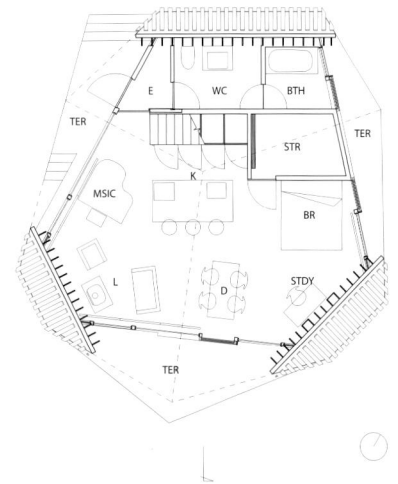

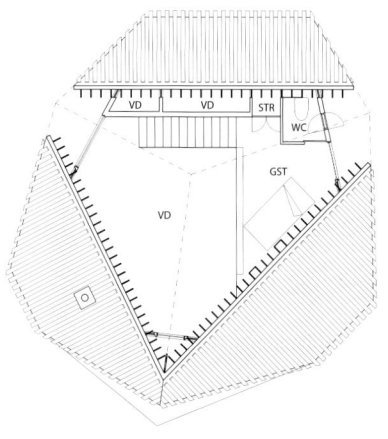

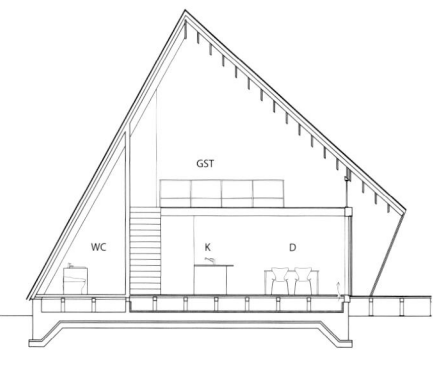

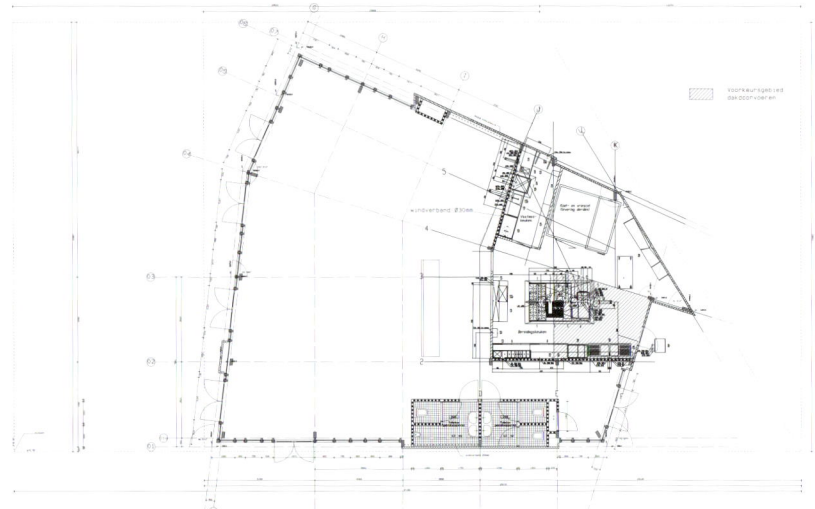

Fuiks Eten en Drinken, 2007
Address: Vuykpark, Capelle aan den IJssel, The
Netherlands. **Client:** Vilusto Vastgoed. **Gross floor
area:** 275 m². **Materials:** wood.

Marine lining and carpentry

ARCHITECTS: MIII architecten

MIII architecten have designed a restaurant on the site
of the former "Vuyk" shipyard in Capelle aan den IJssel.
This distinctive building is an overdue reminder of Vuyk's
long and remarkable tradition of master craftsmanship.
The wooden structure, marine lining and carpentry as
well as the sloped, angular surfaces lends this building
its dynamism and nautical feel. The key concept here
was to envelop a building encased in a wooden coat.
The smooth wooden cladding alludes to the master
carpentry of the past. The open front coping has several advantages above a closed one; for example, wind
can freely flow along the front end of the building and
by doing so, naturally dehydrate these parts while also
ventilating the rear. For the wooden cladding, MIII chose
scraped laths of Oregon pine.

01 Floor plan **02** Detail roof **03** Exterior view **04** Rear view

02

House in Tunquen, 2005
Address: Punta del Gallo, Tunquen, Casablanca, Chile.
Client: private. **Gross floor area:** 140 m². **Materials:** impregnated pine, broad ribbon, fibrocement and glass.

01

A modern ranch house

ARCHITECTS:

Riesco + Rivera Arquitectos Asociados

The concept was to divide the house into three units, distinct in terms of space and utility, but with a unitary reading; each unit can be used separately and each reflects its use. The first space is a communal one, the second for children, while the third unit houses the sleeping quarters. The architects studied the conventional inventory of space utilisation programs and constructive systems (Canadian wood systems). This delimited the use of standard dimensions for each unit in a house of 140 m², as well as defining the materials. The variations to the "standard" and the contrast between spaces defined the character and qualities of the building. In order to increase the space between each unit the architects created horizontal and vertical space through a small patio of that opens and closes perspectives, light and space.

02

04

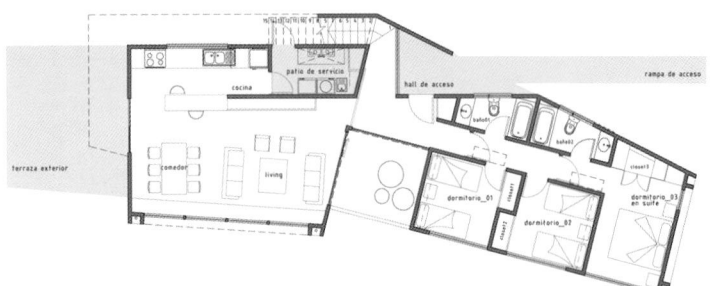

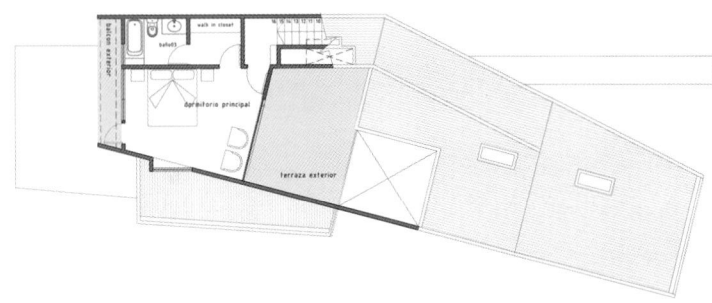

05

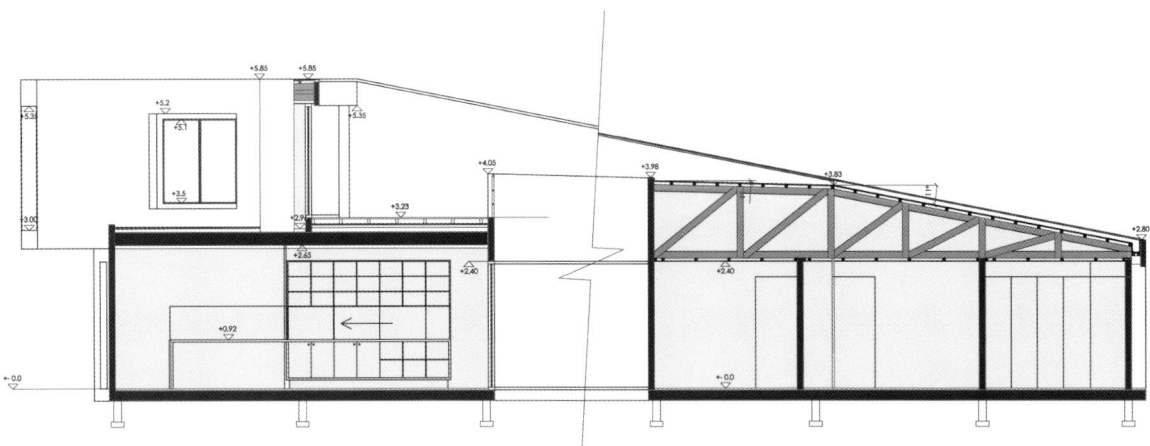

Huski Hotel, 2005
Address: 3 Sitzmark St., Falls Creek, Victoria,
Australia. **Client:** Zacamoco Pty Ltd. **Gross floor area:**
1,346 m². **Materials:** mostly wood.

Snowflake geometry

ARCHITECTS: Elenberg Fraser

Built on a corner site, Huski is a five-story apartment
hotel, open for both the winter and summer seasons
at Falls Creek in the Victorian highlands. The design
for Huski originated in the study of snowflake geometry. These pure yet complex patterns combined with
the influence of Australian timber mountain huts and
international alpine resorts provided the basis for the resulting architectural form. Radial in nature, the building
responds to the delicate surrounding environment while
utilizing the steep site to maximize views of the Kiewa
valley and Mount Spion Kopje, and allowing the scenery
to penetrate every apartment. The modulated planes
of the north façade emphasize the dynamic quality of
the building both in plan and elevation. By contrast, the
subtlety of the worn timber materials is calming and
suggests an affinity with local building typologies. From
afar, Huski addresses the scale of the mountain itself,
not the module of the apartment, causing a shift in ap-
prehension and scale as you approach. Huski's human
inhabitants are like the eyes of statuettes in a baroque
façade – this is not a mask, but a reverberating surface
that both reveals and conceals the activity within; under
scrutiny the surface breaks down.

02

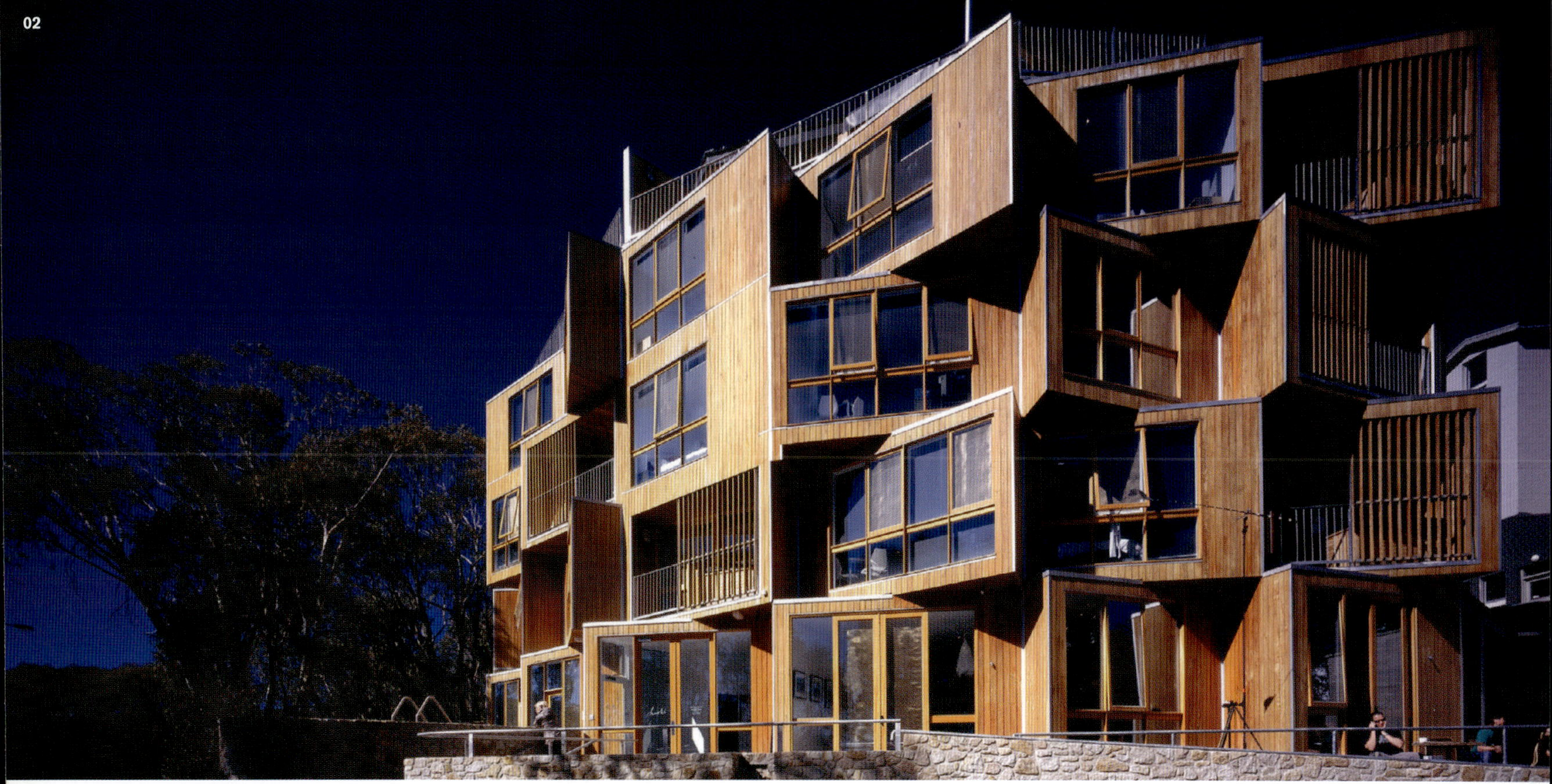

03

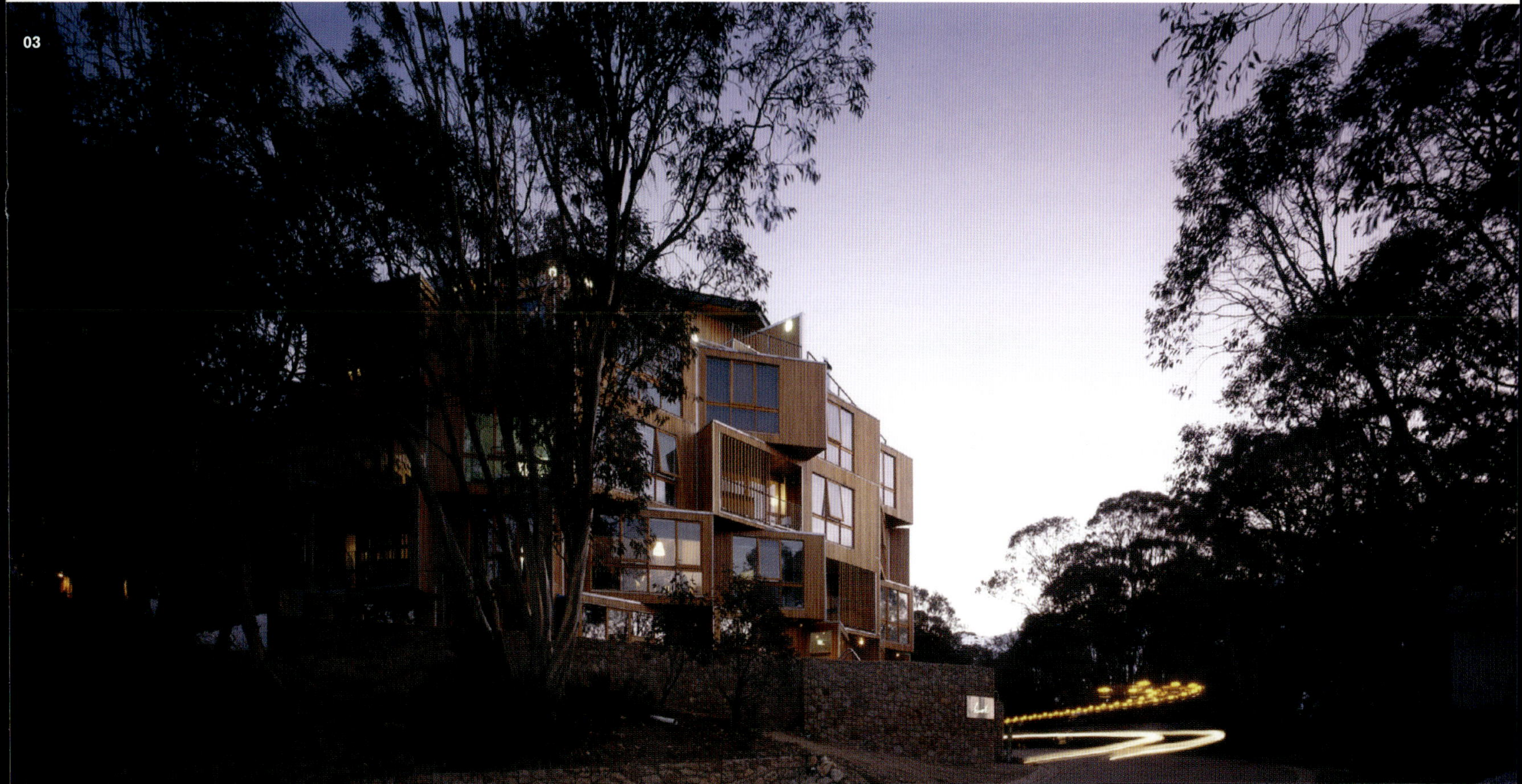

04

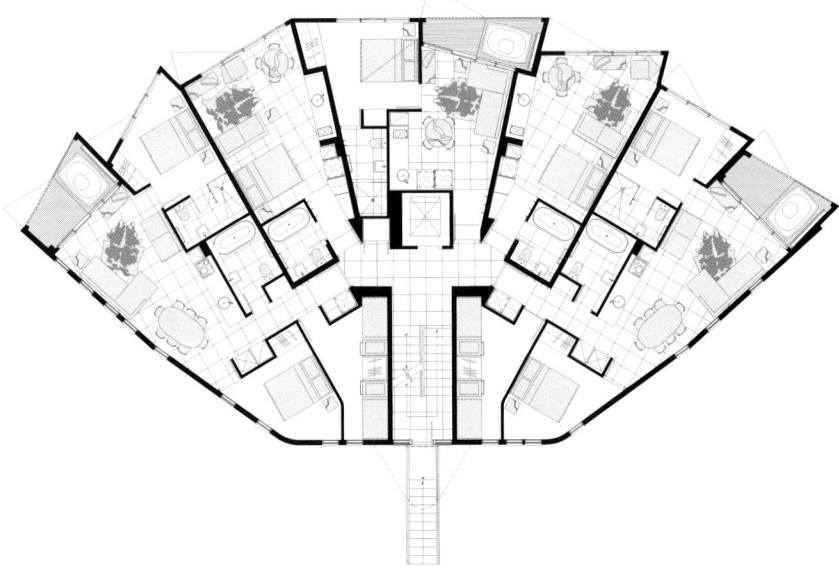

05

06

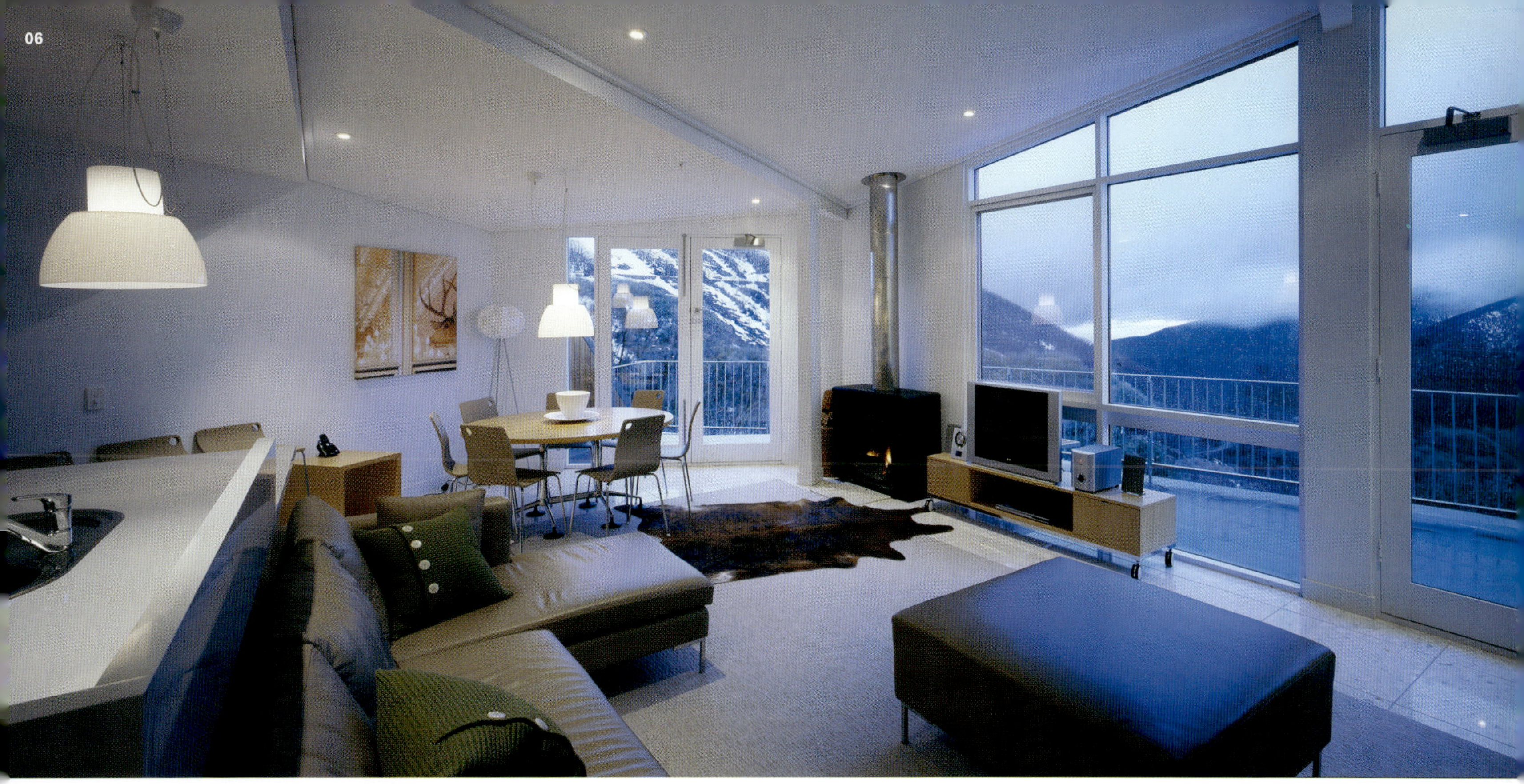

07

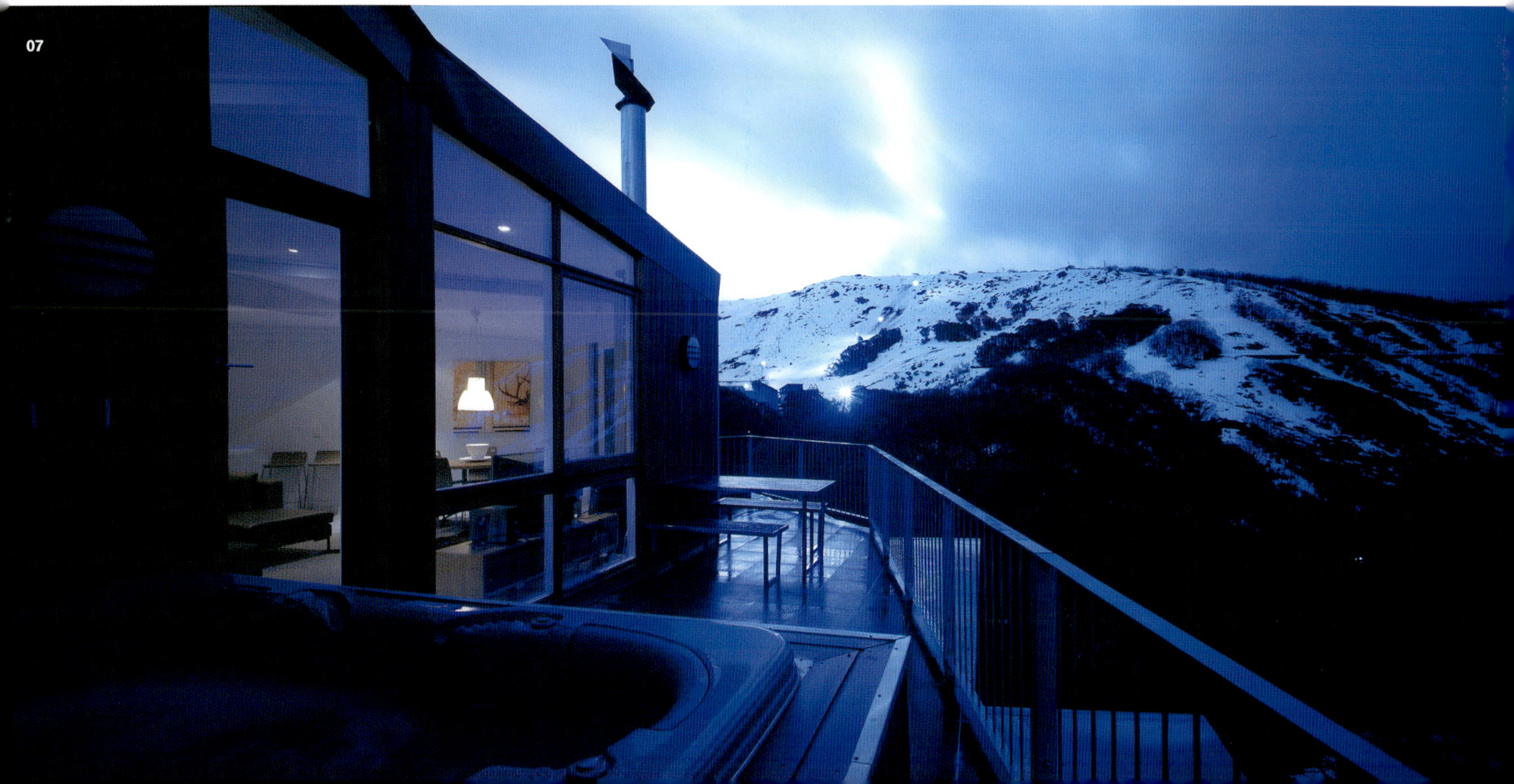

BR House, 2004
Address: Araras, Rio de Janeiro, Brazil. **Gross floor area:** 739 m². **Interior design:** Diana Radomysler + Marcio Kogan. **Project architects:** Lair Reis, Oswaldo Pessano, Paula Moraes, Regiane Lão, Renata Furlanetto, Samanta Cafardo, Suzana Glogowski.

Elegant box

ARCHITECTS: Marcio Kogan with Bruno Gomes

The concept behind this house is of two monolithic cement slabs containing the designed box of the first floor, supported by stilts and a stone box. The wooden façade consists of vertical wooden strips which, on the terraces of the suites, can fold back completely in a shrimp-like manner. At nightfall, this "skin" appears to be fully lit, surrounded by a beautiful mountainous forest. This two-story building, which blends into the forest landscape of the mountain region of Petrópolis near Rio de Janeiro, is made of concrete, steel, wood, aluminum and glass on two floors. The first floor has four suites, guest bathroom, kitchen and living / dining rooms. The ground floor contains a heated pool and a sauna with a large fixed glass wall so that while you sweat you can enjoy views of unspoiled Atlantic rainforest.

04

N

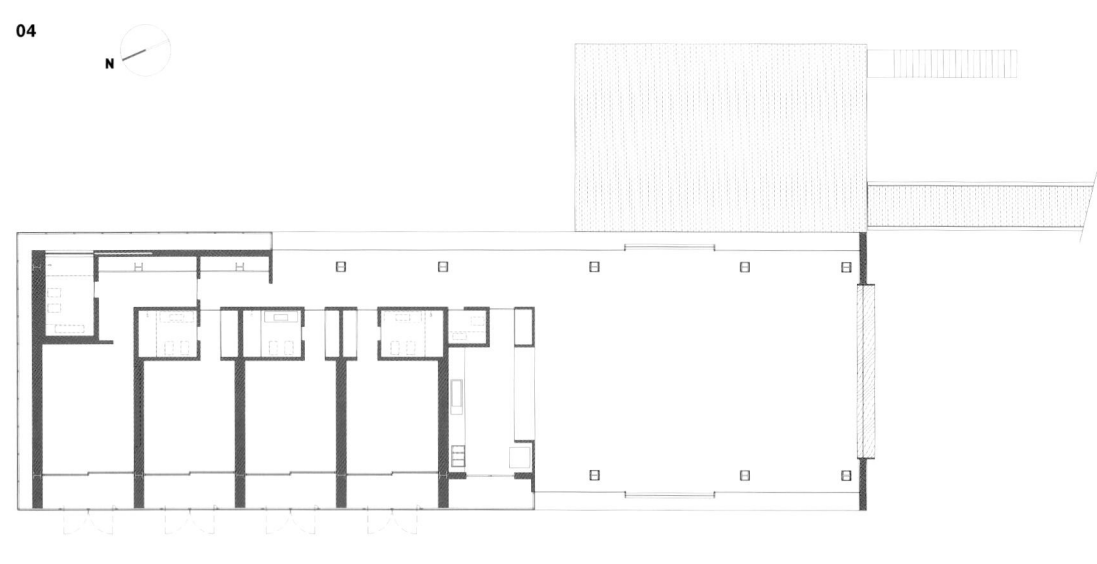

05

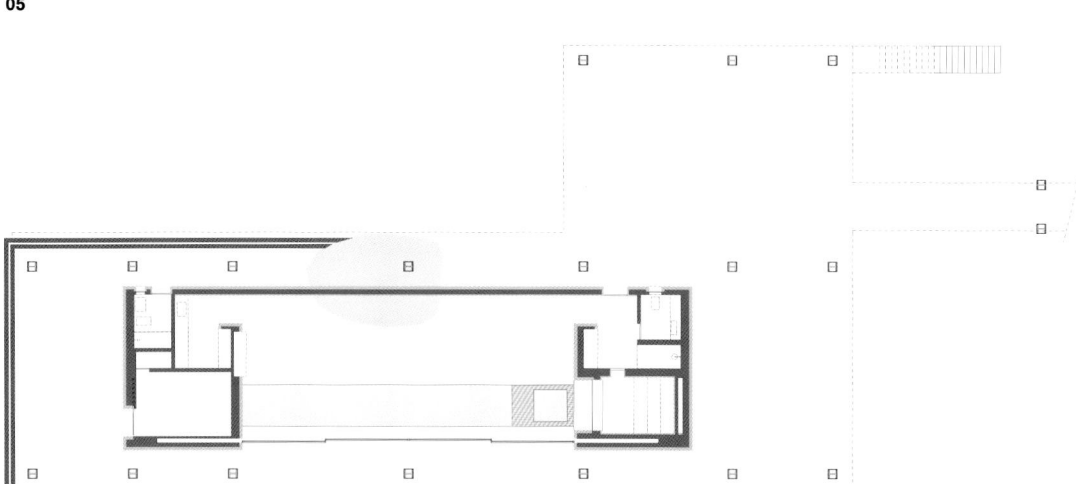

Hotel Kirkenes, 2005
Address: Kirkenes Harbor, Kirkenes, North Norway.
Client: Via Travels. **Gross floor area:** 22 m². **Materials:** wood, aerated concrete.

The natural charm of the North

ARCHITECTS: Sami Rintala

The town of Kirkenes is situated in northern Norway at the intersection of many cultures; here Saami, Russians, Norwegians and Finns have long interacted with one another. This new hotel dispenses with all unnecessary luxuries: there are no satellite TV channels, minibar or brass doorknobs. The idea was simply to create a warm shelter that looks out onto the Barents Sea. A person spending the night in this hotel would still feel that they were in Kirkenes. The hotel was built in ten days with the help of three architecture students and was completed three minutes before its opening. It contains a single room, a double room and a lobby. After all, a hotel should have a lobby for meetings and chance encounters. The hotel was built of timber on an aerated concrete block foundation. The interior was painted white to maximize the natural light and sense of space while the outside is painted black to absorb sunlight and to integrate it into the surrounding dark rocky shorescape.

03

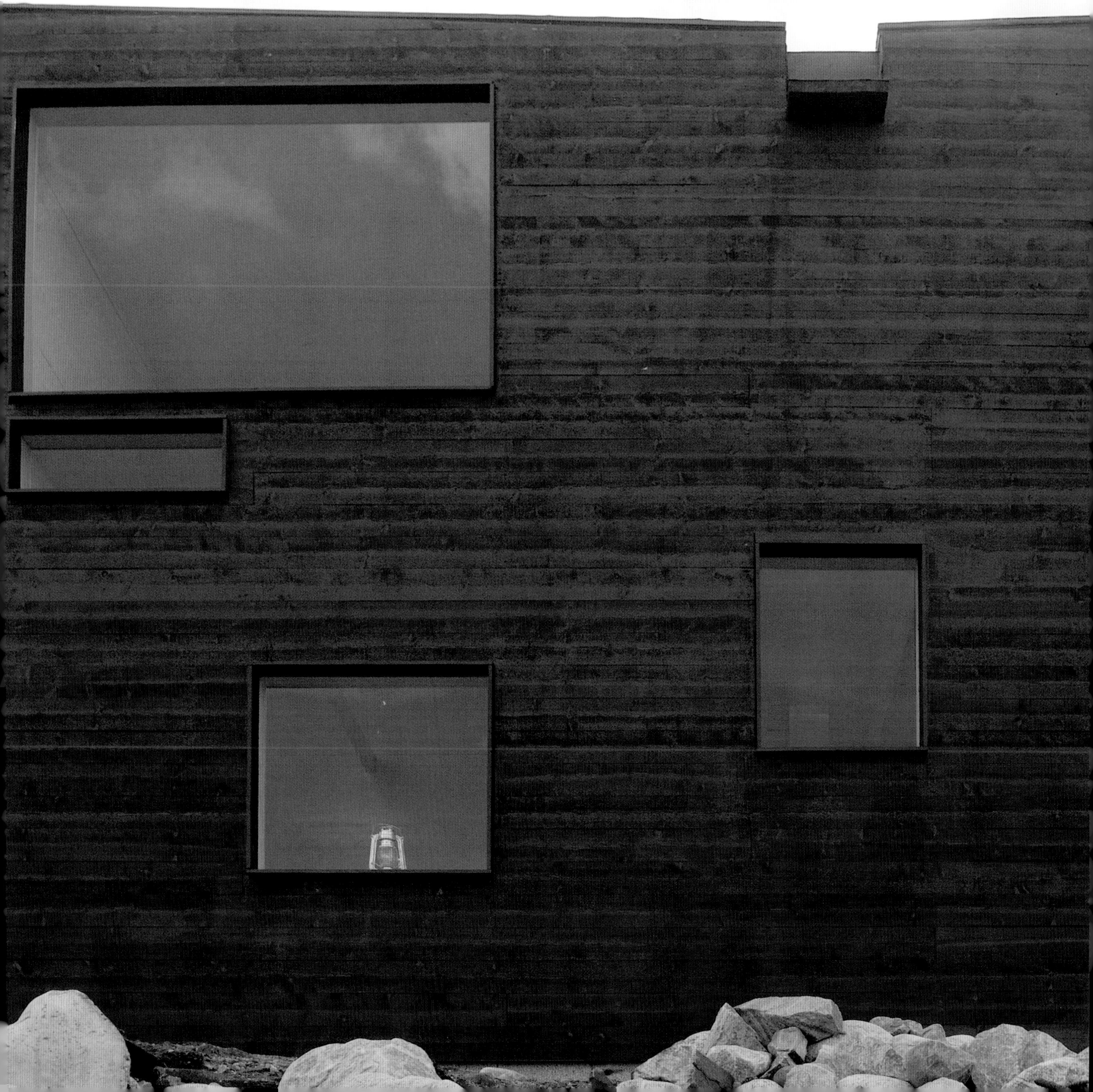

04

05

06

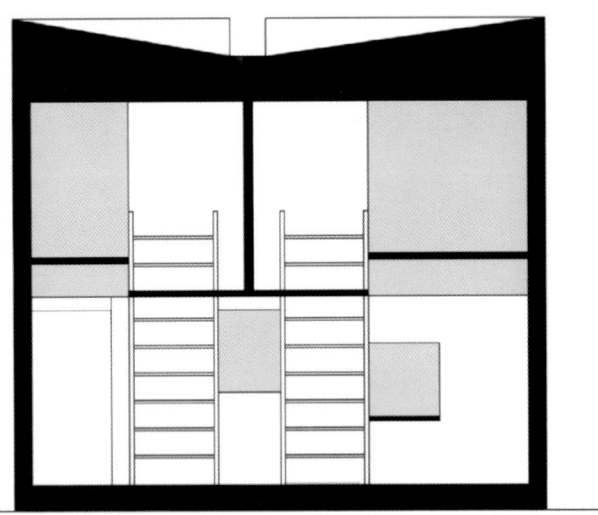

Tenerife School of Dramatic Arts, 2003
Address: Calle Suárez Hernández s/n, El Ramonal, 38009 Santa Cruz de Tenerife, Spain. **Client:** Tenerife Insular Council + Canary Islands Government: Education, Culture and Sports Council. **Gross floor area:** 3,360 m². **Materials:** concrete, wood (ipê, pinewood), glass, HPL panels.

Zigzag

ARCHITECTS: gpy arquitectos

This building presents itself to the city as a platform, an urban stage with the city and surrounding landscape as its backdrop. The interior roofed patio is conceived as a scenic box that opens up towards the city and acts as the building's spatial reference point, a place for inter-action and exchange; where the action, as it unfolds, defines the space of representation. Designed as an inclined surface, the patio also functions as the back-bone for the routes throughout the building – a system of ramps that connects the different scenic spaces of the building via an oblique zigzag geometry. The theatre space is not bound to conventional forms. The stage is not fixed, thus the space can be used in a variety of ways. The wooden stage as scenic space is taken out of its usual context and related to elements of everyday life: the street, the city, the mountains and the sea.

04

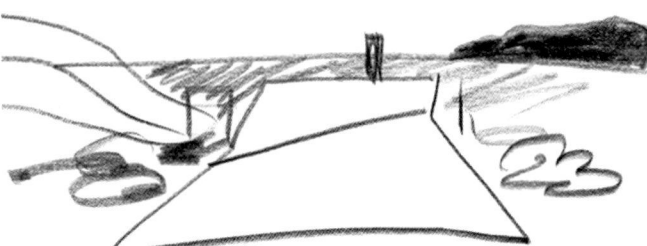

05

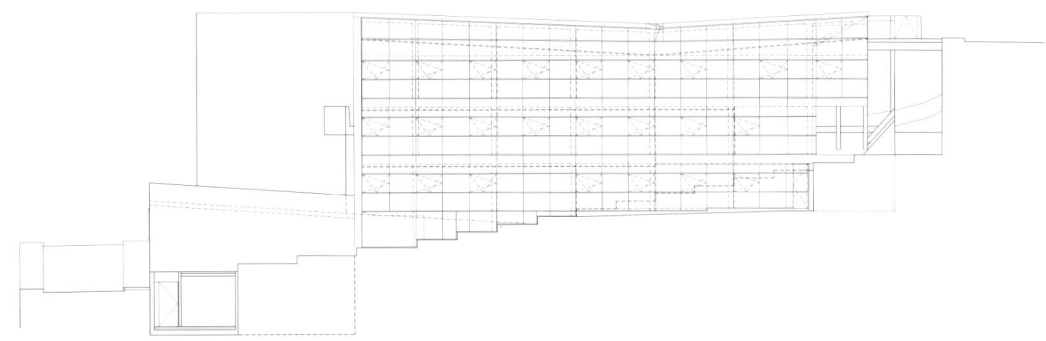

06

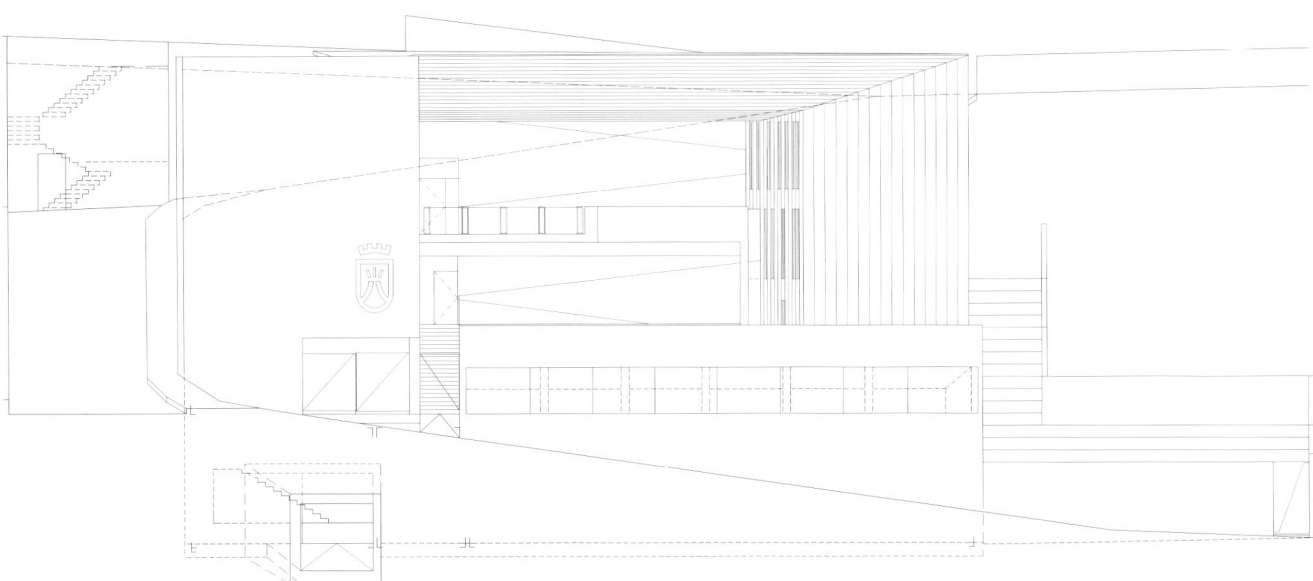

Yokohama International Port Terminal, 2002
Address: Yokohama, Japan. **Client:** Port & Harbour Bureau, City of Yokohama. **Gross floor area:** 48,000 m². **Materials:** steel, wood.

Fluid, uninterrupted and multi-directional space

ARCHITECTS: Foreign Office Architects

Farshid Moussavi, Alejandro Zaera Polo

The Yokohama project aims to produce a new type of transportation space with more urban qualities. The project is generated from a circulation diagram that aims to challenge the linear structure characteristic of piers, and the directionality of the circulation. Starting with the idea of the "no-return pier", the architects aimed to structure the building as a fluid, uninterrupted and multi-directional space, rather than a conventional gateway to flows of fixed orientation. A series of specific interlocking circulation loops allowed them to subvert the traditional structure of this type of building. Rather than conceiving the building as an object on the pier, the project is produced as an extension of its terrain, as a systematic transformation of the lines of the circulation diagram into a folded and bifurcated surface. More than 500 skilled carpenters from all over Japan worked on the project.

03

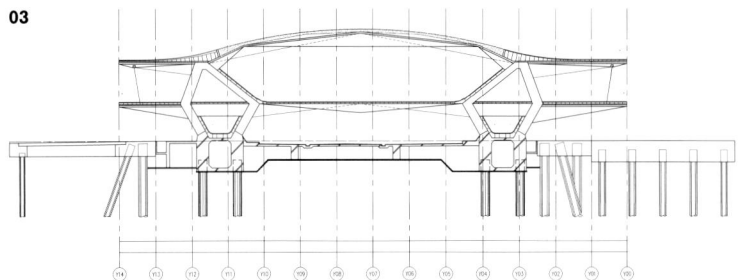

04

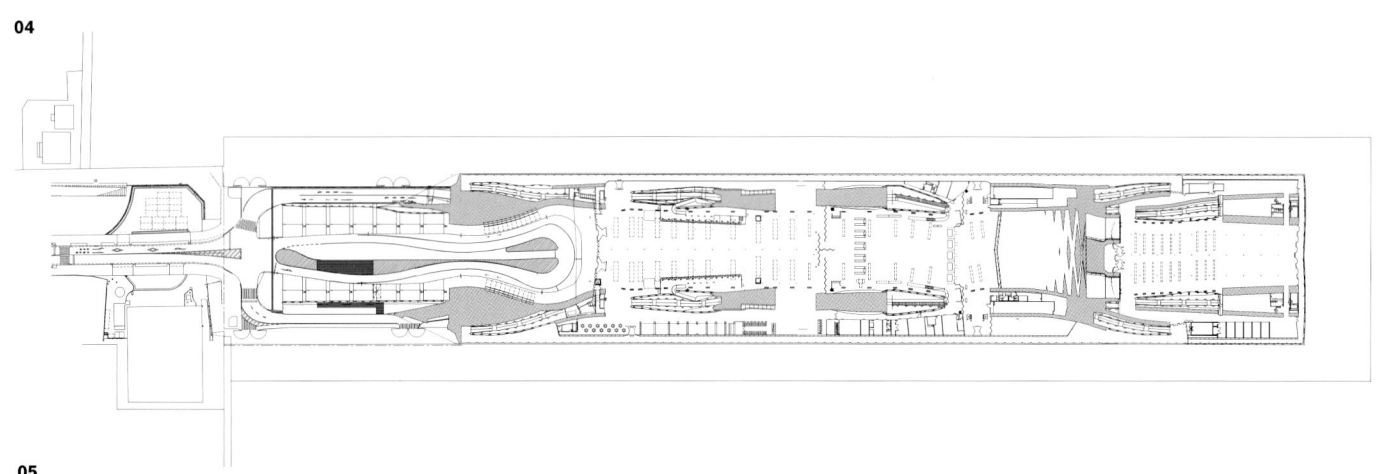

05

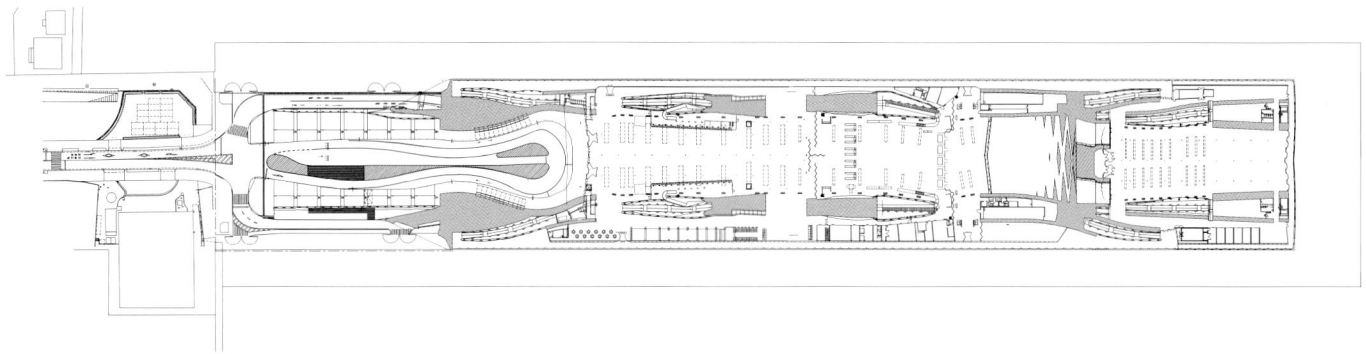

06

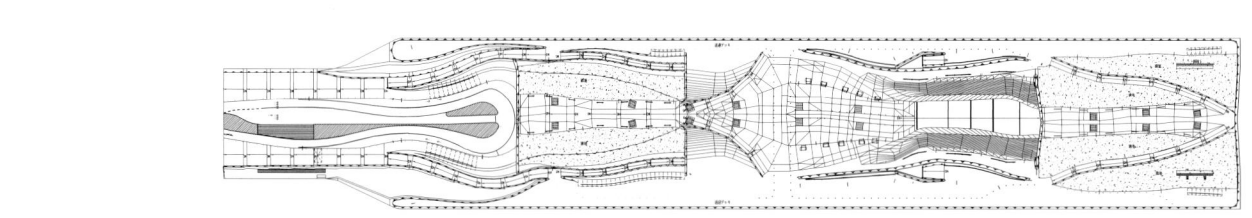

248

07

ARCHITECTS

INDEX

123

3rw architects → 110, 168
Øvre Korskirkesmuget 2a
pb. 1131. 5809 Bergen (Norway)
T +47.5.5365536
F +47.5.5365537
3rw@3rw.no
www.3rw.no

A

Architekturbüro Robert Albertin → 86
Winggel 12
7023 Haldenstein (Switzerland)
T +41.81.25019.66
F +41.81.25019.67
ra@albertin-architektur.ch
www.albertin-architektur.ch

**Arc Architekten
Partnerschaft** → 184
Alfons-Hundsruckerstraße 11
84364 Bad Birnbach (Germany)
T +49.8563.9760.10
F +49.8563.9760.50
info@arcarchitekten.de
www.arcarchitekten.de

**ARCHITEKTUR 109
Mark Arnold + Arne Fentzloff
Freie Architekten BDA** → 216
Hohnerstraße 23
70469 Stuttgart (Germany)
T +49.711.609341
F +49.711.609371
info@architektur109.de
www.architektur109.de

architektur_raum bauer sternberg → 170
Argelanderstraße 81
53115 Bonn (Germany)
T +49.228.24230.10
F +49.228.24230.12
office@bauer-sternberg.de
www.bauer-sternberg.de

B

BattersbyHowat → 142, 180
1441 East Pender Street
Vancouver, British Columbia V5L 1V7
(Canada)
T +1.604.669.9647
F +1.604.669.2010
general@battersbyhowat.com
www.battersbyhowat.com

**baumraum / Andreas Wenning
Dipl.-Ing. Architekt** → 14, 194
Roonstraße 49
28203 Bremen (Germany)
T +49.421.705122
F +49.421.7946351
a.wenning@baumraum.de
www.baumraum.de

Atelier Bow-Wow → 174
8-79 Suga-cho, Shinjuku-ku
Tokyo 160-0018 (Japan)
T +81.3.3226.5336
F +81.3.3226.5366
info@bow-wow.jp
www.bow-wow.jp

Brendeland & Kristoffersen arkitekter AS
→ 100
Fjordgata 50
7010 Trondheim (Norway)
T +47.7.35362.10
F +47.7.35362.01
firma@bkark.no
www.bkark.no

Bucholz McEvoy Architects → 74
Unit C, Mountpleasant Centre, Upper
Mountpleasant Avenue
Rathmines, Dublin 6 (Ireland)
T +353.1.4966.340
F +353.1.4966.341
info@bmcea.com
www.bmcea.com

C

**Jean-Charles CASTRIC
architecte D.P.L.G.** → 134
6a, Route de Brest
29000 Quimper (France)
T +33.2.98955686
F +33.2.98955686
jccastric@free.fr

COAST GbR → 198
Helfferichstraße 1
70192 Stuttgart (Germany)
T +49.711.259854.0
F +49.711.259854.1
coast@coastoffice.de
www.coastoffice.de

cukrowicz nachbaur architekten → 130
Anton-Schneider-Straße 4a
6900 Bregenz (Austria)
T +43.5574.82788
F +43.5574.82688
office@cn-arch.at
www.cn-arch.at

D

**Martin Despang
c/o University of Nebraska-Lincoln
College of Architecture** → 104
238 Architecture Hall West
P. O. Box 880107
Lincoln, NE 68588-0107 (USA)
+1.402.472.9956
+1.402.472.3806
mdespang2@unl.edu
http://archweb.unl.edu

Despang Architekten → 104
Am Graswege 5
30169 Hanover (Germany)
T +49.511.882840
F +49.511.887985
info@despangarchitekten.de
www.despangarchitekten.de

Mari-Aymone Djeribi → 150

Atelier Dreiseitl → 64

E

Eberle Architekten BDA → 60
Burgkmairstraße 14
86152 Augsburg (Germany)
T +49.821.349993.10
F +41.821.349993.11
mail@eberle-architekten.de
www.eberle-architekten.de

Stefan Eberstadt → 54
Landsbergerstraße 191
80687 Munich (Germany)
T +49.89.51739052
F +49.89.51739052
stefan.eberstadt@stefaneberstadt.de

Joachim Eble Architektur → 64
Berliner Ring 47a
72076 Tübingen (Germany)
T +49.7071.96940
F +49.7071.600912
info@eble-architektur.de
www.eble-architektur.de

Eco Design Architects and Consultants
→ 178
4/Fl The Armoury
160 Sir Lowry Rd.
Cape Town, 7925 (South Africa)
T +27.21.4621614
F +27.21.4613198
info@ecodesignarchitects.co.za
www.ecodesignarchitects.co.za

Hermann Eisenköck
Dipl.-Ing. Architekt → 146
Körblergasse 100
8010 Graz (Austria)
T +43.316.323100.35
F +43.316.323100.30
office@archconsult.com
www.archconsult.com

Elenberg Fraser → 230
374 George Street
Fitzroy, Victoria 3065 (Australia)
T +61.39417.2855
F +61.39417.2866
mail@e-f.com.au
www.e-f.com.au

F

Farwick + Grote
Architects & Urban Planners → 38
van-Delden-Straße 15
48683 Ahaus (Germany)
T +49.2561.42960
F +49.2561.429620
info@farwickgrote.de

Markus Fischer Architekt → 82
Pohlstraße 44
10785 Berlin (Germany)
T +49.30.253580.98
F +49.30.253580.99
info@fischer-berkhan.de
www.fischer-berkhan.de

FOA Foreign Office Architects → 246
55 Curtain Road
EC2A 3PT London (United Kingdom)
T +44.207.03398.00
F +44.207.03398.01
press@f-o-a.net
www.f-o-a.net

G

O. Galletti & C. Matter
architectes EPFL, FAS, SIA → 56
Avenue de Montoie 20bis
1007 Lausanne (Switzerland)
T +41.21.6250468
F +41.21.6250469
gm.architectes@bluewin.ch
www.galletti-matter.ch

gmp – Architekten von Gerkan,
Marg und Partner → 10
Elbchaussee 139
22763 Hamburg (Germany)
T +49.40.88151.0
F +49.40.88151.177
hamburg-e@gmp-architekten.de
www.gmp-architekten.de

gpy arquitectos → 242
Calle Castillo 56, 2°d
38003 Santa Cruz de Tenerife (Spain)
T +34.922.244575
F +34.922.151049
estudio@gpyarquitectos.com
www.gpyarquitectos.com

Dipl.-Ing. Architekt Jörg-Henner Gresbrand
c/o Stadt Rotenburg / Wümme, Bauamt, Hoch-
bauabteilung → 114
Große Straße 1
27356 Rotenburg / Wümme (Germany)
T +49.4261.71161
F +49.4261.71271
jh.gresbrand@rotenburg-wuemme.de
www.rotenburg-wuemme.de

H

Mario Hägele
Freier Architekt BDA DWB → 26
Hermann-Kurz-Straße 19
70192 Stuttgart (Germany)
T +49.711.459899.10
F +49.711.459899.19
mario_haegele@mwerk-s.de
www.mwerk-s.de

Halle 58 Architekten GmbH → 136
Hallerstrasse 58
3012 Berne (Switzerland)
T +41.31.302.1030
F +41.31.302.0588
hall58@bluewin.ch
www.halle58.ch

Ville Hara
c/o Avanto Architects → 30
Töölönkatu 38a
00260 Helsinki (Finland)
T +358.503.531095
hara@avan.to
www.avan.to

Helin & Co Architects → 190
Urho Kekkosen katu 3b
P.O. Box 1333
00101 Helsinki (Finland)
T +358.207.577.800
F +358.207.577.801
info@helinco.fi
www.helinco.fi

Picture Credits

All other pictures, portraits and plans
were made available by the architects.

Cover

front side: Tony Miller, St. Kilda West /
Huski, Falls Creek
back side: Jussi Tiainen, Helsinki (l.)
Peter Wildanger (r.)